Foster Children, Rights and the Law

This book discusses child wishes, rights and participation in the foster care system. Making decisions in a foster child's best interest is a widely used, but also widely criticized international legal doctrine. This work discusses the two major legal frameworks, best interest and normalcy, for which foster care decisions are made and how those frameworks might shape how child welfare professionals view and interpret children's rights and participation. Normalcy, the idea that decisions should promote a "normal" life, is a separate legal doctrine which can be in conflict with best interest determinations. However, the concept of normalcy is also theoretically built into best interest decisions and therefore also plays a role in most child welfare systems. Mixing both empirical legal and child welfare research, the book demonstrates the ways in which risk aversion and fear drive best interest decision-making to the detriment of both practitioners and the children they aim to serve. It argues that a children's rights framework starting with normalcy is a better tool for promoting child participation and centering the child within the dependency process. The book will be of interest to academics, researchers and policymakers working in the areas of children's rights law, child welfare and international human rights law.

Matthew Trail is Research Fellow with the Max Planck Institute for Research on Collective Goods, Germany, and a former US legal aid child welfare care attorney.

Foster Children, Rights and the Law

Best Interest, Normalcy and the Welfare System

Matthew Trail

Routledge
Taylor & Francis Group
LONDON AND NEW YORK

First published 2025
by Routledge
4 Park Square, Milton Park, Abingdon, Oxon OX14 4RN

and by Routledge
605 Third Avenue, New York, NY 10158

Routledge is an imprint of the Taylor & Francis Group, an informa business

British Library Cataloguing-in-Publication Data
A catalogue record for this book is available from the British Library

Library of Congress Cataloging-in-Publication Data
Names: Trail, Matthew, author.
Title: Foster children, rights and the law : best interest, normalcy and the welfare system / Matthew Trail.
Description: Abingdon, Oxon [UK] ; New York, NY : Routledge, 2025. | Includes bibliographical references and index. | Contents: The Child Welfare System and Dependency—The Best Interest of Children—Normalcy—Risk, Normalcy, and Best Interest—Decision Making—Childrens Rights and Participation—Best Interest vs Normalcy : How Professionals Respond—Normalcy Charter.
Identifiers: LCCN 2024057663 (print) | LCCN 2024057664 (ebook) | ISBN 9781032829791 (hardback) | ISBN 9781032836201 (paperback) | ISBN 9781003510253 (ebook)
Subjects: LCSH: Foster children—Legal status, laws, etc. | Foster home care—Law and legislation. | Foster children—Care. | Children—Legal status, laws, etc. | Children (International law) | Child welfare.
Classification: LCC K1965 .T73 2025 (print) | LCC K1965 (ebook) | DDC 341.4/8572—dc23/eng/20241202
LC record available at https://lccn.loc.gov/2024057663
LC ebook record available at https://lccn.loc.gov/2024057664

ISBN: 978-1-032-82979-1 (hbk)
ISBN: 978-1-032-83620-1 (pbk)
ISBN: 978-1-003-51025-3 (ebk)

DOI: 10.4324/9781003510253

Typeset in Galliard
by Apex CoVantage, LLC

Contents

Acknowledgments *vi*

1 The Child Welfare System and Dependency 1

2 The Best Interest of Children 21

3 Normalcy 52

4 Risk, Normalcy and Best Interest 72

5 Decision-Making 92

6 Children's Rights and Participation 118

7 Best Interest vs Normalcy: How Professionals Respond 168

8 Normalcy Charter 187

Index *209*

Acknowledgments

Most importantly, to my amazing wife, Elisabeta, for always encouraging all of our journeys together.

To Prof- Dr. Dr. h.c. Christoph Engel, for all of his invaluable wisdom and for taking a chance on a Texas attorney.

To Dr. Dr. Pascal Lagenbach for always making time to guide me through the research process.

To Dr. Emily Keddell for all of the past, present and future advice.

To the Rees Center at the University of Oxford for allowing me access to their collective knowledge.

To Disability Rights Texas and Richard Lavallo for teaching me to be a better advocate for children in care.

To the Florida Guardian Ad Litem's office for their participation and support of my research.

To Jon Sommer, Raychel Johnson, Chris Cudebec, Alicia Guerra and Sabrina Blaylock for their patient help in making my research questions understandable to the rest of the world.

To Laura at Foster Parent Partner for her essential help in reaching so many child welfare professionals.

To Manjola and Greisi Shehu for making Germany feel like home.

To both the Euro and Texas Saints for all of the adventures.

1 The Child Welfare System and Dependency

When the child welfare dockets are being heard, the hallway of the seventh floor of the Harris County Juvenile Justice Center in Houston is a place of barely contained chaos. There are never enough seats; so many people stand. Attorneys, caseworkers, foster parents, biological family, child advocate volunteers and court staff buzz about the place, discussing cases, last-minute case plans and impromptu mediations. Every so often a bailiff steps out of the court room and tells the loudest groups to hush.

Decisions are made in that hallway to reunite families, to separate siblings, to send a child to a new foster home, to terminate the rights of a parent and to alter lives forever. The foster children themselves are only occasionally part of those conversations. The common theme of those decisions, like all child welfare decisions, is that they are all made supposedly in the best interests of the child or children at the center of the case.

The words "best interest" are repeated hundreds of times a day in that hallway and in hallways like it around the United States. Child Protective Services (CPS) create detailed case plans in the child's best interest. Court Appointed Child Advocates (CASA) make recommendations in the child's best interest. Attorneys for each party, on every side argue in the child's best interest and ultimately courts make rulings in the child's best interest. This legal standard has no uniform definition and yet governs essentially all decisions about children in care, but perhaps it should not.

The rights of foster children and the more recent legal requirement of normalcy, how foster children can lead a normal life, are often in conflict with best interests. The poorly defined notion of best interest coupled with the overlapping and sometimes contrasting legal frameworks of normalcy and child rights means that decision-making throughout the child welfare world is often subjective and inconsistent. So, perhaps there are better ways to make decisions under alternative legal frameworks that would lead to better outcomes and ways in which the children themselves can have more say in what happens to them.

In the following chapters, I will discuss the history, use and critiques of legal best interest and normalcy, the rights of children in foster care, what research tells us about decision-making in child welfare and how all of these

DOI: 10.4324/9781003510253-1

different pieces of the child welfare world fit together. I will also discuss what my own study of best interest decision-making found and how we might incorporate these threads of science and law to make better child-centered decisions. Though these topics have been discussed individually by other writers, this book will attempt to tie these branches of empirical and legal research together to give us a complete picture of how we make decisions for children in care. I ultimately will advocate for a Normalcy Charter that combines children's rights, direct legal representation and normalcy as a better approach to our current best interest driven system.

Because it is easy to lose individuals in the stream of large numbers and complex ideas, I have included snippets from case histories with the names and small details changed to protect their anonymity. These stories truly belong to the children themselves and I acknowledge they could each tell them better than me. I include them with respect to each. Each is a child's voice making a request and often being ignored.

The Child Welfare System: Foster Children

Mike had been in care for 8 years when I was first appointed to his case. He was living at a residential treatment facility (RTC) in central Texas after his prior foster placement broke down following mental health issues and multiple stays in psychiatric hospitals. He wanted to live with extended family, but his history of mental health outbursts meant that CPS felt he would be safer at the RTC. He spent most of his time there trying to get other kids to play role playing games with him. He asked to attend a regular school, but was not allowed. The RTC staff made him do farm work around the facility, which he hated. One day when he was frustrated and refused, RTC staff restrained him and broke his arm. Though that injury would have been cause enough for CPS to take him from his parent's home, because there were no open foster homes that would take teenage boys, he stayed at that facility for another six months until a family member was finally approved for placement.

Before we can delve into the minutia of child welfare best interest and normalcy law and related decision-making, it is important to get a general sense of scope of the foster care system and what it looks like on a daily basis for the children and families involved, what the process of foster care consist of and what happens to people caught up in the system. This will by necessity be a superficial summary as each of the topics touched on here have be written about by social science researchers and legal scholars in their own volumes, but hopefully this introduction will give an unfamiliar reader a better overall idea of the child welfare system. Where possible in this chapter, I will include numbers and findings from international sources for comparisons, but as each care system is very different there is a limit to how detailed these can be.

The United States Department of Health and Human Services (HHS) (2023) tracks the national foster care data reported by the states and estimates that more than 3 million children were involved in the child welfare system in

2021 as part of an abuse or neglect investigation or preventive service. HHS (2021) reported that more than 606,000 children were part of the foster care system, meaning that they had been removed from their homes and placed somewhere else, generally a foster home or family home. More than 206,000 children entered foster care during that fiscal year and nearly 215,000 exited the system over the same time. Over the last decade, these numbers have risen and fallen but have always been between 600,000 and 690,000 with the entered and exit numbers fluctuating similarly (Adoption and Foster Care Analysis and Reporting System, 2022). For some perspective, that number is more than the whole population of Wyoming and roughly the size of Detroit or Boston (United States Census Bureau, 2022).

Though these numbers are large enough in their own right to be concerning, estimates of scope of the child welfare system actually show even more exposure. Wildeman and Emanuel (2014) estimated that almost 6 percent of US children would be taken into foster care at some point in their childhood and for Black children the rate was more than 11 percent. In a follow-up paper, Kim et al. (2017) found that more than 37 percent of all US children would be investigated by CPS and more than 50 percent of Black children.

Though worldwide data is difficult to track, some researchers estimated that as many as 2.7 million children around the globe could be living in some form of alternative care (Petrowski et al., 2017). In the EU and UK combined, there are an estimated 758,000 children in care (Eurochild, 2021). UNICEF (2023) estimated that 105 out of every 100,000 children in the world were in some form of residential congregate care facility with Western Europe actually having the highest rates of 294 per 100,000.

The cost for all of these cases and these children are significant. The Congressional Research Service (CRS) (2023) reported that the US spent more than $31 billion on child welfare services, more than half of which comes from state and local budgets. The next largest piece come from federal child welfare programs and the remaining from other federal programs (CRS, 2023). Other nations spend comparable sums on their child protection systems. For example, in recent years Germany spent €14 billion (Kindler, 2023), Austria spent €796 million (Meier & Möstl, 2023) and France €13 billion (Lafourcade & Dartigue, 2023).

Global averages are difficult to come by, but in the United States children tend to be on average about 8 years old, though the highest percentage of children in care are young, with 31 percent being three years or younger and 42 percent being less than six years old (HHS, 2021). They are split reasonably in the middle between boys and girls with boys making 51 percent of the total. The vast majority, nearly 80 percent, live with either a foster family, at 44 percent, or with a kinship family, at 35 percent. The remainder live in group homes, pre-adoptive homes, or institutions like RTCs (HHS, 2021).

In the EU, the children represented are more likely to be boys and tend to be a little older, in their early teens depending on the specific country (European et al., 2020). The reason for the higher age and gender difference does not have a simple answer, but the influx of a large amount of unaccompanied older male youth refugees is one possible answer (European et al., 2020).

Though 43 percent or about 168,000 US foster children are reported as White, a disproportionate amount are Black or Hispanic representing 22 percent from each group or about 171,000 combined, with mixed ethnic background children accounting for an additional 8 percent (HHS, 2021). The Child Welfare Information Gateway (CWIG) (2021) noted that this disproportionate effect encompassed the entire child welfare system, with Black children being more likely to be reported to CPS, more likely to be investigated, more likely to be taken into care. They also spend more time in the foster care system and they are less likely to be reunited with their families (CWIG, 2021).

This minority bias is not limited to the United States, though, and is a common problem throughout the world. As a brief example, the UK takes in a disproportionate amount of Black, Traveler and Roma children (Ahmed et al., 2022). Indigenous children are overrepresented in New Zealand (Cram et al., 2015). Black and Indigenous children are overrepresented in Canada (Ontario Human Rights Commission, 2018). Finally, Roma children are pulled into care at higher rates in Moldova, Bulgaria, the Czech Republic, Romania and Slovakia (Rourke, 2021).

Disabled youth are also over represented within the foster care system both in the US and in Europe and have higher rates of abuse than children without a disability (Slayter, 2016; Fisher et al., 2008; European et al., 2020). Researchers have also shown that foster youth are more likely to have a disability than non-disabled children (Bilaver et al., 2020; Stein et al., 2013). Bilaver et al. (2020) found that 44 percent of foster children met the criteria for having a special health care need, such as behavioral disorders, anxiety, developmental delays and speech and language disorders. Foster children with a disability remain in care longer than their non-disabled peers and have more placement disruptions (Platt et al., 2022). They are also more likely to be prescribe psychotropic medication (Walsh & Mattingly, 2013).

On average in the United States, the children in care stay in the system for almost 22 months, though the median number is closer to 15 months. A plurality of 42 percent of the children are in care for less than year, whereas 18 percent or more than 68,000 children remain in care for more than three years and 6 percent for more than five years (HHS, 2021).

Children's time in care can look vastly different from one another depending on the type of placement, such as kinship home versus group home and their stability within the placements. Stability relates to the number of placements a child has while in the care system, with states counting less than two placements per 12 months as stable, with the majority of children, over 80 percent, who had been in care less than a year meeting that standard (Children's Bureau, 2019). The children that had been in care longer, however, were much less stable with nearly 60 percent of children who had been in care for more than two years having three or more placements (Children's Bureau,

2021). In one longitudinal study of foster youth, Pecora et al. (2005) found that from their participants the average number of placements was 6.5 and that nearly a third had experienced substantial placement instability with more than eight placement changes.

Instability in placement comes with its own set of negative outcomes, such as increased risk of behavioral problems (Rubin et al., 2007), cognitive and physical health delays (Asif et al., 2023), increased risk of juvenile delinquency (Ryan & Testa, 2005) and poor academic performance (Clemens et al., 2018). In an often-cited study of 1200 foster youth, George (1990) found that instability in placement even makes reunification with the family less likely.

Their Homes

CWIG (2023b) reported that many of the children that come into care arrive from homes experiencing poverty at a rate of neglect seven times higher than compared to non-poor families. The lack of affordable child care, the loss of employment and the loss of government benefits all are linked to a child being placed into care as is the additional monitoring of poor communities by CPS (CWIG, 2023b). Chapin Hall (2022) reported that the use of food banks, housing instability and utility shut offs were also predictors of child welfare investigations. Some of the racial disparity inherent in the child welfare system can be linked to poverty as well since in the US, Black, Native American and Hispanic families are more than twice as likely to experience poverty as their White counterparts (Chapin Hall, 2022). This link between poverty and foster care also in prevalent in European countries (European et al., 2020).

Foster children are also more likely to come from homes with substance abuse issues (Cunningham & Finlay, 2013; Sepulveda & Williams, 2019). The HHS (2021) reported that 36 percent of the children removed from their home had a parent involved in drug abuse. Those responsible for the abuse tend to be the child's parents, though more than 14 percent are abused by a non-parent, which can include other family members and the romantic partners of the parents (HHS, 2021).

Parents with disabilities were also significantly more likely to have their children removed than non-disabled parents and parents with disabilities are disproportionately involved with child welfare (National Council on Disability, 2012). Lightfoot and DeZelar (2016) estimated that 19 percent of children removed from their homes had a parent with a disability and that disability was listed as one of the reasons for the removal. However, a study by the National Research Center for Parents with Disabilities (2022) found that when controlled for poverty related factors, a parent's disability was not a factor for long-term risk of child abuse.

All five of the Smith siblings, ages 3 through 15, came into care after the death of their grandmother. They had been living at the grandmother's home with their mother, who had mental health and substance abuse issues. The mother herself had been a foster child once. When the children stopped going to school and lost their housing, CPS took all of them into care. They managed to place the two youngest siblings together in one nearby foster home, but the three oldest were split and placed separately. All of them had to change schools. The two oldest boys asked to stay with their grandfather a couple hours away, but he only had room for one.

Abuse and Neglect

The stories of why they are brought into care are unique to the families, but they are categorized and reported in simpler terms. More than three quarters are brought into the US system because of neglect, with only about 16 percent recorded as being physically abused and another 10 percent identified as sexually abused (HHS, 2023). It is important to note, though, that when recording these numbers, HHS only counts each type of incidence once, so a single child can be neglected multiple times and only appear in the data as one count of neglect. Additionally, the same child can be counted multiple times in the data if they were subjected to multiple forms of abuse (HHS, 2023).

Of course, neglect and abuse have legal definitions which vary in wording from state to state. The federal definition from the Child Abuse and Treatment Act (2010) is a

> recent act or failure to act on the part of a parent or caretaker, which results in death, serious physical or emotional harm, sexual abuse or exploitation, or an act or failure to act which presents an imminent risk of serious harm.
>
> (p. 24)

State definitions tend to be broader with more nuance. The Texas Family Code (2023) states that mental, physical and emotional injury that causes harm or impairs development can all constitute abuse. Texas defines neglect as the "*blatant disregard for the consequences of the act or failure to act that results in harm to the child or that creates an immediate danger to the child's physical health or safety*" and then the statute goes on to list nine specific examples, including failure to provide medical care, food and clothing (Texas Family Code §261.001(4), 2023).

Virginia adds medical neglect as a separate category of abuse and also expands physical abuse to include children being present when a parent or caretaker is making or selling drugs (Virginia Administrative Code, 2020). Florida actually lists specific injuries that might be deemed willful abuse, such as bone fractures, brain damage, bites, asphyxiation and disfigurement (Florida Statute Title V Chapter 39, 2023). California adds a second category of neglect called severe neglect that adds an element of willfulness and or harm to a child to distinguish it from simple neglect (California Penal Code, 2022).

Regardless of the specifics, the broad themes of the law regarding abuse are same. The same acts or omissions that constitute child abuse in Miami generally look like the same behavior in Seattle.

Neglect is a bit more complicated, though. As mentioned above, there are strong connections between poverty and foster care (Williams et al., 2023). Since neglect generally involves the lack of adequate care, it is often wrapped up in measures of poverty and every state includes poverty correlates in their neglect definition, such as lack of food, clothing and basic hygiene. The nation is evenly split regarding exemptions for poverty from the legal definitions of neglect, but in half of the states, simply being poor might be enough to constitute child maltreatment (Williams et al., 2023). In EU Parliament guidance, a distinction is made between intentional, deliberate neglect and the neglect that is linked to poverty (Dimitrova-Stull, 2014).

It is also important to understand that abuse and neglect can lead to the death of children. HHS (2023) reported that more than 1,800 children died in 2021 as a result of maltreatment. Nearly half of those deaths come from infants with Black children having higher fatality rates than White or Hispanic children (HHS, 2023).

Though 15 years of representing foster children and seeing the harm of removal and care has left me deeply suspicious of the child welfare system, it needs to be acknowledged that it does sometimes perform exactly its purpose and protect children. I had clients that were sexually abused by the parents for years, clients that were locked for days inside kitchen counters, clients that were nearly starved to death and clients whose feet bottoms were routinely whipped by coat hangers. The system is greatly flawed, but still needed.

The Court Case

In the US the process for initiating a child abuse case and the steps that follow are also similar across the states. The case generally begins with a report of child abuse or neglect made to the state CPS agency. CPS will determine if the report warrants an investigation or any sort of additional preliminary services to keep the family intact (California Legislative Analysis Office, 1996; Foster Care Review Office, 2017; Youth Law Center, 2018.) If the CPS agency believes that abuse or neglect have occurred and the child or children are in danger, then they will remove the child from the caregiver's home in a process known appropriately enough as removal. Generally, CPS has the power to remove a child in danger without a court hearing, though sometimes CPS will seek court approval prior to a removal (Youth Law Center, 2018; Tennessee Court Improvement Program, 2008; Arkansas Department of Human Services, 2024, p. 76).

Federal law calls for states to have child maltreatment reporting laws that establish mandatory reporters (CWIG, 2023a). These professionals are required by law to report any reasonable suspicion of child abuse or neglect to the state CPS agency. These roles vary by state, but most states require medical professionals, school and education professionals, social workers, police and therapist to report child maltreatment (CWIG, 2023a). HHS (2023) notes that 67 percent of child abuse and neglect reports come through these professional mandated reporters, with most coming from law enforcement, school and medical staff.

Though not every state uses the term, the courts and cases in most states are referred to as dependency. Because it would be both challenging and confusing to describe and summarize the court process for all 50 states, as an example, I will describe the general procedures from Texas and Pennsylvania, as representative of the approximate timelines and types of hearings that are involved in a foster care case. Different states use different names for what are essentially the same hearing and have slightly different rules concerning service of process, appointment of attorneys and the precise timelines for when hearings must take place.

The beginning of the Texas legal case occurs when CPS files a petition within the dependency court seeking court approval for the removal of the child (Children's Commission, 2023). Similarly in Pennsylvania a case commences with a protective order on behalf of the child or the transfer of the case from another jurisdiction (Office of Children and Families in the Court, 2019). Service is issued for both parents and each parent is entitled to an attorney under both Texas and Pennsylvania law (Children's Commission, 2023; Office of Children and Families in the Court, 2019).

In both states if parents cannot afford their own attorney one is taken from a list of available private attorneys maintained by each court. Men married to the biological mother and men that might be the biological father are also included as parties to the case. Potential parties can also include other family member caretakers and fictive kin caretakers (Children's Commission, 2023; Office of Children and Families in the Court, 2019). Children are also considered parties to the case and are appointed an attorney ad litem and a guardian ad litem. The attorney represents the child and the guardian represents the child's best interest (Children's Commission, 2023; Office of Children and Families in the Court, 2019).

As a bit of clarification as regarding attorney and guardian ad litems, the states vary quite a bit on how they approach foster child representation. The National Association of Counsel for Children (NACC) (2023) reports that 13 states do not require any attorney representation at all for children in care. The states that do require attorneys also have different requirements for the type of representation. Some states have client directed representation meaning that foster children guide representation as would an adult client. Some states have pure best interest representation meaning that attorneys act on behalf of the child's best interest, which I will discuss in detail in the best interest chapters. Finally, many states have a hybrid model of representation that allows one attorney to fill both attorney ad litem and guardian ad litem roles so long as there is no conflict between the two (NACC, 2023).

In addition to CPS workers and attorneys, many US jurisdictions also work with an organization known as Court Appointed Special Advocates (CASA), which consist of paid staff and volunteers (Osborne et al., 2020). A CASA volunteers or staff members are appointed by the courts to act as the guardian ad litem of the child and to make recommendations in the child's best interest (Osborne et al., 2020). In some states, CASA attorneys represent foster children as their guardian ad litem best interest lawyer (NACC, 2023).

Returning now to the court process, once a child has been removed by CPS because of safety concerns, Texas requires that an initial hearing be held the following business day after the removal and no later than the third business day (Children's Commission, 2023). Pennsylvania calls the first hearing a shelter hearing and it needs to occur within 72 hours following removal (Office of Children and Families in the Court, 2019). Following the first hearing, the Texas court will hear hold a contested adversary hearing within 14 days with the burden of proof resting on the state CPS agency (Children's Commission, 2023), whereas Pennsylvania courts hold their adjudication hearing within ten days of the shelter hearing (Office of Children and Families in the Court, 2019).

If the case continues, the Texas court must hold a status hearing within 60 days and review the case plan for the child, which includes information on the child's current placement, their education and CPS's plan for the child's permanency (Children's Commission, 2023). Cases in Pennsylvania have an extra hearing not found in Texas called a disposition hearing that is generally concerned with which person or entity will have custody of the child (Office of Children and Families in the Court, 2019).

So long as the child is in temporary custody of the state, both Texas and Pennsylvania courts will hold permanency hearings at least twice a year and children are required to attend these hearings unless waived by the judge (Children's Commission, 2023; Office of Children and Families in the Court, 2019).

Texas requires that a final hearing on the merits of the case regarding the permanent custody of the child by the state to take place within a year of the initial temporary hearing, though courts can extend this time for another 180 days if needed (Children's Commission, 2023). Pennsylvania requires that a petition for termination be filed by CPS for any child that has been in care for 15 of the last 22 months; however, the time for setting the hearing is left open with the understanding that it should not be delayed (Office of Children and Families in the Court, 2019).

In every day practice if the parties needed more time to resolve the case, courts would often commence the trial before the deadline, but then put the trial in recess and reset for a few months in the future. At the final hearing in both states, CPS must show by a clear and convincing evidence standard the parents' rights should be terminated and that efforts were made to reunite the child with their family (Children's Commission, 2023; Office of Children and Families in the Court, 2019).

If the parents' rights are terminated and CPS takes on permanent custody of the child, then the court will continue to have permanency hearings every 180 days so long as the child is in care (Children's Commission, 2023; Office of Children and Families in the Court, 2019). Best practice courts have these permanency hearings more frequently, usually every 90 days and parties are able to request hearings in between.

Texas foster children remain under the automatic jurisdiction of the court until 6 months past their 18th birthday and judges can extend their jurisdiction upon the request of the foster youth until they turn 21 years old (Children's Commission, 2023). In Pennsylvania, foster youth may also remain in care until their 21st birthday upon a finding of the presiding court that they are in an education or employment program or have medical needs that require extended care (Office of Children and Families in the Court, 2019).

With the exception of the actual trial to terminate parental rights, court hearings tend to be reasonably informal with judges granting great leeway in hearsay and evidence rules. Because so much of the information about a child in care comes from teachers, therapists, caregivers, juvenile probation officers, doctors and others than cannot attend every hearing, it would be impossible to get a current picture of the child without waiving a lot of court formality.

Again, the overall court process and timeline varies state by state, but the general requirements are similar throughout the country. However, it is important to note that the laws covering foster child jurisdiction are broader and more complex as there are other types of courts and cases that can also hear evidence about a child in care. Child welfare cases can also be part of child custody and divorce suits, while children with Native American ancestry can be covered by Indian Child Welfare Act, which grants jurisdiction of native children back to tribal courts (DePasquale, 2022). Additionally, some states have developed special dual status courts that hear cases involving foster children who are also in trouble with the juvenile justice system and those courts can make orders in both the child welfare and the juvenile case (Kelly & Haskins, 2021).

Leaving the Care System

The legal case is concluded when the child formally exits the child welfare system and this can be done in multiple ways. The Annie E. Casey Foundation (2021) notes that the most common way for foster children to exit the system is when they return to their family, with approximately 47 percent of cases concluding in reunification. Though that number has been on a slight decline for the last decade. The second most common reason children exit care is through adoption, with roughly a quarter of all foster children being adopted out of care with most of those being adopted by their foster parent and most going to children under 5 years old (Annie E. Casey Foundation, 2023).

According to Annie E. Casey Foundation (2021), children also exited foster care by finding a permanent home with other family members at six percent, living with a non-family permanent guardian at 12 percent and emancipation or ageing out of the system at nine percent. The remaining 2 percent either are sent to another state agency for care, run away from care or die while in care (Annie E. Casey Foundation, 2021).

Research has also identified ways in which individual child and case factors can influence both the timing and the type of exit from care (Connell et al., 2006; Courtney & Wong, 1996; Lloyd Sieger, 2020). Race (LaBrenz et al., 2021) and disability (Connell et al., 2006) of the child can both lead to delayed reunification. Age, gender and race can all be factors that determine if a child is adopted, with Baccara et al. (2014) finding an adoption preference for young, White girls. Johnson et al. (2020) found adoption rates more than 70 percent higher for White children compared to Black and Hispanic children. Children that had been sexually abused and those that were living in group homes were also less likely to be adopted (Connell et al., 2006).

Sharon came into care together with her two young sisters after their mother was arrested for drugs and prostitution. Sharon, who was 15 when she came into the system, never accepted that she belonged anywhere other than with her mother, even though her mother allowed her to be sexually abused by her boyfriends. Sharon bounced from foster home to foster home to residential facility for the next three years and despite court orders to the contrary, she and her mother never stopped communicating through social media and phone calls. The mother, who never made any progress on her reunification plan and tested positive for drugs throughout the case, eventually relinquished her legal parental rights to all three daughters. Fathers were never identified for any of them. On her 18th birthday, Sharon left care and returned to her mother's home.

Adult Outcomes

One of the primary reasons that the child welfare system always seems to be in need of reform is that care experienced adults, the adults who spent time in the foster care system, tend to have such negative outcomes later in life across multiple types of life measurements. In a Casey Family Programs study of care experienced adults from the Northwest, Pecora et al. (2005) found that more than half reported mental health issues, with rates of PTSD more than six times that of other adults. They also struggled with completing education after high school and more than a third were living below the poverty level (Pecora et al., 2005).

In two widely cited influential longitudinal studies, researchers at Chapin Hall looked at outcomes of care experienced adults from the Midwest, the Midwest Study and from California, the CalYOUTH study. In the Midwest Study, Courtney et al. (2011) followed more than 700 young adults until they were 26 years old. In the CalYOUTH study researchers followed another 700 care experienced adults until their 21st birthday (Courtney et al., 2020).

For the Midwest cohort, researchers found that of the former care experienced adults, nearly a third had experienced some form of homelessness or couch surfing (Courtney et al., 2011). CalYOUTH participants also reported that a quarter had been homeless for at least one night, with half of those reporting homelessness of more than a month (Courtney et al., 2020). In a separate study, Fowler et al. (2017) reported a similar high-rate homelessness and noted that care experienced adults that were reunited with family did not experience homelessness rates like those who aged out of care.

Of those that had finished high school more than a third said they had dropped out of their college or trade school programs (Courtney et al., 2011). Okpych and Courtney (2018) found similar results in a separate study of care experienced adults with only 12 percent able to complete their undergraduate college degrees within a six-year span.

The Midwestern study also found that nearly half of the care experienced adults did not have a job and those that did made $18,000 less a year than their adult counterparts (Courtney et al., 2011). Courtney et al. (2020) found similar result to the prior study with care experienced CalYOUTH adults reporting less employment in terms of ever having a job and in fewer total hours worked than their similar adult cohorts. Nearly half of them had some form of economic hardship in the prior year, and nearly 30 percent would be considered food insecure by federal standards (Courtney et al., 2020).

The researchers also found that the women in the Midwest Study were also more likely to have been pregnant at some point during the course of the study at a 90 percent rate compared to their adult cohorts at 55 percent (Courtney et al., 2011). In comparison to other adults, the women tended to be unmarried at the time of their pregnancy and reported that the pregnancy was unplanned (Courtney et al., 2011).

The Midwest care experienced adults were also more likely to be involved with the criminal justice system with more than 80 percent of the men and nearly 60 percent of the women reporting being arrested (Courtney et al., 2011). Similarly in the CalYOUTH study, Courtney et al. (2020) reported that care experienced adults had more involvement with criminal justice than their peers with three time the amount of arrest and nearly six times as likely to have spent a night in jail. Some researchers have found that removal from home and placement in the foster care system alone can be correlated with higher rates of crime later in life (Doyle, 2008); however, this is disputed (Gross & Baron, 2020).

The CalYOUTH study adults had three times the rate of their peers of disability or a health-related condition that limited their daily life (Courtney et al., 2020). This is in line with the findings of Ahrens et al. (2014) that found that care experienced adults had a higher chance of being diagnosed with multiple chronic health conditions than that of the general population, which the researchers suggested was related to the lifelong stress of foster care and insecurity. The CalYOUTH participants were also observed to have mental and behavioral health disorders in their sample with 20 percent reporting suicidal thoughts and nearly 30 percent reporting some mental health issue (Courtney et al., 2020). In their meta-analysis, Kang and Adams (2017) also reported similarly high levels of mental health and behavioral problems with young adults who had aged out of care.

Both the Midwest and the CalYOUTH studies reported incidents of sexually risky behaviors. Eleven percent of the Midwest adults reported being paid for sex (Courtney et al., 2011) and 10 percent in the CalYOUTH group (Courtney et al., 2020). Other studies have also found links between in foster care and being sex trafficked (Gerassi, 2015; Nixon et al., 2002).

These negative trends are persistently found throughout the years as the Annie E. Casey Foundation (2023) reports that homelessness, early pregnancy, arrests and unemployment all remain at similarly high levels for care experienced adults in the most recent federal data. Each of these issues comes with its own set of accompanying and related problems, which tend to compound to create worse outcomes. Some research has even suggested mere CPS involvement in a child's life has strong correlations with negative life outcomes, such as higher rates of mental health issues and having problems with their education (Evangelist et al., 2023). Trivedi (2019) wrote that the mere act of removal might lead to lifelong trauma and can be linked to separation and attachment disorders.

Combs et al. (2018) found similar rates of pregnancy and parenthood among care experienced women as other studies, but they noted also correlations between pregnancy, homelessness, economic insecurity and poorer education and employment outcomes. Lee et al. (2023) found that care experienced adults with an emotional disability had higher rates of +homelessness and incarceration. For adults that were part of both the foster care and the juvenile justice system, even compared to their care experienced peers, they had higher rates of unemployment, subsequent criminal activity and housing insecurity (Culhane et al., 2011; Coulton et al., 2015). This has led some scholars to label the connection between foster care, juvenile delinquency and adult crime as the foster care to prison pipeline (Yamat, 2020).

In their systemic review of care experienced adult outcomes, Lindner and Hanlon (2024) wrote that the way a youth left the foster care system had an impact on their adult experience. Those youth that were adopted tended to have better health, employment, education and crime related outcomes than those that aged out or were reunified and that adults that had stable foster placements also had better outcomes than those that were exposed to instability (Linder and Hanlon).

One of the biggest challenges in trying to understand the negative outcomes associated with child welfare system exposure is separating the possible neglect and abuse prior to CPS involvement with the trauma of removal and placement in a new home. This is especially complicated by other factors, such as poverty, disability and substance abuse that are often correlated with CPS cases.

There are a few studies that have attempted to make the separation. Font and Maguire-Jack (2020) attempted to control for CPS involvement by testing food stamp recipient families that were investigated by CPS and those that were not. They excluded families that had children removed and found that those children that had been investigated by CPS had worse adult outcomes regarding employment, school and crime than those who experienced similar levels of poverty but were not investigated (Font & Maguire-Jack, 2020). In a cohort study, Currie and Widom (2010) found that adults that were abused or neglected as children had worse education, employment and fewer assets than their non-abused peers.

In their comprehensive review of the literature connecting poverty, child maltreatment and CPS involvement the National Academies of Sciences and Medicine (2023) ultimately concluded that the causal links between poor adult outcomes cannot be separated as there are simply too many confounding individual family and case factors.

Other research has also attempted to place an economic figure behind these outcomes. Peterson et al. (2018) applied monetized quality of life and statistical value of life calculations to estimate the economic toll child maltreatment had on the US economy. They wrote that substantiated cases alone of abuse costs nearly $430 billion and that if they included investigations, that number was $2 trillion (Peterson et al., 2018). An older UK report attempted a similar analysis and found that the cost in 1996 was more than £730 million (Williams, 1996).

Though a direct causal effect may never be fully understood because of the complex nature of the families involved and the system itself, the final results, the outcomes of adults are well established and dire.

Lamont was funny and easygoing. He aged out of the foster care system at 18 and refused to extend care despite the many requests from his CASA volunteer to stay until he at least finished high school. Because of a juvenile conviction for assault that he picked up while in the foster care system, he was never able to find a stable placement as most homes did not want a Black teenage boy on probation. He spent his last two years in care living at a residential treatment facility with another dozen other teenage boys. He got in fights there as well after one of them took his iPod. The fight was a violation of his probation, so he spent some time in the juvenile jail. He went to live with family when he turned 18, but was kicked out within a few weeks. He started breaking into empty homes shortly thereafter to find a place to sleep. He could have gone back into care, but he preferred being homeless to the RTC. He never finished high school and has been arrested multiple times as an adult.

The System

Though I hope that this short bird's eye view of the child welfare system will give those readers new to this world some basic understanding of the children, families, systems and processes involved, it is by no means comprehensive. A foster child is at the nexus of an overlapping and complex system of systems. Arguably foster children touch more government public systems than any other type of citizen.

On any given day, my former clients might be qualifying under federal law for special education through the public school system. They might be receiving Social Security benefits or going to therapy paid for by Medicaid. They might be qualifying for housing support through United States Department of Housing and Urban Development. They might be testifying in as witnesses regarding trafficking cases or they might be attending a Job Corps vocational program. They might be caught up in the US immigration system and seeking special protection and fast track residency as dependent children. This is just a small fraction of the US federal programs and laws that might impact a foster child. The state and local community programs would be even higher and run the gamut from youth support groups to state prisons.

A small army of adults from these programs are assembled in the supposed support of the child. Social workers, CASA guardians, school staff, therapists, foster parents, doctors and judges all work and interact directly with foster children and generally each one of those people is backed by an agency or support staff that work indirectly. All are tasked with making decisions in the child's best interest, even those that have never met the child.

At the core of all of these programs and laws, though, is an individual child, a child that has their own voice and their own understanding of what constitutes their best interest and what a normal life would look like for them.

References

Adoption and Foster Care Analysis and Reporting System. (2022). *The AFCARS report.* U.S. Department of Health and Human Services, Administration for Children and Families, Children's Bureau. https://www.acf.hhs.gov/sites/default/files/documents/cb/trends-foster-care-adoption-2012-2021.pdf

Ahmed, N., James, D., Tayabali, A., & Watson, M. (2022). *Ethnicity and children's social care.* UK Department of Education. Retrieved February 12, 2024, from https://assets.publishing.service.gov.uk/media/628666598fa8f556165a1e4b/Ethnicity_and_childrens_social_care.pdf

Ahrens, K. R., Garrison, M. M., & Courtney, M. E. (2014). Health outcomes in young adults from foster care and economically diverse backgrounds. *Pediatrics, 134*(6), 1067–1074. https://doi.org/10.1542/peds.2014-1150

The Annie E. Casey Foundation. (2021). *KIDS count data center.* https://datacenter.aecf.org/data/tables

The Annie E. Casey Foundation. (2023). *Child welfare and foster care statistics.* Blog. https://www.aecf.org/blog/child-welfare-and-foster-care-statistics

Arkansas Department of Human Services. (2024). Division of Children & Family Services Policy & procedure manual. https://humanservices.arkansas.gov/wp-content/uploads/Policy-Manual-January-2024.pdf

Asif, N., Breen, C., & Wells, R. (2023). Influence of placement stability on developmental outcomes of children and young people in out-of-home care: Findings from the pathways of care longitudinal study. *Child Abuse & Neglect*, 106145. https://doi.org/10.1016/j.chiabu.2023.106145

Baccara, M., Collard-Wexler, A., Felli, L., & Yariv, L. (2014). Child-adoption matching: Preferences for gender and race. *American Economic Journal: Applied Economics, 6*(3), 133–158. https://doi.org/10.1257/app.6.3.133

Bilaver, L. A., Havlicek, J., & Davis, M. M. (2020). Prevalence of special health care needs among foster youth in a nationally representative survey. *JAMA Pediatrics, 174*(7), 727–729. https://doi.org/10.1001/jamapediatrics.2020.0298

CA Penal Code § 11165.2. (2022). https://law.justia.com/codes/california/2022/code-pen/part-4/title-1/chapter-2/article-2-5/section-11165-2/

California Legislative Analyst Office. (1996). *Child abuse and neglect in California part I.* https://lao.ca.gov/1996/010596_child_abuse/cw11096a.html

Chapin Hall. (2022). *Child and family well-being system: Economic and concrete supports as a core component.* https://www.chapinhall.org/wp-content/uploads/Economic-Supports-deck.pdf

Child Abuse and Treatment Act Reauthorization Act of 2010 (P.L. 111–320), 42 U.S.C. §5101, Note (§3). https://www.congress.gov/111/plaws/publ320/PLAW-111publ320.pdf

Child Welfare Information Gateway. (2021). *Child welfare practice to address racial disproportionality and disparity.* U.S. Department of Health and Human Services, Administration for Children and Families, Children's Bureau. https://www.childwelfare.gov/resources/child-welfare-practice-address-racial-disproportionality-and-disparity/

Child Welfare Information Gateway. (2023a). *Mandatory reporting of child abuse and neglect.* U.S. Department of Health and Human Services, Administration for Children and Families, Children's Bureau. https://www.childwelfare.gov/resources/mandatory-reporting-child-abuse-and-neglect/

Child Welfare Information Gateway. (2023b). *Separating poverty from neglect in child welfare.* U.S. Department of Health and Human Services, Administration for Children and Families, Children's Bureau. https://www.childwelfare.gov/pubs/bulletins-povertyneglect

Children's Bureau. (2019). *Report to Congress on state child welfare expenditures.* Children's Bureau. https://www.acf.hhs.gov/cb/report/cwo-2019

Children's Bureau. (2021). *Child welfare outcomes report data. Outcome 6: Placement stability.* https://cwoutcomes.acf.hhs.gov/cwodatasite/sixOneLessThan12/index

Children's Commission. (2023). *Texas child welfare law bench book.* https://www.texaschildrenscommission.gov/media/dfxpfdl5/2023-child-welfare-bench-book-final-online.pdf

Clemens, E. V., Klopfenstein, K., Lalonde, T. L., & Tis, M. (2018). The effects of placement and school stability on academic growth trajectories of students in foster care. *Children and Youth Services Review*, *87*, 86–94. https://doi.org/10.1016/j.childyouth.2018.02.015

Combs, K. M., Begun, S., Rinehart, D. J., & Taussig, H. (2018). Pregnancy and childbearing among young adults who experienced foster care. *Child Maltreatment*, *23*(2), 166–174. https://doi.org/10.1177/1077559517733816

Congressional Record Services. (2023). *Child welfare: Purposes, federal programs, and funding.* Retrieved February 6, 2024, from https://sgp.fas.org/crs/misc/IF10590.pdf

Connell, C. M., Katz, K. H., Saunders, L., & Tebes, J. K. (2006). Leaving foster care: The influence of child and case characteristics on foster care exit rates. *Children and Youth Services Review*, *28*(7), 780–798. https://doi.org/10.1016/j.childyouth.2005.08.007

Coulton, C., Crampton, C., Cho, Y., & Kim, S. (2015). Effects of foster care and juvenile justice involvement on early adult outcomes: A study of Cleveland's youth. In *Case Western Reserve, center on urban poverty and community development, Jack, Joseph, and Morton Mandel school of applied social sciences.* Center on Urban Poverty and Community Development, Case Western Reserve University. https://case.edu/socialwork/povertycenter/sites/default/files/2018-09/2.pdf

Courtney, M., Brown, A., Katz, C., Love, K., & Klodnick, V. (2011). *Midwest evaluation of the adult functioning of former foster youth: Outcomes at age 26.* https://www.chapinhall.org/wp-content/uploads/Midwest-Eval-Outcomes-at-Age-26.pdf

Courtney, M. E., Okpych, N. J., Harty, J., Feng, H., Park, S., Powers, J., Nadon, M., Ditto, D. J., & Park, K. (2020). *Findings from the California Youth Transitions to Adulthood Study (CalYOUTH): Conditions of youth at age 23.* Chapin Hall at the University of Chicago. https://www.chapinhall.org/wp-content/uploads/CY_YT_RE1020.pdf

Courtney, M. E., & Wong, Y.-L. I. (1996). Comparing the timing of exits from substitute care. *Children and Youth Services Review*, *18*(4), 307–334. https://doi.org/10.1016/0190-7409(96)00008-4

Cram, F., Gulliver, P., Ota, R., & Wilson, M. (2015). Understanding overrepresentation of indigenous children in child welfare data: An application of the Drake risk and bias models. *Child Maltreatment*, *20*(3), 170–182. https://doi.org/10.1177/1077559515580392

Culhane, D., Byrne, T., Metraux, S., Moreno, M., Toros, H., & Stevens, M. (2011). *Young adult outcomes of youth exiting dependent or delinquent care in Los Angeles County*. https://shnny.org/uploads/Young-Adult-Outcomes-LA-2011.pdf

Cunningham, S., & Finlay, K. (2013). Parental substance use and foster care: Evidence from two methamphetamine supply shocks. *Economic Inquiry*, *51*(1), 764–782. https://doi.org/10.1111/j.1465-7295.2012.00481.x

Currie, J., & Widom, C. S. (2010). Long-term consequences of child abuse and neglect on adult economic well-being. *Child Maltreatment*, *15*(2), 111–120. https://doi.org/10.1177/1077559509355316

DePasquale, S. (2022). *Abuse, neglect, dependency, and termination of parental rights proceedings in North Carolina*. The School of Government at the University of North Carolina. Retrieved February 1, 2024, from https://www.sog.unc.edu/sites/default/files/full_text_books/All%20chapters.pdf

Dimitrova-Stull, A. (2014). *Violence towards children in the EU*. European Parliamentary Research Service. Retrieved February 12, 2024, from https://www.europarl.europa.eu/RegData/etudes/IDAN/2014/542139/EPRS_IDA(2014)542139_EN.pdf

European Commission, The Directorate-General for Employment, Social Affairs and Inclusion, Lerch, V., & Nordenmark Severinsson, A. (2020). *Feasibility study for a child guarantee: Target group discussion paper on children in alternative care*. Publications Office of the European Union. https://doi.org/doi/10.2767/461907

Doyle, J. J., Jr. (2008). Child protection and adult crime: Using investigator assignment to estimate causal effects of foster care. *Journal of Political Economy*, *116*(4), 746–770. https://doi.org/10.1086/590216

Eurochild. (2021). *Better data for better child protection systems in Europe: Mapping how data on children in alternative care are collected, analysed and published across 28 European countries*. Technical Report of the Datacare Project. Retrieved February 12, 2024, from https://eurochild.org/uploads/2022/02/UNICEF-DataCare-Technical-Report-Final-1.pdf

Evangelist, M., Thomas, M. M. C., & Waldfogel, J. (2023). Child protective services contact and youth outcomes. *Child Abuse & Neglect*, *136*, 105994. https://doi.org/10.1016/j.chiabu.2022.105994

Fisher, M., Hodapp, R., & Dykens, E. (2008). Child abuse among children with disabilities: What we know and what we need to know. *International Review of Research in Mental Retardation*, *35*, 251–289. https://doi.org/10.1016/S0074-7750(07)35007-6

Florida Statute Title V Chapter 39. (2023). http://www.leg.state.fl.us/statutes/index.cfm?App_mode=Display_Statute&URL=0000-0099/0039/Sections/0039.01.html

Font, S. A., & Maguire-Jack, K. (2020). It's not "just poverty": Educational, social, and economic functioning among young adults exposed to childhood neglect, abuse, and poverty. *Child Abuse & Neglect*, *101*, 104356. https://doi.org/10.1016/j.chiabu.2020.104356

Foster Care Review Office. (2017). *Local review board member guide book*. https://fcro.nebraska.gov/pdf/2017-guide-book-abuse-neglect.pdf

Fowler, P. J., Marcal, K. E., Zhang, J., Day, O., & Landsverk, J. (2017). Homelessness and aging out of foster care: A national comparison of child welfare-involved adolescents. *Children and Youth Services Review*, *77*, 27–33. https://doi.org/10.1016/j.childyouth.2017.03.017

George, R. M. (1990). The reunification process in substitute care. *Social Service Review*, *64*(3), 422–457. https://doi.org/10.1086/603780

Gerassi, L. (2015). From exploitation to industry: Definitions, risks, and consequences of domestic sexual exploitation and sex work among women and girls. *Journal of Health and Human Behavior*, *25*(6), 591–605. https://doi.org/10.1080/10911359.2014.991055

Gross, M., & Baron, E. J. (2020). Temporary stays and persistent gains: The causal effects of foster care. *PSN: Other Social Welfare Policy (Topic)*. https://max-gross.github.io/website_documents/foster_care.pdf

Johnson, L., Slayter, E., & Livingstone, A. (2020). Locating the intersections of disability, race and ethnicity in adoption rates among foster children introduction. *Adoption Quarterly*, *23*, 1–25. https://doi.org/10.1080/10926755.2020.1719252

Kang-Yi, C. D., & Adams, D. R. (2017). Youth with behavioral health disorders aging out of foster care: A systematic review and implications for policy, research, and practice. *The Journal of Behavioral Health Services & Research*, *44*(1), 25–51. https://doi.org/10.1007/s11414-015-9480-9

Kelly, B., & Haskins, P. (2021). Dual system youth: At the intersection of child maltreatment and delinquency. *NIJ Journal*, *283*. https://nij.ojp.gov/topics/articles/dual-system-youth-intersection-child-maltreatment-and-delinquency

Kim, H., Wildeman, C., Jonson-Reid, M., & Drake, B. (2017). Lifetime prevalence of investigating child maltreatment among US children. *American Journal of Public Health*, *107*(2), 274–280. https://doi.org/10.2105/ajph.2016.303545

Kindler, H. (2023). *Mapping child protection systems in the EU (27) Germany*. Retrieved February 12, 2024, from https://fra.europa.eu/sites/default/files/fra_uploads/de_-_report_-_mapping_child_protection_systems_-_2023.pdf

LaBrenz, C. A., Findley, E., Graaf, G., Baiden, P., Kim, J., Choi, M. J., & Chakravarty, S. (2021). Racial/ethnic disproportionality in reunification across U.S. child welfare systems. *Child Abuse & Neglect*, *114*, 104894. https://doi.org/10.1016/j.chiabu.2020.104894

Lafourcade, M., & Dartigue, G. (2023). *Mapping child protection systems in the EU (27) France*. Retrieved February 12, 2024, from https://fra.europa.eu/sites/default/files/fra_uploads/fr_-_report_-_mapping_child_protection_systems_-_2023.pdf

Lee, J. S., Gimm, G., Mohindroo, M., & Lever, L. (2023). Assessing homelessness and incarceration among youth aging out of foster care, by type of disability. *Child and Adolescent Social Work Journal*, *40*(6), 743–759. https://doi.org/10.1007/s10560-022-00817-9

Lightfoot, E., & DeZelar, S. (2016). The experiences and outcomes of children in foster care who were removed because of a parental disability. *Children and Youth Services Review*, *62*, 22–28. https://doi.org/10.1016/j.childyouth.2015.11.029

Lindner, A. R., & Hanlon, R. (2024). Outcomes of youth with foster care experiences based on permanency outcome – Adoption, aging out, long-term foster care, and reunification: A systematic review. *Children and Youth Services Review*, *156*, 107366. https://doi.org/10.1016/j.childyouth.2023.107366

Lloyd Sieger, M. H. (2020). Foster care factors and permanency for children with substance-related removals. *Families in Society*, *102*(1), 91–103. https://doi.org/10.1177/1044389420947225

Meier, L., & Möstl, M. (2023). *Mapping child protection systems in the EU (27) Austria*. Retrieved February 12, 2024, from https://fra.europa.eu/sites/default/files/fra_uploads/at_-_report_-_mapping_child_protection_systems_-_2023.pdf

The National Academies of Sciences, Engineering, and Medicine. (2023). *Reducing intergenerational poverty*. The National Academies Press. https://doi.org/10.17226/27058

National Association of Counsel for Children. (2023). *State models of children's legal representation*. https://counselforkids.org/wp-content/uploads/2023/05/Model-of-Rep-Chart-2023.pdf

National Council on Disability. (2012). *Rocking the cradle: Ensuring the rights of parents with disabilities and their children*. https://www.ncd.gov/publications/2012/Sep272012

National Research Center for Parents with Disabilities. (2022). *Recurrence of substantiated reports of child maltreatment by low-income parents with disabilities: The importance of poverty and race*. Brandeis University. https://heller.brandeis.edu/parents-with-disabilities/data-hub/child-welfare-family-law-rights/recurrence.html

Nixon, K., Tutty, L., Downe, P., Gorkoff, K., & Ursel, J. (2002). The everyday occurrence: Violence in the lives of girls exploited through prostitution. *Violence Against Women*, *8*(9), 1016–1043. https://doi.org/10.1177/107780120200800902

Office of Children and Families in the Court, Administrative Office of Pennsylvania Courts. (2019). *Pennsylvania dependency benchbook*. Retrieved February 6, 2024, from https://ocfcpacourts.us/wp-content/uploads/2020/05/2019-Pennsylvania-Dependency-Benchbook-3rd-Edition-Interactive-002427.pdf

Okpych, N. J., & Courtney, M. E. (2018). Barriers to degree completion for college students with foster care histories: Results from a 10-year longitudinal study. *Journal of College Student Retention: Research, Theory & Practice*, *23*(1), 28–54. https://doi.org/10.1177/1521025118791776

Ontario Human Rights Commission. (2018). *Interrupted childhoods: Over-representation of Indigenous and Black children in Ontario child welfare*. Retrieved February 12, 2024, from https://www.ohrc.on.ca/en/interrupted-childhoods

Osborne, C., Warner-Doe, H., LeClear, M., & Sexton, H. (2020). The effect of CASA on child welfare permanency outcomes. *Child Maltreatment*, *25*(3), 328–338. https://doi.org/10.1177/1077559519879510

Pecora, P., Kessler, R., Williams, J., O'Brien, K., Downs, A., English, D., White, J., Hiripi, E., White, C., Wiggins, T., & Holmes, K. (2005). *Improving family foster care: Findings from the Northwest Foster Care Alumni study*. https://psycnet.apa.org/doi/10.1016/j.childyouth.2006.04.003

Peterson, C., Florence, C., & Klevens, J. (2018). The economic burden of child maltreatment in the United States, 2015. *Child Abuse & Neglect*, *86*, 178–183. https://doi.org/10.1016/j.chiabu.2018.09.018

Petrowski, N., Cappa, C., & Gross, P. (2017). Estimating the number of children in formal alternative care: Challenges and results. *Child Abuse & Neglect*, *70*, 388–398. https://doi.org/10.1016/j.chiabu.2016.11.026

Platt, C., & Gephart, S. M. (2022). Placement disruption of children with disabilities in foster care. *Journal of Pediatric Nursing*, *66*, 30–35. https://doi.org/10.1016/j.pedn.2022.05.004

Rourke, B. (2021). *Blighted lives: Romani children in state care*. European Roma Rights Centre. Retrieved February 12, 2024, from http://www.errc.org/uploads/upload_en/file/5284_file1_blighted-lives-romani-children-in-state-care.pdf

Rubin, D. M., O'Reilly, A. L., Luan, X., & Localio, A. R. (2007). The impact of placement stability on behavioral well-being for children in foster care. *Pediatrics*, *119*(2), 336–344. https://doi.org/10.1542/peds.2006-1995

Ryan, J. P., & Testa, M. F. (2005). Child maltreatment and juvenile delinquency: Investigating the role of placement and placement instability. *Children and Youth Services Review*, *27*(3), 227–249. https://doi.org/10.1016/j.childyouth.2004.05.007

Sepulveda, K., & Williams, S. (2019). One in three children entered foster care in 2017 because of parental drug abuse. *Child Trends*. https://www.childtrends.org/blog/one-in-three-children-entered-foster-care-in-fy-2017-because-of-parental-drug-abuse

Slayter, E. (2016). Youth with disabilities in the United States Child Welfare System. *Children and Youth Services Review*, *64*, 155–165. https://doi.org/10.1016/j.childyouth.2016.03.012

Stein, R. E., Hurlburt, M. S., Heneghan, A. M., Zhang, J., Rolls-Reutz, J., Silver, E. J., Fisher, E., Landsverk, J., & Horwitz, S. M. (2013). Chronic conditions among children investigated by child welfare: A national sample. *Pediatrics*, *131*(3), 455–462.

TennesseeCourt Improvement Program. (2008). *Child dependency benchbook* (6th ed.). https://www.tncourts.gov/sites/default/files/docs/child_dependency_benchbook.pdf

Tex. Fam. Code § 261.001(1). (2023). https://statutes.capitol.texas.gov/Docs/FA/htm/FA.261.htm

Trivedi, S. (2019). The harm of child removal. *New York University Review of Law & Social Change*, *43*, 523. https://scholarworks.law.ubalt.edu/all_fac/1085/

UNICEF. (2023). *Children in alternative care*. Retrieved February 12, 2024, from https://data.unicef.org/topic/child-protection/children-alternative-care/

United States Census Bureau. (2022). *US Census quickfacts, population estimates, July 2022*. https://www.census.gov/quickfacts/geo/chart/ID/PST045222

U.S. Department of Health and Human Services (HHS). (2021). *The AFCARS report #29*. Retrieved February 1, 2024, from https://www.acf.hhs.gov/sites/default/files/documents/cb/afcars-report-29.pdf

U.S. Department of Health & Human Services, Administration for Children and Families, Administration on Children, Youth and Families, Children's Bureau. (2023). *Child maltreatment 2021*. https://www.acf.hhs.gov/cb/data-research/child-maltreatment

Virginia Administrative Code. (2020). *22VAC40-705-30*. https://law.lis.virginia.gov/admincode/title22/agency40/chapter705/section30/

Walsh, W., & Mattingly, M. (2013). Psychotropic medication use among children in the child welfare system. *The Carsey School of Public Policy at the Scholars' Repository*, *187*. https://scholars.unh.edu/carsey/187

Wildeman, C., & Emanuel, N. (2014). Cumulative risks of foster care placement by age 18 for U.S. children, 2000–2011. *PLoS One*, *9*(3), e92785. https://doi.org/10.1371/journal.pone.0092785

Williams, G. (1996). *Childhood matters: Report of the National Commission of Inquiry into the Prevention of Child Abuse* (Vol. 1). Report. The Stationery Office.

Williams, S., Dalela, R., & Vandivere, S. (2023). In defining maltreatment, nearly half of states do not specifically exempt families' financial inability to provide. *Child Trends*. https://www.childtrends.org/blog/in-defining-maltreatment-nearly-half-of-states-do-not-specifically-exempt-families-financial-inability-to-provide

Yamat, M. (2020). The foster-care-to- prison pipeline. *Justice Policy Journal*. Retrieved February 12, 2024, from https://www.cjcj.org/media/import/documents/the_foster_care_to_prison_pipeline.pdf

Youth Law Center. (2018). *Overview of the foster care system in California*. https://ylc.org/wp-content/uploads/2018/11/Foster-Care-Overview-FACT-SHEET-040116.pdf

2 The Best Interest of Children

Back in the seventh floor courtroom, best interest is the core discussion in front of the bench. Lawyers might argue that it is best for this child to be adopted and for that child to age out. It is best for the child to have parental visits even though mom still test positive for drugs. It is best for the child to be placed with their sibling. It is best for the child to be removed from the home. It is best for the child to go to be in therapy. It is best for the child to stay in their original school. It is best for the child to be on psychotropic medication.

After witness testimony and argument, the court would on most occasions make a ruling for a written order. This court finds that it is in the child's best interest to . . . suspend visits with family, to undergo a new psychological test, to extend foster care jurisdiction until they turn 21. But what exactly does best interest even mean?

In a nutshell, best interest refers to factors related to the child's stability in their placement, their time in the child welfare system, their physical, emotional and living needs, their safety considerations, their wishes and the individual characteristics that are important to their identity. This amalgamation of a best interest definition is my attempt to simplify a complex legal doctrine, but it is far from including the full scope of best interest. I will spoil the ending of the chapter and say that I am one of many that have strong criticisms of best interests as a legal framework for decision-making. Before I move to the critiques though, I will attempt to explain what best interest of the child means for governments, courts, the child welfare system and the individuals within. Though be prepared because best interest and simple definitions have long been enemies.

In the US there is no standard definition and states are free to define best interest in whatever way they see fit, with some codifying multiple best interest factors and some pulling them only from case law (CWIG, 2020). Though there is some majority agreement with factors such as health and safety mentioned in more than half of US jurisdictions and family preservation and permanency listed in about 20, most jurisdictions work with their own factors (CWIG, 2020).

The Oregon Statute (2022) has six factors and identifies the emotional ties of the child. The Alabama Code (2022) also has six factors and includes the goal of reunification of families. Texas lists the child's desires and age and

DOI: 10.4324/9781003510253-2

notes that its factors are non-exhaustive and courts are free to consider factors not mentioned in the law (Children's Commission, 2023). Tennessee courts have nine statutory factors and states that conflict between the rights of the parent and the best interest of the child should be made in favor of the child (Tennessee Court Improvement Program, 2008). Nevada Code (2022) highlights some negative factors, such as exposure to domestic violence and family violence related crimes being against a child's best interest.

The above cited examples are taken from state laws that courts and judges might cite in their rulings. There are also best interest factors and standards found throughout CPS agency guidelines that are applied every day, but do not have the same legal weight. The Missouri's CPS manual links child best interest with the least restrictive placement (Missouri Department of Social Services, 2021). Michigan CPS instructs its staff to consider the impact of trauma when making a placement in the child's best interest (Michigan Department of Health and Human Services, 2023). Kansas CPS holds a best interest staffing for children that can be adopted and considers factors, such as the child willingness to be adopted and their understanding of their legal circumstances (Kansas Department for Children and Families, 2022). Washington CPS in their permanency planning guidelines list medical issues and the developmental needs of the child as factors in determining their permanency best interest (Washington State Department of Children Youth and Families, 2022).

In their book on best interest in foster care Font and Gershoff (2020) wrote that while permanency, stability and safety are generally identified as factors these alone are not enough to produce a healthy child and later a healthy adult and that social and emotional factors were at least as important. They wrote that the underpinning legal presumption of the US foster care system is that it is in children's best interest to remain with their parents (Font & Gershoff, 2020).

Interestingly, both the proponents of strengthening families to take fewer children into care and those that advocate for earlier removals for the safety of the child, both use the language of best interest in their arguments (Font & Gershoff, 2020). This becomes especially complicated in issues of neglect, which often does not have the immediacy of risk that abuse cases do. However, Font and Gershoff (2020) wrote that delaying foster care even in neglect cases comes with its own associated risk to the child from greater exposure to maltreatment.

As mentioned before, there are multitudes of court cases discussing best interest both in a child custody and in a foster care context. Because the primary reasons state high courts review best interest decisions is when parental rights are terminated, the vast majority of case law deals with courts applying best interest to termination proceedings. For example, the Tennessee Supreme Court (2017) in *In Re Gabriella D. et al.* ruled that all nine statutory best interest factors had to be considered, but that a best interest decision was more than simply weighing the factors against each other. The Maine Supreme Judicial Court (2023) ruled in *In re Children of Quincy A.* that a child's need for permanency alone was not sufficient for best interest termination. Contrastingly, the Arizona Supreme Court (2018) held in *Alma S. v. Department of*

Child Safety that a child adoptability could be the deciding best interest factor when terminating a parent's right. These cases are just a few illustrations, as thorough discussion of state case law on best interests could fill a bookshelf on its own. Still even a bookshelf worth of case law would not contain a consensus on best interest.

The United States Supreme Court has also heard repeated cases with best interest implications, such as *Smith v. Organization of Foster Families*, 431 U.S. 816 (1977), *Santosky v. Kramer*, 455 US 745 (1982), *Reno v. Flores*, 507 US 292 (1993), *Troxel v. Granville*, 530 U.S. 57 (2000), *Fulton v. Philadelphia*, 593 US ___ (2021), *Haaland v. Brackeen*, 599 US ___ (2023). None of those cases produced a federal standard definition of best interests or even a particularly useful guideline.

Briefly, it should also be noted that best interests of the child standard has moved beyond just custody and foster care decisions and has been adapted into other foster care adjacent domains.

The federal, Every Student Succeeds Act (2015) (ESSA), applies best interest language to foster children with a mandate that child welfare and child education agencies must work together to determine if a staying in their original school is in the best interest of a child that has come into care. ESSA (2015) factors include school relationships, academic needs, but also case permanency goals.

US immigration law also has adapted the best interest standard for certain classes of juvenile asylum seekers (Harvard Law Review, 2021). Minors with no parents that have been abandoned, abused or neglected may apply for a special immigration class known as Special Immigrant Juvenile Status so long as it is determined that returning to their country of origin would not be in their best interest. However, the US specifically rejects best interests as a standard for most refugee children (Harvard Law Review, 2021).

The best interest of the child has also found its way into medical practice with pediatricians being asked to make medical decisions in the child's best interests (Bowyer, 2016). März (2022) wrote that best interests is perhaps the principal internationally accepted guideline for making ethical medical decisions and included child capacity and medical treatment team and family decision-making as factors that should be considered. Best interest for child patients should be a balance between the proposed benefits of treatments versus the burdens that those treatments might entail (Weise et al., 2017). Best interest in medical decisions for children also has crossover with foster care best interest in that doctors can use it to overrule parental judgment (Racine et al., 2013) and they can use it to overrule child patient objections (Wasserman et al., 2019).

International Perspective of Best Interest

Perhaps most importantly the best interest of the child has become a pillar of international law. Though the previous focus of this chapter has been on the United States child welfare system, best interest is the global standard for decisions regarding children. This is exemplified most famously in the United Nations Convention on the Rights of the Child, which (CRC) (1989) places best interest of significant importance. Article 3 of the CRC states "*In all actions concerning children, whether undertaken by public or private, social welfare institutions, courts of law, administrative authorities or legislative bodies, the best interests of the child shall be a primary consideration*". Best interest is mentioned seven more times in the CRC (1989) in Articles 9, 18, 20, 2, 37 and 40. The CRC has also been signed by ever country on the planet except the United States, making it a truly universal standard (Skivenes & Sørsdal, 2018).

The UN Committee on the Rights of the Child (2013) in their discussion of best interest note that it is a concrete substantive right, a legal principle open to interpretation and a specific procedural rule for individual cases. In their 21-page analysis of best interests under the CRC, the committee never establishes a full definition, but the authors do write that it is a complex, but flexible legal notion that needs to be applied on an individual specific case basis. They go on to write that best interest should be the primary consideration for all child related decisions and the most important for any decision involving adoptions. Finally, they establish that best interest are in alignment with other portions of the CRC, such as the right to be free from discrimination, the right to life and the right to be heard (UN Committee on the Rights of the Child, 2013). Though not defined in either treaty, best interest of the child is also identified in both the Charter of Fundamental Rights of the European Union and the Council of Europe Convention on the Protection of Children against Sexual Exploitation and Sexual Abuse (European Union Agency for Fundamental Rights, 2022).

The former Commissioner for Human Rights Council of Europe argued that while bets interests are not directly defined, the sum total guidance of the CRC provides a useful framework for understanding the concept (Hammarberg, 2008). Therefore, all of the norms mentioned in the CRC are what constitutes best interests. So the right to a family, the right to education, the right to be heard, the right to be free from violence, the right to be free from exploitation as well the other rights listed on the 41 human right CRC articles are all together in a child's best interest (Hammarberg, 2008).

This idea that a collection of human rights of the child constitutes best interests has garnered support among the literature on the topic (Degol & Dinku, 2011; Logan, 2008; Juhlin, 2023; Sormunen, 2020) and is supported by UN commentary (Ruggiero, 2022). However, UN bodies have been careful not to rank and order the rights as they are supposed to exist equally and to encompass both the child's present situation and their future with the understanding that an adult's opinion of best interest cannot be used to extinguish the child's fundamental rights (Ruggiero, 2022).

The Council of Europe (COE) (2011) in its guidance to its member state identified best interest as a fundamental principal in providing services to children, but again they did not provide a definition, only guidelines as to what best interest services might include. They recommended services that promote inclusion, discourage discrimination, respect the child's dignity and promote independence (COE, 2011).

In a further effort to clarify the term, the COE (2016) would go on to produce a 162-page book with 21 authors each discussing a portion of best interest as it related to a different aspects of child welfare and decision-making. Though the term is never precisely identified in the book, Llorenz (2016) wrote that it should be objective and that

> the best interests of five different children should prompt us to make five different determinations (given that no two children are alike in the same circumstances and in the same situation). But the assessment and determination of one child's best interests made by five adults individually in the adoption of a decision should arrive at the same result.
>
> (p.12)

In addition to domestic child welfare, because of the CRC and subsequent treaties, best interest has also become the standard for most international child refugee law (McAdam, 2007). As is the case in other areas of the law, the term is applied and understood differently depending on the individual context and the nation making the decisions. Still, high courts across the globe routinely use best interest of the child language in making refugee decisions (McAdam, 2007) and it has been argued that the standard actually provides superior refugee protection than international refugee law (Pobjoy, 2015).

As there is significant overlap between child refugee and child protection populations, it is helpful to also look at how best interest is considered in the refugee context. UN High Commissioner for Refugees (UNHCR) (2021) in its nearly 200-page guidance on understanding and applying best interest describes a complex six step best interest procedure process that includes both a best interest assessment, a best interest determination and a best interest determination review that each includes information about the child's history, family, living conditions, health, safety and daily activities. The European Asylum Support Office (EASO) (2019) in its 48-page guide, instructed workers to balance and weigh the various rights of the child along with the individual case factors. The EASO identified 12 key, but non-exhaustive, best interest factors, such as nondiscrimination, family unity, health and school needs, the child's capacity, identity and needs and the child's vulnerability and safety. Coupled with these factors is the admonishment that they all must be considered in light of the child's gender, ethnic, national, socioeconomic and political identity (EASO, 2019).

As a brief aside, the fact that these organizations need book length documents to explain what five words mean, should give some indication of the coming criticisms of best interests. There are whole courses in law school covering an entire area of law that require less explanation.

Best interest also has been adopted in treaties globally, the African Unions' African Charter on the Rights and Welfare of the Child (1999) makes best interest of the child the primary consideration and title of Article 4. It mentions best interest eight more times throughout the treaty regarding children's rights to participate, to freedom and to family matters. The South Asian Association for Regional Cooperation incorporates best interest as one of the guiding principles of its Convention on Regional Arrangements for the Promotion of Child Welfare in South Asia (2002). Additionally, best interest of the child has made its way into numerous national constitutions, such as Norway, Belgium, Malta, Ireland (Sloth-Nielsen & Oliel, 2019), South Africa (Skelton, 2019) and Zimbabwe (Moyo, 2019).

The adoption of the CRC meant that individual nations also began using best interest language and best interest determinations in the child welfare systems; however, even similar Western nations do not have precise agreement on what best interest actually means (Skivenes & Sørsdal, 2018). When researchers compared the best interest factors of 14 wealthy countries, they found that the only common factor was that all had procedural requirements incorporated into best interest decision-making. The majority had factors related to child participation, child's needs, permanency and child protection, but other factors had less agreement. The researchers also divided the countries along what they labeled weak and strong discretion and noted that fewer factors in the best interest definition meant that the decision-makers were more responsible for forming their own intrinsic idea of what best interest meant (Skivenes & Sørsdal, 2018). Relatedly, in a COE study of European dependency law, Wenke (2021) wrote that in court proceedings best interest is still not well understood or implemented in member states and recommended that courts and practitioners needed guidance for making better decisions.

International courts have also had a hand in shaping best interest discussions. The European Court of Human Rights (ECtHR) has heard multiple cases involving the intersection of the termination of parental rights and best interest with most of those cases turning on interpretations of Article 8 of the European Convention on Human Rights (ECHR), which establishes a right to family integrity (Turković, 2013).

ECtHR case law begins with the assumption that the child's best interests are first found within the family environment, but best interest shifts once that home is deemed to be unsafe (Norwegian National Human Rights Institute, 2021). The ECtHR has also not adopted a standard definition for best interest but in the case *Y.C. v. United Kingdom* (2012), the court broadly adopted the language from UK law as the nine elements that would need to be weighed when making a best interest determination. These elements will likely sound familiar as they include the child's wishes, needs, background and relationships.

History Best Interest Child Welfare

It is also helpful at this point to understand that best interest as a legal doctrine has a long history and that its meaning has changed over time. Kohm (2008) traced the history of best interest from 18th century American and British common law and found that early American laws regarding adoption and even juvenile justice embraced best interest as a legal concept. Kohm (2008) argued that this best interest of the child doctrine is a distinctly American concept that arose out of the industrial revolution and new philosophical beliefs about the purpose of childhood that placed less emphasis on children as workers and more on their emotional well-being.

For most of history the law considered children to be the property of their fathers; however, the law eventually began to embrace a notion known as tender years, which identified young children as being better cared for by their mothers (Carbone, 2014) The first actual use of the term best interests in American case law comes from an 1815 Pennsylvania child custody case where the court wrestled with the competing notion of father's rights and the tender years doctrine (Kohm, 2008). Best interest developed from these early child custody cases that focused on abusive or non-supportive fathers as a legal reason for judicial intervention. This eventually led to the use of best interest as the legal standard for all custody cases and from there to other child related decisions (Carbone, 2014).

The adoption of best interest into the CRC led to its spread around the world and to its spread beyond custody disputes and adoption, which Kohm (2008) argued is the origin of the legal doctrine of children's rights.

So where does all of this leave us in our understanding of what best interest actually means? It depends on the country, on the individual jurisdiction, on the facts of the case, on the type of case, on the context to which it is being applied, the person and their role making the decision, the legal factors that may or may not exists to guide decision-makers, the weight and rank they give the factors and which factors they actually consider. Despite being more than three centuries old and being used almost universally for child welfare related decisions, the legal definition of best interest is still imprecise, unclear and subject to debate.

Kensie was 16-years-old and had spent the last two years as a runaway from care. She had been living with her boyfriend and selling drugs. She had a long history of substance abuse before she ran from care, but when they broke up, she called CPS and was placed first in an emergency shelter and then a few days later at her grandmother's home. That placement broke down within a couple of weeks as Kensie and her grandmother fought over her continued marijuana use. CPS returned her to the emergency shelter, but she requested to live with a family friend named Clark. Clark owned his own home, had known Kensie since she was a baby, lived in the school district Kensie preferred and was willing to take her in, but he had a decade old drug possession arrest. CASA and CPS refused to place her with Clark saying it was not in her best interest and began looking for a placement at an RTC. When Kensie learned that she would be moved to an RTC, she cut her wrist and attempted suicide. Emergency shelter staff found her bleeding out on the floor of her room. She was taken to the hospital where she stayed overnight. Because of her history with drugs, running away and now a suicide attempt, CASA and

CPS thought her best interests were to be in a locked down facility. Kensie said she would rather die and would hurt herself again if CPS attempted to place her in an RTC. Her best interest was to live in a normal home with someone that knew her.

How Courts and Attorneys View Best Interest

Given the nebulous legal definition of best interests, it is helpful to next try to get a sense of how professionals in the child welfare field think about the concept. Unfortunately, this is not well researched question despite the surplus of material about best interest as a legal representational model and legal concept.

In a qualitative interview study of 50 New York child welfare professionals that included 19 child welfare attorneys and 8 judges, Banach (1998) asked each participant to read a short best interest definition and then reflect about a recent case in which best interest was considered. The participants identified three broad categories of best interest factors that influenced their decisions (Banach, 1998).

The first category was precipitating events such as those changes in the family that led to removal (Banach, 1998). Secondly were guiding principles of limiting the amount of time a child was in care, preserving the family, the family's culture and how to limit future harm to the child. Lastly were specific case variables about the family, the child, the alternative caregiver and the child welfare system itself. The researcher wrote that while there was some general agreement among participants about the factors, each participant reported that they must be considered on an individual case basis. However, there was no agreement on best interest guidelines and each decision was subjective (Banach, 1998).

Unfortunately, lawyers and judges are not separated in this study, so it is impossible to tell if their opinions differ from other child welfare professionals. Given that lawyers and judges make up the bulk of the participants, it seems reasonable, though, to include these findings here.

Another bit of research that might help make some sense of the legal community's understanding of best interest comes from a vignette study that asked Norwegian judges to determine if it was in the best interest of a foster child should be adopted or kept in care. Helland (2020) identified six factors the judges used when making the determination. While the judges considered the child's attachment and permanency needs, they placed the greatest weight on the child's age and their time in care (Helland, 2020).

Another Norwegian study examined the best interest decisions of three contested foster care adoption decisions from the Norwegian Supreme Court (Skivenes, 2010). A document analysis of the similar cases revealed that the court made its best interest adoption decisions based on notions of stability and permanence, contact and relationship with both the biological and adoptive families and the child's views. However, Skivenes (2010) identified great variation in how these factors were considered by the court and what evidence they gave weight to in each case with the ultimate conclusion by the researcher that the case decisions were all rather arbitrary.

In a follow-up to the Skivenes study, Helland (2021) examined four more Norwegian Supreme Court foster care adoption cases using a document analysis approach. The author wrote that the court centered it best interest decisions around four guiding arguments. The court weighed between the child's right to a new family, the child's right to their birth family, the time they had been in care and finally, the notion that a child is vulnerable and requires safety and stability. Unlike the prior study, children's views were not considered prominently in the analysis. Helland (2021) also identified inconsistency in how the court applied these arguments.

Finally, in a systemic case study analysis of best interests in both the Supreme Court of Finland and ECtHR cases between 2001and 2014, Sormunen (2021) found significant discrepancies in how both courts approach the standard. The Finnish court often applied best interests to child immigrant, education and welfare cases, but did not apply the term in all of the cases and applied it inconsistently among the types of cases. Similarly, the ECtHR also applied essentially a different best interest standard on child welfare than child immigration cases with the courts weighing child wishes, family unity and child age differently. For example, the ECtHR emphasized family preservation in child welfare cases, but not immigrant cases (Sormunen, 2021).

Best Interest as a Representational Model

Though the research is limited regarding how the legal community weighs best interests, best interests as a representational model has been the subject to a great deal of debate among lawyers for many decades (Duquette et al., 2021; Miller et al., 2020). As I touched on briefly in the prior chapter, attorney representation of foster youth in the US tends to fall along three lines, direct representation, best interest representation and hybrid representation. These models and the debate around them have correlates in other parts of the world as well (Tempesta, 2019), but for simplicity's sake, I will limit my discussion to the United States.

In the US, children first acquired the right to counsel through the Supreme Court decision *In ReGault*, which dealt with the right of a juvenile defendant to an attorney during criminal proceedings (Malempati, 2014). This decision changed the view of children being the property of their parents to having their own independent rights. While the Supreme Court has never held that children in dependency proceedings have a right to counsel, Congress in the 1974 Child Abuse and Prevention Act (CAPTA) did tie federal funding to a requirement that dependent children have representation. However, the law did not require attorneys per se, which has led to a mix of representational models throughout the states (Malempati, 2014).

The American Bar Association (ABA) (2011) in their Model Act Governing the Representation of Children in Abuse, Neglect and Dependency

Proceedings was clear that foster children should receive direct representation like any other client and while attorneys could serve as a best interest advocate if court appointed in that role, this is not the same as an actual attorney client relationship, which all foster children should have. This recommendation falls in line with the federal guidance developed in response to a Clinton era foster care initiative that urged states to allow each child in care to have an independent attorney (Duquette et al., 1999). This was also the advice of two expert panels spaced a decade apart and convened by Fordham University that have been influential in the legal community (Duquette et al., 2021). In fact, direct representation over best interest has been the recommendation of most professional and academic writing (Duquette et al., 2021).

In their endorsement of a direct representational model, the ABA (2011) goes so far as to admonish attorneys against applying a personal best interest standard to their client. The ABA (2011) does allow attorneys whose child clients insist on an outcome that would represent a substantial danger to act against the expressed wishes of the client for that unique situation and make limited disclosures to other professionals on the case who can act to limit the danger.

As a real-world example of this, a teenage client of mine once refused to get a rabies shot after being bitten by a street dog. Despite my best counsel, he continued to refuse and my ethical duty to make sure he did not die of rabies, meant that I alerted his guardian ad litem and an emergency court hearing was set to order the medical procedure.

The ABA (2011) acknowledges in its model rules that because of a child's young age or diminished capacity that there might be some instances where an attorney might use their substitute judgment on behalf of a child client. However, substitute judgment must be done with what the attorney believes the child would request and it has to be issue specific, so that direct representation can continue on all other matters (ABA, 2011). The National Association for Counsel of Children (NACC) (2022) in their recommendations for child welfare representation also favor a direct representation model and note that even when attorneys must use substitute judgment, that is not the same as a best interest decision. This limited exception to direct representation is the legal communities attempt to balance the real concern that zealous representation of a child client's wishes might actually result in harm to the child, like in the rabies example above.

In an analysis of when attorneys might be forced to make a best interest decision Peters (1996, p. 1566) cautioned that "*nothing about legal training or traditional legal roles qualifies lawyers to determine best interests.*" Still attorneys would need to develop a deep understanding of the concept because that it the framework from which all of the other parties to the case are making decisions. Peters (1996) suggested that best interest decisions by attorneys should still be guided as much as possible by the child's wishes and that factors like family relationships, expert opinions and if alternative proposals for the child are an actual improvement for their life even if the current circumstances might not be in the child's best interest.

Malempati (2014) argued that a best interest model risks violating attorney ethical rules as this put the lawyer in the role of a court advisor and not an advocate. Additionally, best interest risk diminishing a child client's voice and participation as their position on an issue might not be what adults believe is the right and therefore best choice. Ultimately, the dual role required by best interest is counter to legal advocacy in every other area of law (Malempati, 2014).

In one of the very few studies to actually question US child welfare attorneys about their beliefs about their representation, Miller et al. (2020) surveyed more than 900 attorneys asking about the impact and quality of their advocacy, the communication, contact and relationship with their client and finally their own competence to represent children. One of the principal findings was that attorneys who worked under a best interest model of representation scored significantly lower on all measurements but competence than attorneys in a hybrid or direct representational model. The authors speculated that these lower scores might come about because a best interest model of representation does not require the same level of client engagement (Jay Miller et al., 2020).

Professional boards seem to favor direct representation, but state governments seem less enthusiastic. Of the states that require an attorney be appointed, only 13 mandate a direct representation model, while 23 promote a hybrid or best interest approach (NACC, 2023). There are studies that show that legal representation can benefit a foster child in finding permanency (Zinn & Slowriver, 2008), reunification, educational gains and stability (Washington State Center for Court Research, 2021). However, when the Florida Legislature commissioned a literature review of attorney representation studies, the Office of Program Policy Analysis and Government Accountability (2021) reported that the models and methods were too different to draw any conclusions about which worked best in practice. So there remains an open question if best interest, hybrid or direct representation produce the best outcomes.

In actual every day practice, even direct representation is often not a clear bright line. It more resembles a sliding scale depending on the age, capacity and desire of the client. It should be obvious that representing a toddler is different from representing a teenager. For my clients that could tell me what they wanted, I often did not agree with them, but that is no different than many of my adult clients as well. I also represented a number of non-verbal children with developmental disabilities that could provide little to no direct guidance for their case. My representation in those cases was under a limited substitute judgment standard generally focused on how to make sure that my client had a stable and permanent family home.

Taken as a whole though, the legal community continues to struggle with best intertest, not only in simply defining the term, but also in applying it to the traditional duties and ethics of representing a client. Attorneys do not understand best interest, we do not understand if the best interest representation model is better or worse and the decades long argument continues.

Child Welfare Professionals and Researchers

In addition to attorneys, there are obviously dozens of other professionals in foster child's life that are also making best interest decisions on their behalf and a whole field of researchers trying to understand those decisions. How these professionals interpret best interest and what factors they consider is of significant importance then to the child welfare community. Perhaps usurpingly at this point, there is not a consensus opinion, but there are some studies that help guide our understanding.

One of the ways that researchers have attempted to quantify the best interest standard is through the use of a best interest questionnaires and scales. Developed in the Netherlands for use on child asylum and juvenile placement cases, the Best Interest of the Child Questionnaire (BIC-Q) is a six-page CRC children's rights-based form that aims to measure the social, developmental, family and risk factors that would either promote or hamper the well-being of a child (Zijlstra, 2012). The BIC-Q asks questions that rate the child's family environment, physical and home environment, their social network, their education, their interest and their peers from unsatisfactory to good. It asks not only about the present, but also requires the examiner to answer the same questions about the future. Finally, the BIC-Q also requires the examiner to note any violations of the CRC for each of these questions (Zijlstra, 2012). Overall, the BIC-Q has been found to have good reliability related to measuring child rearing (Kalverboer et al., 2011), and predicting child internalizing behavior (Zijlstra et al., 2013), but the results can differ depending on the cultural factors of the examiners (Zevulun et al., 2019).

In an effort to better understand best interest from the child's perspective, the BIC-Q form was adapted into the Best Interest of the Child Self-Report Questionnaire (BIC-S) (Ten Brummelaar et al., 2014) that included similar items related to the child's past, present and future family situation, their larger social network, including school and their current and long-term stability. One of the strengths of the BIC-S was that it actually included children in the design process (Ten Brummelaar et al., 2014). When tested on well-being measures, the BIC-S is also reliable in rating the child-rearing environment within the context of the child's rights (Zijlstra et al., 2023).

While the two questionnaires are an interesting attempt to assign and standardize definitive factors to best interest and measure them, they do not really get us any closer to understanding how people within child welfare perceive them.

The other ways in which researchers have attempted to explain best interest in by studying child welfare workers and parents. In one qualitative study of ten Brazilian foster parents, Baldini (2021) conducted a series of interviews with each participant to understand how they viewed the best interest of the children in their care. From the interviews several themes emerged. Firstly, the foster parents all agreed that the children's best interest were better served in a foster home setting than in some form of congregate care (Baldini, 2021).

They also identified caring relationships as a best interest factor, but that relationship was predicated on an idea of children's vulnerability and dependence, therefore other family relationships that were not direct care oriented were less important (Bandini, 2021). They also acknowledged children's wishes and participation as a factor, but most also routinely ignored or overruled those wishes when they disagreed. Bandini (2021) noted that one of the most salient findings from the study was the amount of discretion that foster care givers had when making best interest decisions even when those decisions ran counter to official government guidelines.

In another study of New Zealand social workers, Keddell (2017) conducted structured interviews with 22 social workers and 15 child welfare stakeholders, such as parents and foster parents. The participants discussed a difficult case in which they believed a positive outcome had been achieved (Keddell, 2017).

Participants routinely rated family preservation as the most important outcome and that children's best interest was directly related to children's needs. These needs were generally identified as emotional and psychological. The researcher noted that social workers often viewed best interest through the lens of a simplified version of attachment theory, where the early failures of stable emotional attachments led to problematic behavior later in the child's life that caused them problems. Social workers also emphasized that children's wishes were an important component in their best interest. In contrast, parent participants did not give as much weight to children's wishes and identified physical safety as being in the child's best interest (Keddell, 2017).

Keddell (2017) argued that the use of attachment theory for best interest decision-making by social workers removed their decision-making process from some of the more grounded realties of the lived experience of families that are living within the child welfare system. It also supported cultural norms about families and childhood that could be detrimental to minority groups (Keddell, 2017).

In the same Norwegian best interest study of judges and adoption discussed previously, Helland (2020) also presented 556 child welfare workers with a vignette of a 4-year-old boy whose foster parents wanted to adopt him. The workers identified eight factors related to the boy's best interest, including his attachment to his foster parents, lack thereof to his birth parents, and his needs for stability and permanence. Workers considered the boys' bond to his foster parent as the most influential factor with 67 percent of the participants listing it (Helland, 2020).

However, there was substantial divergence among the individuals for which factors they considered and which they found most weighty (Helland, 2020). The researcher suggested this could be from a lack of clear policy guidance as to what factors are important or due to unique characteristics of the workers themselves (Helland, 2020).

Another study to specifically question child welfare case workers about best interest decision-making specifically comes from the Czech Republic. In that work, researchers noted the inherent potential conflict between children's wishes and children's best interest (Hloušek et al., 2020).

The researchers focused on the questions of how social workers and legal professionals understood the legal concept of best interest and how that was implemented in their child welfare practice. Using qualitative semi-structured interviews with 13 Czech Republic children's social workers, the researchers recorded 90-minute interviews with each of the participants and then coded their responses (Hloušek et al., 2020).

The participants regularly stressed the individual nature of their cases and the unique aspects of each decision, with individual family circumstances, age of the child and ethnic and cultural factors all being important. The researchers noted that this is generally in keeping with the requirements of Czech family law and the UN Convention on Children's Rights (Hloušek et al., 2020).

Participants were also likely to give a formal answer that mirrored the legal language that they had in their training handbooks. However, most emphasized that this formal definition had to be tempered by common sense and experience from working in the field (Hloušek et al., 2020). The social workers also tended to give rankings to the various best interest factors with protection and safety generally receiving the highest weight. While most at least mentioned the child's wishes as part of a best interest calculation, they did not believe that it was as important as other factors (Hloušek et al., 2020).

Though these studies point to interesting results with some overlap in terms of children's safety and participation, unfortunately, none of the studies is definitive enough to make any final conclusions about how social workers weigh best interest factors when making a best interest decision. They also are from four different parts of the world with different histories, cultures, norms and laws, so making any comparisons even on the issues of overlap is problematic. If anything, the studies do show how truly universal the best interest decision has become and how poorly understood it is everywhere.

Layla, age 6 and Monica age 8 came into care when their mother was arrested for drug possession and prostitution. Their mother quickly relinquished her rights to both girls, and the two became permanent wards of the state. CPS was able to find a foster home willing to take them both in as a sibling pair, but Layla's behaviors made her a difficult child. Violent tantrums that left the room in tatters along with behaviorally related enuresis and encopresis not only impacted the foster home, but Monica as well. Monica's behavior began to deteriorate and CPS determined that it was in both their best interest to remove Layla from the home and separated the two. Monica thrived in the home alone and eventually requested to stop visits with her sister altogether.

Why Best Interests May Not Be the Best

On any given day in my former practice, CPS or CASA would tell me about something being in the best interest of my client, often something that my client objected to. On Monday, CPS caseworker would tell me that a parent's positive drug test meant that my client could only have supervised visits at the CPS office. On Tuesday, a different CPS worker would tell me that drug use would not prevent unsupervised visits for another similar aged client. To me, best interest was always a post hoc rationale for whatever CPS had already decided. It is broad, vague, inconsistent, subjective, culturally insensitive, racially loaded, fraught with bias, too risk averse and prone to error.

It should be of no surprise that best interest as a legal doctrine and as a decision-making framework has come under a great deal of criticism from researchers, practitioners and legal scholars for at least a half century. In perhaps the most influential work of best interest critique, Mnookin (1973) laid out what would become some of the most common arguments against the standard. Firstly, in the context of child removal, best interest requires judges or other decision-makers to have access to a huge amount of information about the child, the child's family and their homelife, while also generally having very little information about what the child's future placement and stability might be. This in turn means that judges have to make flawed predictions about not only what is best for the child in the present moment, but also what might be best for the child in the future (Mnookin, 1973).

Even assuming judges have superhuman predictive powers Mnookin (1973) goes on to argue that judges must then decide what values to bring to the decision.

> Should the judge be concerned with happiness? Or should he or she worry about the child's spiritual goodness or economic productivity? Is stability and security for a child more desirable than intellectual stimulation?
>
> (Mnookin, 1973, p. 618)

Because the standard is so broad, judges ultimately rely on their own intrinsic values which opens the door to a number of biases especially regarding race and class (Mnookin, 1973). This also leads to inconsistent decisions across child welfare as different judges with different values come to different conclusions under the same case facts because of their opinions about sex, the LGBTQ community or religion. Finally, Mnookin (1973) argued that best interest makes removal into care too simple of a decision because it does not well take into count the future damage of the foster care system itself might inflict on a child.

Fifty years later in Harris County, Mnookin's criticisms are still on point. Attorneys often were anxious to transfer their child welfare cases from the elected family law courts to the appointed specialist child welfare courts. The family law judges tended to have much less experience with the child welfare system, were less willing to allow children to participate and were much more differential to the opinions of CPS and the CASA. The best interest of the child would literally change the moment a case transferred to the child welfare court.

Dolgin (1996) wrote that best interest was just a judicial invocation to acknowledge that a child is part of the case, but that generally the rights and positions of other parties were more important. The durability of the standard comes from its vagueness, which Dolgin (1996) argued allowed it to be flexible enough to allow its meaning to change over the centuries, but more importantly because it invokes a moral order of protecting children even if it fails to do so.

In many ways, the basic criticisms that Mnookin laid out are repeated by others and disputed by some for the next five decades. Though there is a lot of overlap among the critiques, it is worth attempting to divide them for discussion to gain a better understanding of the individual complaints.

Indeterminacy

Perhaps the most common criticism of best interest is its indeterminate and vague nature, which even its defenders acknowledge is a source of problems with the standard that leads to unpredictable case outcomes (Sutherland, 2016). Parker (1994) argued that one type of inherent indeterminacy stems from rational choice theory. Under rational choice theory, a decision-maker would need to know all of the options, the outcomes, the probabilities of those outcomes along with the weighted value of each of these. Because most of these factors are unknown and impossible to quantify, Parker (1994) wrote that no two decision-makers will necessarily come up with the same answer.

Because decisions throughout child welfare are made through a best interest lens, this indeterminacy is found throughout the legal process. Gupta-Kagan (2022) wrote that broad definitions and lack of hierarchies in care proceedings lead to indeterminate outcomes at every stage of the case. In a national guidance for judges, the US Children's Bureau actually flat out rejected the best interest standard for rulings and stated

> Should a court be concerned with the child's physical well-being, intellectual development, material comforts, emotional stability? What weight should be placed on each of these? Should a court determine whether the child is more likely to become delinquent, go to college, have close, warm relationships with an adult, grow up "happy" in his/her own home or in some other placement? Should courts consider the likely impact of each possible disposition on each of these variables, or on any other variables; and compare the home to each one to see which one has the most pluses? Are they to determine the child's best interest in the short run or the long run?
>
> (Davidson et al., 1981, p. 212)

Pepe (2022) argued that much of this indeterminacy, at least in the United States comes from the lack of federal standards, noting that when the term appears in a handful of federal laws, it is never defined. As noted in the prior section, states are free to determine their own best interest standards and their own factors to consider. With no consistent guideline, it is no wonder that best interest outcomes can be so unpredictable. However, as the questions in the quote above lay out, the guidelines would need to be very comprehensive and they would come with their own internal value judgments.

The standard has sometimes been compared to the old Justice Stewart quote about obscenity "*I know it when I see it*" (Funderburk, 2013; Wayne, 2008), but this is obviously not the language of legal standard that should rule the lives of children. This vagueness, Funderburk (2013) argued ultimately leads decision-makers to apply a personal subjective standard of what they believe is good for a child even though best interest and good should not be used interchangeably.

Within US constitutional jurisprudence there exist the concept that a law or statue can be struck down if it is too vague to be understood (Vornholt, 1980). While I could find no US cases where the best interest standard itself is challenged as vague, Vornholt (1980) wrote that vagueness has been used to challenge state parental termination cases but with mixed results depending on the jurisdiction.

The US Supreme Court has been critical of the standard, though, for its vagueness and in *Lassiter v. Department of Social Svcs.*, 452 U.S. 18 (1981) Justice Blackburn in wrote

> This Court more than once has adverted to the fact that the "best interests of the child" standard offers little guidance to judges, and may effectively encourage them to rely on their own personal values.
>
> (p. 18)

Likewise in *Reno v. Flores*, the Court wrote that best interest does not even represent the relationship between parents and child, writing,

> Similarly, "the best interests of the child" is not the legal standard that governs parents' or guardians' exercise of their custody: So long as certain minimum requirements of child care are met, the interests of the child may be subordinated to the interests of other children, or indeed even to the interests of the parents or guardians themselves.
>
> 507 US 292, 304 (1993)

The High Court of Australia in *Secretary, Department of Health and Community Services v JWB and SMB* 1992 also leveled a similar critique with Justice Brennan writing that

> the best interests approach does no more than identify the person whose interests are in question: it does not assist in identifying the factors which are relevant to the best interests of the child . . . That is because the best interests approach offers no hierarchy of values which might guide the exercise of a discretionary power.
>
> (p.32)

The Supreme Court of Canada in the 2004 *Canadian Foundation for Children, Youth and the Law v. Canada* case went even further and specifically rejected best interests as a fundamental principle of justice partially because it failed to meet the requirement that the concept is "*capable of being identified with some precision*" (p.95). The Court concluded

> Its application is inevitably highly contextual and subject to dispute; reasonable people may well disagree about the result that its application will yield, particularly in areas of the law where it is one consideration among many.
>
> (p. 95)

Discretion and Inconsistency

Closely related to vagueness is the concept of discretion. Because best interest is such a vague and imprecise standard, it allows judges to make decisions with virtually no restrictions leading to widely different outcomes.

In *Troxel v. Granville*, 530 U.S. 57 (2000), the US Supreme Court overturned a Washington state ruling that allowed grandparent visitation to be in the child's best interest. Justice Souter wrote that the standard was viewed *"as placing hardly any limit on a court's discretion to award visitation rights"* (p. 77). Souter wrote that while discretion in a particular case is not per se unconstitutional, but if every case allows unrestrained discretion, then a law could be invalid. Unfortunately, the *Troxel* court only critiqued best interest as it applied to this particular law, but did not tackle it as a universal standard.

In a recent Michigan Supreme Court case, In re G. M. DIXSON, Minor (2022) Chief Justice McCormick wrote in her dissent that

> the best-interests standard is capacious, allowing for individual, subjective biases about parenting to drive decision-making. This isn't a new observation, which makes it all the more frustrating.
>
> (p. 8)

European courts have also struggled with applying the concept consistently. In Klaassen and Rodrigues (2017) examination of child family reunification case before the Court of Justice of the European Union (CJEU), they found the court was inconsistent in how and when it applied best interest to cases from different member states and to litigants from different parts of the world.

In a similar analysis that compared ECtHR child refugee first entry and expulsion cases Smyth (2015) found that while the court considered multiple factors in each type of cases, the ECtHR weighed them differently in different types of case. For example, age and family unity where give nearly opposite values depending if the case involved first entry or expulsion. Smyth (2015) wrote

> what the Court infers from these factors varies significantly from case to case, and for every line of apparently established jurisprudence there is an exception. This inconsistency in the jurisprudence hints that the Court's

> approach to identifying and analysing the best interests of the child is not entirely principled.
>
> (p. 85)

Outside of the courts, legal scholars have also faulted the judicial discretion of best interest. Pepe (2022) wrote that the law "shapeshifts" (p.499) and that there nothing standard about its application. Kohm (2008) argued that while best interest has served some purpose in the past,

> The application of this standard, however, has turned toward near pure judicial discretion in contemporary judging, causing litigators and advocates to have no rule of law to rely upon.
>
> (p. 3)

In another critique, Sankaran (2022) wrote that it is

> not a standard at all, but simply unfettered discretion disguised as a legal principle. This phrase simply allows a juvenile court judge to do whatever they please without constraint. It allows them to govern their fiefdom in whatever manner they chose, with little to no appellate oversight . . . . Giving judges this level of unfettered discretion is dangerous, especially if we pretend that they are actually applying some sort of legal standard when doing so.
>
> (para 4, 5, 6)

This same problem was pointed out by Mnookin (1973) who wrote

> As long as the best interests standard or some equally broad standard is used, it seems inevitable that petitions will be filed and neglect cases will be decided without any clear articulation or consistent application of the behavioral or moral premises on which the decision is based.
>
> (p. 619)

Bias

As a vague standard that places no restraint on judicial decision-making, it should be no surprise that best interest is also subject to biases regarding poverty, race, disability and culture. Justice Brennan made this exact point in *Smith v. Organization of Foster Families*, 431 U.S. 816 (1977) writing,

> social workers of middle-class backgrounds, perhaps unconsciously, incline to favor continued placement in foster care with a generally higher-status family rather than return the child to his natural family, thus reflecting a bias that treats the natural parents' poverty and lifestyle as prejudicial to the best interests of the child.
>
> (p. 834)

As explained in the prior chapter, the US child welfare system has a large volunteer organization known as CASA that is appointed to individual cases as a child's guardian ad litem and they are tasked with making best interest recommendations on behalf of a foster child. When Mulzer and Urs (2017) examined the CASA program they found that it was primarily made of older educated White women and that cases with CASA volunteers were less likely to result in reunification with the parent and they spent less time with Black children than with White children. When Osborne et al. (2020) examined the Texas CASA program they found similar results that children with CASA volunteers were less likely to achieved permanency, less likely to be reunified with family, less likely to be placed with family and more likely to be adopted. They also found significant racial differences with Black and Hispanic children in comparison to White children (Osborne et al., 2020). Mulzer and Urs (2017) argued that best interest allows a charitable class of wealthy White women to inflict their own cultural value system over poor and often minority parents.

As noted, child welfare systems worldwide have a problem with disproportionality and racial bias. In the US, courts have used best interest as a reason to separate families because of race (Park, 2023). Historically the standard has also been used to justify the removal Native American children and lower socioeconomic class immigrant children (Greensmith, 2019).

Usurpingly best interest as a tool of racial bias is not limited to the United States. Cripps (2012) wrote that in the Australian context, best interest has been used as a legal excuse to control Indigenous Aboriginal people. White, straight, married motherhood was used to judge the best interests of Indigenous families and as many as one third of Indigenous families had children removed (Cripps, 2012). This best interest approach was also used in the Canadian context to justify the removal of First Nations children and to ignore the kinship, cultural and identity bonds of those families (Lynch, 2001).

> The abstraction of First Nations and Aboriginal children from their families and communities both reflects and reinforces the law's normative construction of the "ideal environment" for the upbringing of a child; namely, an environment involving two biological parents, a stable home, and financial security.
>
> (Lynch, 2001, p. 521)

In addition to race and culture, the best interest standard has also been used to justify discrimination against people's sexual orientation and gender identity. In the recent past, Courts across the United States routinely denied parent's custody of their children because of the sexual orientation of the parents (Rittenhouse, 2011). It was deemed to be not in the child's best interest to be exposed to a LGBTQ parent even though research has shown there were no harmful effects to children (Rittenhouse, 2011). Though this practice has been eliminated in the US following the *Obergefell v. Hodges*, 576 US 644

(2015) Supreme Court decision that banned same-sex marriage restrictions, the best interest standard has now been turned to the trans community.

Anti-trans bills have appeared in nearly US state as well as numerous federal bills before the US Congress (Trans Legislation Tracker, 2024). A recent Wyoming House Bill 156 (2024) actually stated that,

> in determining the best interests of the child under this article, there shall be a conclusive presumption that it is not in the best interests of the child to undergo any gender transition or gender reassignment procedures.
> (HB 156 Section 1. W.S. 3-2-113)

While the language of best interest is not always invoked within the bills, conservative lawmakers (Figueroa, 2023) and policy groups (Vertuno, 2023) have both expressly used best interest of the child to promote anti-trans legislation. Texas even went so far as to direct the state CPS agency to investigate families whose children were receiving gender affirming care (Perez, 2022).

Harkening back to the vagueness and discretionary arguments, the COE Parliamentary Assembly (2015) in contrast, directed its member nations to guarantee the best interest of the child would be paramount when protecting transgender children. Canadian courts and legislation have also used best interest to support gender affirming treatment and the rights of trans children (Houston, 2020).

A final way in which best interest can be biased comes from its application to people with disabilities. As noted in the prior chapter, parents with disabilities are more likely to have their children removed than those without (Fersch, 2023). In their report on the problem, The National Council on Disability (NCD) (2012) wrote that because several US states include some test as to the parents mental and physical health in their dependency best interest statues and all states consider disability as a custody factor, the standard has an outright bias against people with disabilities. The NCD noted that the best interest presumption of children remaining with their parents is often flipped for people with disabilities so that they must show why their disability is not against their child's best interest (NCD, 2012).

Before moving on to the final type of criticism regarding the legal community's use of best interest, it is worth noting that medical professionals have also criticized the use of best interest as a pediatric standard (Waligora et al., 2018). Rhodes and Holzman (2014) echoed the arguments of legal critics that best interest in pediatrics is also vague, culturally insensitive, misleading and fraught with justice concerns related to the provision of scarce medical resources.

Conflicting Rights

An additional critique of best interest is that it is in conflict with both the rights of parents and the rights of children. Cantwell (2017) argued that best interest evolved as a useful way of making child-centered decisions prior to the establishment of children's rights. It is the lack of well-established and enforced rights that allows best interest to be interpreted so broadly with so much discretion. Today, the best interest standard actually obscures and confuses the recognition of the actual rights of the child as it is invoked in the same language "*Best interests become a problem when the concept is invoked pointlessly, that is, when reference to a right would or should suffice.*" (Cantwell, 2017, p. 66). In Chapter 6, I will discuss children's rights in much greater detail, but for now it will suffice to remember that children's rights have grown across legal frameworks worldwide primarily since the passage of the CRC.

Usurpingly, best interest of the child often is in conflict with parental rights which are established as a 14th Amendment constitutional right in the US as discussed in the *Troxel* case and are also understood to be encompassed in Article 9 of the CRC and Article 8 of the ECHR. As Font and Gershoff (2020) discussed, it is understood that states have the power and duty to protect children from harm, so parental rights have obvious limitations. However, because best interest is vague, indeterminate, prone to bias and subject to extreme judicial discretion, parental rights can be impacted or terminated purely because of a single judicial best interest decision. For instance, the North Carolina Supreme Court in *Routten v. Routten,* 374 NC 571, 843 S.E.2d 154 (NC, 2020) held that it was constitutional for a trial court to deny all visitation with a parent if it was in the child's best interest. In addition to the problems above, the subjective nature of best interest means that controversial, but legal protected behavior or speech on the part of the parent could also be used against them in a best interest decision.

Another conflict inherent in best interest, is that "a child" and "children" might have different interests. One example is Hague Convention on International Child Abduction that is designed to quickly return children back to their country of origin often after being taken by a parent or relative to a new country (Daly, 2017). While the Hague Convention is intended to serve the greater best interest of children by promoting their return and discouraging relative from taking them, an individual child's best interest might better be served in the new country (Daly, 2017). This conflict is also part of dependency proceedings as the best interests of siblings are often not aligned. For instance, it might be in all siblings' best interest to live with each other and continue their sibling relationship, but only one sibling is ready to be reunified with the parents or to be adopted.

The final conflict critique argued by Weinstein (1997) is whether the courts systems' adversarial approach to resolving child cases can be squared with a best interest approach. The adversary system with its focus on each side winning a particular outcome means that the court only hears the evidence that each side wants to present. Layered onto this the lawyer duties of zealous advocacy and client confidentiality, then the entire process is geared towards a limited picture of the family that does not take into context cultural and extended family ties and also forces non-adversarial witness, such as teachers and therapists into choosing a side (Weinstein, 1997). While this criticism does not fault the best interest standard itself, it does illustrate another conflict inherent in its actual implementation.

Tanya, who was 16, had lived in the same foster home with her sister, 15 and brother, 18 for more than 12 years. Though she had some learning difficulties and the occasional behavioral outburst, she and her siblings were considered very stable in a caring home. Tanya and her siblings were Black and her foster mother was white. As Tanya grew older, she began having more contact with her extended birth family and eventually began staying the weekends with her father after CPS approved the visits. Her behavior at school and at home began to worsen and she even had a brief stay in the psychiatric hospital. She fought often, sometimes violently, with her siblings, who asked that CPS find another place for Tanya to live. Tanya asked to live with her father, whose rights had been terminated more than a decade ago. CPS initially said that would not be in her best interests, but their only other suggestion was for Tanya to move to an RTC, to which she strongly objected. When they run out of other ideas, CPS often can convince themselves that an RTC is in a child best interest. In this case, CPS refused to approve the move to her father, so a court order was needed to make the change. Ultimately, she was allowed to move and while her school performance never improved, both she and her siblings said they were better off with her in a new home.

Conclusion

So we have a centuries old legal standard that no one can or has ever been able to truly define. Attempts at definitions have some broad overlap, but jurisdictional, regional, cultural and national ideas of best interests are often widely different so that the same case heard across a jurisdictional boundary will have a different definition applied and probably a different outcome, even though regional governing bodies like the EU have produced literal volumes trying to explain the concept.

We also have evidence that best interest of the child changes even within the same jurisdiction when applied to different types of cases, such as custody, dependency, asylum and deportation. So even within jurisdictions there is no universal understanding or application of best interest.

We know that lawyers and child welfare practitioners themselves have mixed and conflicting ideas of best interest so that they often identify different factors when coming to their best interest decisions.

Best interest has been criticized by scholars and courts included national supreme courts on grounds that it is vague, indeterminate, biased and subject to unfettered judicial discretion. It has historically been used against minority and marginalized people. It has been used against native peoples and against the LGBTQ community. It is being harnessed now as a weapon against trans parents and children. It assumes a White, Christian, Western female notion of family and judges others by those standards. It is in conflict with guaranteed rights of parents and of children and continues to hamper the adoption of children's rights today.

What is especially telling is that Mnookin (1973) identified almost all of these flaws more than 50 years ago and that each of them is still an ongoing problem and he could have written the same paper today without needing to change any of the core critiques. In that same time, US constitutional rights have come and gone and human rights on the world stage have expanded. Yet, undefined discretionary best interest remains with us.

In practice best interest meant whatever anyone wanted it to mean. For CPS best interest often meant what was the safest choice for the agency, what was less likely to get them a headline in the paper. For CASA, best interest looked the most like the place with the most services even if that meant that the child was left in an RTC and not reunited with family. For attorneys, best interest was whatever position their client advocated. For judges, best interest was whichever of the above they found the most persuasive that day or perhaps their own subjective judgment brought to the individual case.

As I stated at the beginning of this chapter, I am no fan of best interest, though I should note that there are plenty of scholars, lawyers, judges and child welfare workers that find less fault with it. I believe the difference often comes down to how we view children and children's rights. It is comparable with the dispute about attorney representation models of direct representation versus best interests and why I included that discussion in this chapter.

Do you believe that children are humans with their own rights and autonomy or do you believe that children have fewer rights than adults and adults must protect and act on their behalf? Like all true debates, the question is not quite as binary as presented, but where you fall on that spectrum, I would argue will say much about how you view the best interest standard.

Those who favor child protection and paternalism are more comfortable with a "know it when you see it" indeterminate, discretionary approach to best interest. I can see the appeal as this is somewhat how adults approach children in an everyday approach. Telling kids to be safe, to eat healthy, to study for school are all common ways in which parents might promote a child's best interest and these are situational and unique to the context of each family. Best interest as a parenting strategy is probably good enough. However, we are not speaking of best interest as parents we are talking about how society, governments and courts interact and interfere in the lives of families and children. When human and legal rights are at stake, we can do better than best interest.

References

African Unions' African Charter on the Rights and Welfare of the Child. (1999). https://au.int/sites/default/files/treaties/36804-treaty-african_charter_on_rights_welfare_of_the_child.pdf

Alabama Code. (2022). *Title 12*. Courts § 12–15-101 Alabama Juvenile Justice Act. https://law.justia.com/codes/alabama/2014/title-12/chapter-15/

American Bar Association. (2011). *The model act governing the representation of children in abuse, neglect, and dependency proceedings*. https://niwaplibrary.wcl.american.edu/wp-content/uploads/aba_model_act_2011.pdf

Arizona Supreme Court. (2018). *Alma S. v. department of child safety.*

Banach, M. (1998). The best interests of the child: Decision-making factors. *Families in Society, 79*(3), 331–340. https://doi.org/10.1606/1044-3894.992

Bandini, M. H. (2021). *Perceptions from foster care practitioners on the best interest of children and teenagers within the Brazilian strategy for reforming out-of-home care.* https://www.diva-portal.org/smash/get/diva2:1599677/FULLTEXT01.pdf

Bowyer, L. (2016). The ethical grounds for the best interest of the child. *Cambridge Quarterly of Healthcare Ethics, 25*(1), 63–69. https://doi.org/10.1017/S0963180115000298

Canadian Foundation for Children, Youth and the Law v. Canada (Attorney General). (2004). SCC 4 (CanLII), [2004] 1 SCR 76.

Cantwell, N. (2017). Are 'best interests' a pillar or a problem for implementing the human rights of children? In *The United Nations convention on the rights of the child.* Brill|Nijhoff. https://doi.org/10.1163/9789004295056_006

Carbone, J. (2014). Legal applications of the "best interest of the child" standard: Judicial rationalization or a measure of institutional competence? *Pediatrics, 134*(Suppl 2), S111–S120. https://doi.org/10.1542/peds.2014-1394G

Child Welfare Information Gateway. (2020). *Determining the best interests of the child.* U.S. Department of Health and Human Services, Administration for Children and Families, Children's Bureau. https://www.childwelfare.gov/topics/systemwide/laws-policies/statutes/best-interest/

Children's Commission. (2023). *Texas child welfare law bench book.* https://www.texaschildrenscommission.gov/media/dfxpfdl5/2023-child-welfare-bench-book-final-online.pdf

Council of Europe. (2011). *Council of Europe Recommendation on children's rights and social services friendly to children and families.* Retrieved February 7, 2024, from https://search.coe.int/cm/Pages/result_details.aspx?ObjectID=09000016805afddf

Council of Europe. (2015). 6 Resolution 2048(2015) 'discrimination against transgender people in Europe'. Retrieved February 26, 2024, from https://assembly.coe.int/nw/xml/xref/xref-xml2html-en.asp?fileid=21736

Council of Europe. (2016). *The best interests of the child: A dialogue between theory and practice.* Retrieved February 7, 2024, from https://book.coe.int/en/children-s-rights-and-family-law/6862-the-best-interests-of-the-child-a-dialogue-between-theory-and-practice.html

Cripps, K. (2012). Indigenous children's 'best interests' at the crossroads. *International Journal of Critical Indigenous Studies, 5*, 25–35. https://doi.org/10.5204/ijcis.v5i2.88

Daly, A. (2017). *Children, autonomy and the courts: Beyond the right to be heard.* Brill|Nijhoff. https://doi.org/10.1163/9789004355828

Davidson, H., Horowitz, R., Marvell, T., & Ketchum, O. (1981). *Child abuse and neglect a manual for judges.* U.S. Children's Bureau. Retrieved February 20, 2024, from https://www.ojp.gov/pdffiles1/Digitization/108679NCJRS.pdf

Degol, A., & Dinku, S. (2011). Notes on the principle "best interest of the child": Meaning, history and its place under Ethiopian law. *Mizan Law Review, 5*, 319–337.

Dolgin, J. (1996). Why has the best interest standard survived?: The historic and social context. *Children's Legal Rights Journal, 16*, 2. https://scholarlycommons.law.hofstra.edu/faculty_scholarship/433

Duquette, D. N., Dean, C. P., Hardin, M., & United, S. (1999). *Guidelines for public policy and state legislation governing permanence for children.* Department of Health and Human Services, Administration for Children and Families, Administration on Children, Youth and Families, Children's Bureau. https://catalog.hathitrust.org/Record/003544625

Duquette, D. N., Orlebeke, B., Zinn, A., Pott, R., Skyles, A., & Zhou, X. (2021). *Children's justice: How to improve legal representation of children in the child welfare system*. https://repository.law.umich.edu/books/107/

European Asylum Support Office. (2019). *EASO practical guide on the best interests of the child in asylum procedures*. Retrieved February 16, 2024, from https://euaa.europa.eu/sites/default/files/Practical_Guide_on_the_Best_Interests_of_the_Child_EN.pdf

European Union Agency for Fundamental Rights. (2022). *Handbook on European law relating to the rights of the child*. Retrieved February 14, 2024, from https://fra.europa.eu/en/publication/2022/handbook-european-law-child-rights

Every Student Succeeds Act, 20 U.S.C. § 6301. (2015). https://www.govinfo.gov/content/pkg/PLAW-110publ351/pdf/PLAW-110publ351.pdf

Fersch, P. (2023). Does the best interests standard prejudice disabled parents in custody disputes? *Forbes*. Retrieved February 26, 2024, from https://www.forbes.com/sites/patriciafersch/2023/06/20/does-the-best-interests-standard-prejudice-disabled-parents-in-custody-disputes/

Figueroa, A. (2023). Parents have no right to allow their children's gender transition, Republicans say. *New Jersey Monitor*. Retrieved February 26, 2024, from https://newjerseymonitor.com/2023/07/28/parents-have-no-right-to-allow-their-childrens-gender-transition-republicans-say/

Font, S. A., & Gershoff, E. T. (2020). Current use of the "best interests of the child" standard in foster care policy and practice. In *Foster care and best interests of the child: Integrating research, policy, and practice* (pp. 21–37). Springer International Publishing. https://doi.org/10.1007/978-3-030-41146-6_2

Funderburk, C. (2013). Best interest of the child should not be an ambiguous term. *Children's Legal Rights Journal*, *33*, 229. https://lawecommons.luc.edu/clrj/vol33/iss2/3

Greensmith, H. (2019). *Best interests: How child welfare serves as a tool of white supremacy*. Political Research Associates. Retrieved February 23, 2024, from https://politicalresearch.org/2019/11/26/best-interests-how-child-welfare-serves-tool-white-supremacy

Gupta-Kagan, J. (2022). Confronting indeterminacy and bias in child protection law. *Stanford Law & Policy Review*, *33*, 217. https://scholarship.law.columbia.edu/faculty_scholarship/3856

Hammarberg, T. (2008). *The principle of the best interest of the child: What it mean and what it demands from adults*. Council of Europe, Commissioner for Human Rights. Retrieved February 13, 2024, from https://rm.coe.int/16806da95d

Harvard Law Review. (2021). In the best interests of the child asylum-seeker: A threat to family unity. *Harvard Law Review*, *134*(4), 1456–1476.

Helland, H. S. (2020). Tipping the scales: The power of parental commitment in decisions on adoption from care. *Children and Youth Services Review*, *119*, 105693. https://doi.org/10.1016/j.childyouth.2020.105693

Helland, H. S. (2021). In the best interest of the child? Justifying decisions on adoption from care in the Norwegian Supreme Court. *The International Journal of Children's Rights*, *29*(3), 609–639. https://doi.org/10.1163/15718182-29030004

Hloušek, J., Kappl, M., & Smutková, L. (2020). The best interest of the child and its application in the practice of social workers in the Czech Republic. *Postmodern Openings*, *11*(2), 175–192. https://doi.org/10.18662/po/11.2/169

Houston, C. (2020). Respecting and protecting transgender and gender-nonconforming children in family courts. *Canadian Journal of Family Law*, *33*(1), 103. https://ssrn.com/abstract=3707382

Jay Miller, J., Donahue-Dioh, J., & Owens, L. (2020). Examining the legal representation of youth in foster care: Perspectives of attorneys and attorney guardians ad litem. *Children and Youth Services Review*, *115*, 105059. https://doi.org/10.1016/j.childyouth.2020.105059

Juhlin, A. (2023). *The best interest of the child under international law: The right to respect for private and family life in the formation, malfunctioning, and disruption of a family* [Dissertation]. https://urn.kb.se/resolve?urn=urn:nbn:se:su:diva-218200

Kalverboer, M., Ten Brummelaar, M., Post, W., Zijlstra, E., Harder, A., & Knorth, E. (2011). The best interest of the Child-Questionnaire, reliability and validity: Preliminary data on the question "where to live after detention or secure treatment?" *Criminal Behaviour and Mental Health*, *22*(1), 41–52. https://doi.org/10.1002/cbm.825

Kansas Department for Children and Families. (2022). *Department of PPS policy and procedural manual.* https://www.dcf.ks.gov/services/PPS/Documents/PPM_Forms/Policy_and_Procedure_Manual.pdf

Keddell, E. (2017). Interpreting children's best interests: Needs, attachment and decision-making. *Journal of Social Work*, *17*(3), 324–342. https://doi.org/10.1177/1468017316644694

Klaassen, M., & Rodrigues, P. (2017). The best interests of the child in EU Family Reunification Law: A plea for more guidance on the role of article 24(2) Charter. *European Journal of Migration and Law*, *19*(2), 191–218. https://doi.org/10.1163/15718166-12340007

Kohm, L. M. (2008). Tracing the foundations of the best interest of the child standard in American jurisprudence. *Journal of Law and Family Studies*, *10*, 504.

Lassiter v. Department of Social Svcs. 452 U.S. 18 (1981). https://supreme.justia.com/cases/federal/us/452/18/

Llorenz, J. C. (2016). Presentation of General Comment No. 14: Strengths and limitations, points of consensus and dissent emerging in its drafting. In *The best interests of the child: A dialogue between theory and practice* (pp. 11–17). Council of Europe. Retrieved February 7, 2024, from https://book.coe.int/en/children-s-rights-and-family-law/6862-the-best-interests-of-the-child-a-dialogue-between-theory-and-practice.html

Logan, E. (2008). *The child's best interest: A generally applicable principle.* Council of Europe. Retrieved February 13, 2024, from https://rm.coe.int/16806da904

Lynch, P. (2001). Keeping them home: The best interests of indigenous children and communities in Canada and Australia. *The Sydney Law Review*, *23*(4), 501–542. https://search.informit.org/doi/10.3316/ielapa.200200413

Maine Supreme Judicial Court. (2023). *In re children of quincy A.* https://www.courts.maine.gov/courts/sjc/lawcourt/2023/23me049.pdf

Malempati, S., (2014). Ethics, advocacy, and the child client. *Cardozo Public Law, Policy, and Ethics Journal*, *12*, 633. http://dx.doi.org/10.2139/ssrn.2318020

März, J. W. (2022). What does the best interests principle of the convention on the rights of the child mean for paediatric healthcare? *European Journal of Pediatrics*, *181*(11), 3805–3816. https://doi.org/10.1007/s00431-022-04609-2

McAdam, J. (2007). *Complementary protection in international refugee law.* Oxford University Press. https://doi.org/10.1093/acprof:oso/9780199203062.001.0001

Michigan Department of Health and Human Services. (2023). *Placement selection and standards.* https://dhhs.michigan.gov/OLMWEB/EX/FO/Public/FOM/722-03.pdf

Missouri Department of Social Services. (2021). *Child welfare manual section 4, chapter 2 (placements): Overview.* https://dssmanuals.mo.gov/child-welfare-manual/section-4-chapter-2-placements/

Mnookin, R. H. (1973). Foster care: In whose best interest? *Harvard Educational Review*, *43*(4), 599–638. https://doi.org/10.17763/haer.43.4.unm6691p3u1n450v

Moyo, A. (2019). The legal status of children's rights in Zimbabwe. In A. Moyo (Ed.), *Selected aspects of the Zimbabwean Constitution and the Declaration of Rights.* Retrieved February 15, 2024, from https://zimlii.org/akn/zw/doc/book-chapter/2020-06-30/chapter-9-the-legal-status-of-childrens-rights-in-zimbabwe/eng@2020-06-30/source.pdf

Mulzer, A., & Urs, T. (2017). However kindly intentioned: Structural racism and volunteer CASA programs. *City University of New York Law Review*, *20*, 23.

The National Association for Counsel of Children. (2022). *Recommendations for legal representation of children and youth in neglect and abuse proceedings*. https://nacc-childlaw.org/wp-content/uploads/2024/01/NACC-Recommendations-Final.pdf

National Association of Counsel for Children. (2023). *State models of children's legal representation*. https://counselforkids.org/wp-content/uploads/2023/05/Model-of-Rep-Chart-2023.pdf

National Counsel on Disabilities. (2012). *Rocking the cradle: Ensuring the rights of parents with disabilities and their children*. Retrieved February 26, 2024, from https://www.ncd.gov/assets/uploads/reports/2012/ncd-rocking-the-cradle.pdf

Nevada Code. (2022). *Chapter 432B: Protection of children from abuse and neglect*. https://www.leg.state.nv.us/nrs/nrs-432b.html

Norwegian National Human Rights Institute. (2021). *Day of general discussion: "Children's rights and alternative care" – Written submission from the Norwegian National Human Rights Institution*. The Committee on the Rights of the Child. Retrieved February 14, 2024, from https://www.ohchr.org/sites/default/files/documents/hrbodies/crc/discussions/2021/submissions/subm-2021-day-general-nhri-chil-righ-comm-norwegian-national-hr-institut.pdf

Office of Program Policy Analysis and Government Accountability. (2021). *Literature review of studies on the effectiveness of advocacy models for children in dependency*. https://oppaga.fl.gov/Documents/Reports/21-07.pdf

Oregon Revised Statute. (2022). *§ 107.137 Factors considered in determining custody of child*. https://oregon.public.law/statutes/ors_107.137

Osborne, C., Warner-Doe, H., LeClear, M., & Sexton, H. (2020). The effect of CASA on child welfare permanency outcomes. *Child Maltreatment*, *25*(3), 328–338. https://doi.org/10.1177/1077559519879510

Park, J. (2023). In no one's "best interest": The hidden racialized impact of the family regulations system. *Columbia Undergraduate Law Review*. Retrieved February 23, 2024, from https://www.culawreview.org/journal/in-no-ones-best-interest-the-hidden-racialized-impact-of-the-family-regulations-system

Parker, S. J. (1994). The best interests of the child: Principles and problems. *International Journal of Law, Policy and the Family*, *8*, 26–41.

Pepe, V. L. (2022). Conceiving consistency: Giving birth to a uniform "best interests of the child" standard. *Hofstra Law Review*, *50*(2), Article 8. https://scholarlycommons.law.hofstra.edu/hlr/vol50/iss2/8

Perez, J. (2022). Abbott orders Texas probe of medical procedures for transgender children. *Politico*. Retrieved February 26, 2024, from https://www.politico.com/news/2022/02/23/texas-governor-orders-probe-of-abusive-procedures-for-transgender-children-00011057

Peters, J. K. (1996). The roles and content of best interests in client-directed lawyering for children in child protective proceedings. *Fordham Law Review*, *64*, 1505. https://ir.lawnet.fordham.edu/flr/vol64/iss4/14

Pobjoy, J. M. (2015). The best interests of the child principle as an independent source of international protection. *The International and Comparative Law Quarterly*, *64*(2), 327–363. http://www.jstor.org/stable/24760683

Racine, E., Bell, E., & Shevell, M. (2013). Chapter 21: Ethics in neurodevelopmental disability. In J. L. Bernat & H. R. Beresford (Eds.), *Handbook of clinical neurology* (Vol. 118, pp. 243–263). Elsevier. https://doi.org/10.1016/B978-0-444-53501-6.00021-4

Reno v. Flores, 507 U.S. 292, 113 S. Ct. 1439 (1993).

Rhodes, R., & Holzman, I. R. (2014). Is the best interest standard good for pediatrics? *Pediatrics*, *134*(Suppl 2), S121–S129. https://doi.org/10.1542/peds.2014-1394H

Rittenhouse, D. (2011). What's orientation got to do with it?: The best interest of the child standard and legal bias against gay and lesbian parents. *Journal of Poverty, 15*(3), 309–329. https://doi.org/10.1080/10875549.2011.589260

Routten v. Routten, 374 N.C. 571, 843 S.E.2d 154 (N.C. 2020). https://www.nccourts.gov/documents/appellate-court-opinions/routten-v-routten-0

Ruggiero, R. (2022). Article 3: The best interest of the child. In Z. Vaghri, J. Zermatten, G. Lansdown, & R. Ruggiero (Eds.), *Monitoring state compliance with the UN convention on the rights of the child: An analysis of attributes* (pp. 21–29). Springer International Publishing. https://doi.org/10.1007/978-3-030-84647-3_3

Sankaran, V. (2022). Best interests standard is a judicial false idol. *The Imprint, Youth and Family News*. Retrieved February 22, 2024, from https://imprintnews.org/opinion/best-interests-standard-judicial-false-idol/236509

Secretary, Department of Health and Community Services v JWB and SMB. (1992). https://www.austlii.edu.au/cgi-bin/viewdoc/au/cases/cth/HCA/1992/15.html

Skelton, A. (2019). Too much of a good thing? Best interests of the child in South African jurisprudence. *De Jure Law Journal, 52*, 557–579. http://www.scielo.org.za/scielo.php?script=sci_arttext&pid=S2225-71602019000200007&nrm=iso

Skivenes, M. (2010). Judging the child's best interests: Rational reasoning or subjective presumptions? *Acta Sociologica, 53*(4), 339–353. http://www.jstor.org/stable/25782154

Skivenes, M., & Sørsdal, L. M. (2018). The child's best interest principle across child protection jurisdictions. In A. Falch-Eriksen & E. Backe-Hansen (Eds.), *Human rights in child protection: Implications for professional practice and policy* (pp. 59–88). Springer International Publishing. https://doi.org/10.1007/978-3-319-94800-3_4

Sloth-Nielsen, J., & Oliel, M. (2019). *Constitutionalising children's rights and domestic courts of member states of the Council of Europe*. Deutsches Kinderhilfswerk. Retrieved February 15, 2024, from https://www.kinderrechte.de/fileadmin/Redaktion/1_Unsere_Arbeit/1_Schwerpunkte/2_Kinderrechte/2.17_Kinderrechte_ins_Grundgesetz/Schriftenreihe_Constitutionalising_Rights_EN.pdf

Smith v. Organization of Foster Families, 431 U.S. 816. (1977). https://supreme.justia.com/cases/federal/us/431/816/

Smyth, C. (2015). The best interests of the child in the expulsion and first-entry jurisprudence of the European Court of Human Rights: How principled is the court's use of the principle? *European Journal of Migration and Law, 17*(1), 70–103. https://doi.org/10.1163/15718166-12342072

Sormunen, M. (2020). A focus on domestic structures: Best interests of the child in the concluding observations of the UN Committee on the Rights of the Child. *Nordic Journal of Human Rights, 38*(2), 100–121. https://doi.org/10.1080/18918131.2020.1770428

Sormunen, M. (2021). *The best interests of the child in human rights practice: An analysis of domestic, European and International Jurisprudence* [Doctoral Thesis, University of Helsinki]. http://urn.fi/URN:ISBN:978-951-51-6990-7

South Asian Association for Regional Cooperation. (2002). *Convention on regional arrangements for the promotion of Child Welfare in South Asia*. Author.

Sutherland, E. E. (2016). Article 3 of the United Nations Convention on the Rights of the Child: The challenges of vagueness and priorities. In L.-A. Barnes Macfarlane & E. E. Sutherland (Eds.), *Implementing article 3 of the United Nations Convention on the Rights of the Child: Best interests, welfare and well-being* (pp. 21–50). Cambridge University Press. https://doi.org/10.1017/9781316662977.003

Tempesta, C. (2019). *Legal representation as a critical aspect of the realization of the child's right to be heard*. Leiden University Faculty of Law. Retrieved February 15, 2024, from https://www.universiteitleiden.nl/binaries/content/assets/rechtsgeleerdheid/instituut-voor-privaatrecht/jeugdrecht/legal-representation-as-a-critical-aspect-of-the-childs-right-to-be-heard.pdf

Ten Brummelaar, M. D. C., Kalverboer, M. E., Harder, A. T., Post, W. J., Zijlstra, A. E., & Knorth, E. J. (2014). The Best Interest of the Child Self-Report Questionnaire (BIC-S): Results of a participatory development process. *Child Indicators Research, 7*(3), 569–588. https://doi.org/10.1007/s12187-013-9225-3

TennesseeCourt Improvement Program. (2008). *Child dependency benchbook* (6th ed.). https://www.tncourts.gov/sites/default/files/docs/child_dependency_benchbook.pdf

Tennessee Supreme Court. (2017). *In Re Gabriella D., Et Al.* https://tncourts.gov/courts/supreme-court/opinions/2017/09/29/re-gabriella-d-et-al

Trans Legislation Tracker. (2024). *2024 anti-trans bills tracker.* Retrieved February 26, 2024, from https://translegislation.com/

Troxel v. Granville, 530 U.S. 57. (2000). https://supreme.justia.com/cases/federal/us/530/57/

Turković, K. (2013). *The case-law of the European Court of Human Rights relevant to the protection the rights of the child in relation to alternative care settings* [PowerPoint Slides]. Retrieved February 14, 2024, from https://rm.coe.int/regional-discussion-presentation-ksenija-turkovic/1680a2cbb5

UN Committee on the Rights of the Child (CRC), General Comment No. 14. (2013). *On the right of the child to have his or her best interests taken as a primary consideration (art. 3, para. 1), 29 May 2013, CRC/C/GC/14.* Retrieved January 30, 2024, from https://www.refworld.org/docid/51a84b5e4.html

UN High Commissioner for Refugees. (2021). *UNHCR best interests procedure guidelines: Assessing and determining the best interests of the child.* Retrieved February 16, 2024, from https://www.refworld.org/policy/opguidance/unhcr/2021/en/122648

United Nations Convention on the Rights of the Child. (1989). https://www.ohchr.org/en/instruments-mechanisms/instruments/convention-rights-child

Vertuno, J. (2023). Texas high court allows law banning gender-affirming care for transgender minors to take effect. *PBS News Hour.* Retrieved February 26, 2024, from https://www.pbs.org/newshour/politics/texas-high-court-allows-law-banning-gender-affirming-care-for-transgender-minors-to-take-effect

Vornholt, R. P. (1980). Application of the vagueness doctrine to statutes terminating parental rights. *Duke Law Journal, 2*, 336–359. https://doi.org/10.2307/1372273

Waligora, M., Strzebonska, K., & Wasylewski, M. T. (2018). Neither the harm principle nor the best interest standard should be applied to pediatric research. *American Journal of Bioethics, 18*(8), 72–74. https://doi.org/10.1080/15265161.2018.1485762

Washington State Center for Court Research, (2021). *Evaluation of the Washington state dependent child legal representation program.* Administrative Office of the Courts.

Washington State Department of Children Youth and Families. (2022). *4305: Policies and procedures permanent and concurrent planning.* Retrieved February 6, 2024, from https://www.dcyf.wa.gov/4300-case-planning/4305-permanent-and-concurrent-planning

Wasserman, J. A., Navin, M. C., & Vercler, C. J. (2019). Pediatric assent and treating children over objection. *Pediatrics, 144*(5). https://doi.org/10.1542/peds.2019-0382

Wayne, R. H. (2008). The best interests of the child: A silent standard – Will you know it when you hear it? *Journal of Public Child Welfare, 2*(1), 33–49. https://doi.org/10.1080/15548730802237262

Weinstein, J. (1997). And never the twain shall meet: The best interests of children and the adversary system. *University of Miami Law Review, 52*, 79. https://repository.law.miami.edu/umlr/vol52/iss1/3

Weise, K. L., Okun, A. L., Carter, B. S., & Christian, C. W. (2017). Guidance on forgoing life-sustaining medical treatment. *Pediatrics*, *140*(3). https://doi.org/10.1542/peds.2017-1905

Wenke, D. (2021). *Feasibility study of a legal instrument on the protection of the best interests of the child in domestic law proceedings by public authorities to limit parental responsibilities or place a child in care*. Council of Europe. https://rm.coe.int/cj-enf-ise-2021-08b-feasibility-study-best-interests-care-proceedings-/1680a342d3

Wyoming House Bill 0156. (2024). *Best interests of a child-gender affirming treatments. Section 1. W.S. 3-2-113 (Wyoming, 2024)*. Retrieved February 26, 2024, from https://wyoleg.gov/Legislation/2024/HB0156

YC V United Kingdom. (2012). 55 EHRR 967.

Zevulun, D., Post, W. J., Zijlstra, A. E., Kalverboer, M. E., & Knorth, E. J. (2019). The best interests of the child from different cultural perspectives: Factors influencing judgements of the quality of child-rearing environment and construct validity of the Best Interests of the Child-Questionnaire (BIC-Q) in Kosovo and Albania. *Child Indicators Research*, *12*(1), 331–351. https://doi.org/10.1007/s12187-018-9543-6

Zijlstra, A. E. (2012). *In the best interest of the child: A study into a decision-support tool validating asylum-seeking children's rights from a behavioural scientific perspective* [Thesis Fully Internal (DIV), University of Groningen].

Zijlstra, A. E., Kalverboer, M. E., Post, W. J., Ten Brummelaar, M. D. C., & Knorth, E. J. (2013). Could the BIC-Q be a decision-support tool to predict the development of asylum-seeking children? *International Journal of Law and Psychiatry*, *36*(2), 129–135. https://doi.org/10.1016/j.ijlp.2013.01.005

Zijlstra, A. E., Post, W. J., Hopman, M., De Jong, A., & Kalverboer, M. E. (2023). The Best Interests of The Child Self-Report (BIC-S): Psychometric properties of the adapted version of the BIC-S used as a monitoring instrument to measure the quality of the children's rearing environment from a children's rights perspective. *Child Indicators Research*, *16*(3), 1341–1361. https://doi.org/10.1007/s12187-023-10010-8

Zinn, A. E., & Slowriver, J. (2008). *Expediting permanency: Legal representation for Foster Children in Palm Beach County*. Chapin Hall Center for Children at the University of Chicago.

3 Normalcy

For my clients in Texas, normalcy was often about after school. High school football, high school basketball, a boxing class, an LGBTQ club, marching band and even after-school tutoring were common requests. For clients in permanent, stable foster home placements, these requests were generally accommodated, but for the less stable populations who were moved from home to home or for those forced to live in an RTC, normalcy was far from guaranteed. Some of my clients in RTCs were never allowed off their facility as the "school", a room with computers for virtual learning, was located in the same complex.

Sometimes when the court would order CPS to allow a child in an RTC or less stable home some normalcy activity, the foster home or the RTC would simply terminate the child's placement and force CPS to find an alternative home. Providing a normal youth activity for a child was simply too much of a hassle for some placements that it was preferable to simply kick them out. So while normalcy seems like the simplest of concepts from which to improve the lives of foster youth, in practice it remains difficult to implement.

In its simplest terms normalcy is the idea that allows and encourages foster parents, CPS agencies and courts to allow foster youth to engage in activities that a normal youth would do. It is about impromptu sleepovers, learning to drive, going on dates, attending school and community events, participating in clubs and sports, staying out until curfew, having a phone with internet access and being allowed on social media. It is about promoting a normal life, a life that encourages foster youth to express their own desires and a life that encompasses both risk and mistake. It is that last part that makes it so challenging for best interest focused individuals and institutions to accept, but it is also the part that might make it a better framework for foster youth decision-making and participation.

Origins

Normalcy as a legal concept in foster care has a relatively short lifespan, really only becoming commonplace in the last decade. The first hint of a normalcy doctrine is sometimes credited from early 2004 California legislation that

DOI: 10.4324/9781003510253-3

sought to make sure that foster children had access to the same educational services and after-school activities as their non-foster peers (Blackshere, 2013). California later added in 2011 to its child Welfare and Institutions Code language that allowed foster children to take part in normal community activities and even forbade its agencies from preventing children to do so (Jacobson, 2016). At this point, California also introduced the concept of the reasonable prudent parent standard (Jacobson, 2016). I will return to a deeper discussion and explanation of the reasonable prudent parent standard and its relation to best interest and normalcy in the next chapter, but for now it is enough to know that its primary function is as a tort liability standard to protect caregivers from accident or injury to a child under their care.

The next state to take on normalcy was Florida, which in 2013 created the "Let Kids Be Kids" law that empowered foster parents to make decisions on behalf of children in their care without seeking CPS permission (Florida GAL, 2014). The law in part stated

> (b) *The Legislature finds that when a caregiver makes decisions, he or she must consider applicable laws, rules, and regulations to safeguard the health and safety of a child in out-of-home care and that those rules and regulations have commonly been interpreted to prohibit children in out-of-home care from participating in extracurricular activities.*
>
> (c) *The Legislature further finds that participation in these types of activities is important to the child's well-being, not only emotionally, but in developing valuable life-coping skills.*
>
> (Fla. Stat. § 39.4091 (b) and (c))

The law was passed partially because of the efforts of the former and current foster youth led group, Florida Youth Shine (FYS) that provided extensive testimony to the legislature about the abnormal lives they had in care (Perlmutter, 2017). Children testified to the absurd levels of safety inspired bureaucracy that prevented them from leading normal lives, such as CPS requiring finger prints and background checks of friend's parents so they were not allowed to spend time at their friend's home. Though normalcy policy guidelines had been implemented at the state CPS agency level since 2005 that would have alleviated much of the problem, these guidelines were routinely ignored and thus a state law was needed (Perlmutter, 2017).

The law also adopted the concept of the reasonable prudent parent standard for decisions regarding normalcy activities replacing the previous tort liability standard for foster parents and caregivers (Florida GAL, 2014).

> The foster care system, which has historically been focused on safety and concerned about liability, often creates huge barriers to the normalcy of a child's experiences growing up, causing children in care to miss out on many rites of passage common to their peers.
>
> (Perlmutter, 2017, p. 158)

Perlmutter (2017) argued that the law not only reduced tort liability to foster caregivers, but it also accomplished the state's policy goal of reducing the state liability for injury and negligence to children under their care.

The Florida law also prevented CPS from interfering in a caregiver's decision, so long as it did not violate a prior court order and even empowered the Florida GAL (2014) office to identify systemic and policy barriers to allowing normalcy activities.

Following California and Florida's lead, Ohio, Utah and Washington all passed versions of normalcy laws (Jacobson, 2016). It was "Let Kids Be Kids" thought that would become the primary inspiration for the normalcy requirement in the federal law Preventing Sex Trafficking and Strengthening Families Act (PSTSFA) that spread normalcy as a legal standard to the rest of the country (Perlmutter, 2017).

Preventing Sex Trafficking and Strengthening Families Act

As the title of the 2014 law suggest, the PSTSFA was aimed at tackling many children and family related problems only a portion of which involved normalcy. Still, Section 111 of the Act, titled "Supporting Normalcy for Children in Foster Care" laid out for the first time a federal framework and standard for normalcy in foster care. The PSTSFA required states to adopt a reasonable prudent parent standard to give caregivers the freedom to

> allow the child to engage in social, extracurricular, enrichment, cultural, and social activities, including sports, field trips and overnight activities lasting 1 or more days, and to decisions involving the signing of permission slips and arranging of transportation for the child to and from extracurricular, enrichment, and social activities.
>
> (Title 1 Subtitle B § 111(a)(2)(c)(2014)

The PSTSFA also required that states train caregivers in normalcy, the reasonable prudent parent standard and provide liability protection to caregivers within a year or risk losing federal funding (Jacobson, 2016).

Following the federal mandate, states began passing their own normalcy and reasonable prudent parent laws and began issuing their own state specific guidance. For instance, Hawaii's guide for caregivers specifically mentioned surfing and bodyboarding as activities covered by normalcy (Hawaii Department of Human Services, 2016). Many states developed elaborate checklists and guides covering as specifically as possible the activities that caregivers could approve and those that only CPS could. The Illinois Department of Children and Family Services (n.d.) allowed caregivers to approve of school photos but not photos in the media. The North Carolina Division of Social Services (2015) allowed children to ride with caregivers on jet skis, motorcycles and ATV's, but were not allowed to ride on lawnmowers. North Carolina (2015) also only approves of cellphones usage with coordination of the CPS, whereas California allows foster youth to use cell phones so long as a court has not ordered otherwise (Youth Law Center, 2018). Arizona's Department of Children and Families (2022) gave caregivers the ability to allow two-night stays away from home or for the caregiver to travel out of state for two nights, but any more required CPS approval. Though there is more overlap than in best interest definitions, the minutia of normalcy does change depending on the jurisdiction.

From the courtroom perspective, judges and attorneys were encouraged to make normalcy part of their ordered case plans and advocacy. In the ABA's guidelines for courts, Pokempner (2016) wrote that judges needed to set the standard for normalcy, which in some courts meant a cultural shift away from providing judicial orders for every activity. Normalcy findings that indicate that the caregivers my exercise the reasonable prudent parent standard should be part of a case permanency orders. Finally, judges need to ask questions about normalcy activities for all foster children, but should give special focus on those that might have barriers to normalcy such LGBTQ youth or youth that are placed in institutional settings (Pokempner, 2016).

In practice even good judges may struggle to promote normalcy for the youth before the bench. Foster parents often cited lack of transportation and money as reasons why the children under their care could not participate in an activity and courts are reluctant to routinely order overworked CPS caseworkers to accommodate every after-school activity. For children in congregate care, like RTCs, the situation is even worse as the youth there are generally locked away from the public and facility rules often conflict with normal activities. For every RTC and unfortunately for many foster parents, foster youth are their primary source of income and the fear of losing their licensing, means that they still defer most decisions to CPS and err on the side of saying no to foster youth requests.

Grace, a 17-year-old, Hispanic female and had been in care for five years after she was removed following sexual abuse by her family. She had been living in the home of Karen and Gladys, two older white sisters. Grace was an average student who often got bored in school, but never got in trouble. She found a job at a fast-food restaurant near her high school, so she could work after school and her caregivers always drove her home. She participated in the school's band, had a cell phone and friends. When she came out as a lesbian to her conservative Christian caregivers, she was no longer allowed to be alone with friends, and they refused to transport her to a local LGBTQ youth club. Instead of staying in the home while she went to college as she had previously planned, she left after graduation and began living with a friend.

Why Normalcy

While on first glance each of the normalcy activities might be a small thing, in totality they essentially represent the life of the child. Normalcy is bigger than simply a youth going on a date or having a social media account, it is inherently the ability to choose their friends, to choose how they spend their free time, to speak and be listened to, to take chances, to fail, to ultimately decide the trajectory of who they will become. Normalcy is about human rights and human freedom. When foster children are denied normalcy, we are denying them both.

The Annie E. Casey Foundation (2015) noted that normalcy is a significant part of foster youth well-being. Normal growing up activities provide youth with the developmental skills to form relationships and life patterns that will help them become stable adults. They need the space to be able to practice adult skills (Annie E. Casey, 2015).

For adolescents, these normal activities are more than just practice, they are fundamental to the development of their brain (Jim Casey Youth Opportunities Initiative, 2011). In fact, brain development is as important for older youth as it is for young children. It is during this time that greater plasticity of the brain allows young people to form and strengthen new neural connections, but those connections can be lost when they are not used. This is a critical time for the formation in the brain of adult social and emotional skills and is a time when exposure to normal activities can help heal the trauma of their past (Jim Casey Youth Opportunities Initiative, 2011).

Pokempner et al. (2015) wrote that the denial of normalcy has negative consequences for foster youth. They can leave care without the life skills to maintain relationships, find work or manage their own lives. As noted in the first chapter, youth that transition out of foster care have particularly bad outcomes. Some of this is related to the fact that they are not allowed to make any decisions on their own throughout their time in care and then when they finally leave, they are unprepared for any level of adult decision-making. This is compounded by the fact that they do not have the family or social support network that a non-foster youth would develop (Pokempner et al., 2015).

Foster youth themselves have often expressed their frustrations with the lack of normalcy in their lives. The National Foster Care Youth & Alumni Policy Council [Council] (2013) an organization of foster care experienced youth and alumni reported that many of their members were not allowed overnight stays with friends or allowed to get a job while in foster care. The Council (2013) reported that members felt as so much of their lives were restricted, that a normal life was denied to them. The Council wrote,

> We should be allowed to experience the same opportunities as our non-foster youth peers in the most normal, healthy and safest method possible. We believe normalcy is a critical component to establishing well-being and normalcy for foster youth deserves a greater degree of consideration and legitimacy by policymakers, practitioners, caregivers, and other stakeholders of the child welfare system.
>
> (Council, 2013, p. 1)

One of the most compelling calls for normalcy comes from New England Youth Coalition (NEYC), which is also made up primarily of current and former foster youth. The NEYC (2016a) defined how they envisioned normalcy to be a combination of six factors, "*families, social and peer inclusion, community inclusion, cultural awareness, age-related milestones and decision-making*" (p.1). For each of the factors, the NEYC emphasized youth participation and youth empowerment. They noted that youth should be able to define their own definition of family, that they should not be restricted because of preconceived ideas about the abilities of children in care (NEYC, 2016a).

Expanding on this the NEYC (2016b) released a Normalcy Bill of Rights that reads,

> *Every foster child:*
>
> 1. *Shall have regular visits with their families and siblings regardless of "good" behavior.*
> 2. *Shall be educated on the components of healthy romantic relationships through guidance from a supportive adult.*
> 3. *Shall be able to participate in activities that build a supportive social network, and have a curfew that allows for such activities.*
> 4. *Shall be allowed to build relationships with peers regardless of gender or sex.*
> 5. *Shall have opportunities to build relationships within their home and school communities equal to their peers not in care.*
> 6. *Shall be taught how to use tools such as personal e-mail, social media, and cell phones in a safe and healthy way that promotes an inclusivity with their communities, peers, and family.*
> 7. *Shall be able to express their identity as they choose, with guidance from supportive adults, because all people have the right to safety regardless of their circumstances.*
> 8. *Shall not be restricted in practicing religious or cultural customs, listening to their choice of music, wearing their preferred style of clothing etc.*
> 9. *Shall be showed respect for their religious and cultural beliefs and shall be able to participate in any activities associated with their religious beliefs.*
> 10. *Shall be allowed to discover and express their gender and sexual identity regardless of placement, and shall not be subjected to discrimination or fear for their safety because of their gender or sexual identity.*
> 11. *Shall be supported to reach age-related milestones including but not limited to obtaining a driver's license, opening a bank account, celebrating birthdays, graduations, etc.*
>
> (NEYC, 2016b, p. 1)

I include the whole NEYC Normalcy Bill of Rights because it is one of the very few examples where current and former foster youth create their own guidelines for how they should be allowed to experience their own lives. A second foster youth led group, the Pennsylvania Youth Advisory Board (2016), also issued their own set of recommendations for what they believed normalcy should entail. They referred to normalcy as "developmentally appropriate freedoms" (DAG) and noted that staff and caregivers needed better understanding and training of why these are important for youth development. The board also recommended that normalcy activities should be implemented using the Teen Success Agreement (Pennsylvania Youth Advisory Board, 2016). The agreement, which was also helped created by foster youth, is a 16-page contract of sorts that lays out youth and caregiver responsibilities and expectations and age-appropriate normalcy activities (Juvenile Law Center, 2013).

All three of these documents promote a more encompassing, holistic view of normalcy than either that of the PSTSFA or state legislatures. It is also notable that the words "best interest" are not to be found anywhere in any of the text.

Another telling portion is that the NEYC felt compelled to include the idea that visits with family could not be excluded because of behavior, as this is one of the reasons that foster children are often denied normalcy activities. Huggins (2019) wrote of her time in care that many foster youth with behavioral problems were not allowed to participate in normalcy activities and that her own activities were allowed because she was "good".

Perlmutter (2017) also noted that when Florida legislators were hearing testimony from foster youth about the need for normalcy, they were only hearing from those more typical youth.

> The members did not have a chance to engage with other children who do not participate in sports or join clubs. They may be loners or nonjoiners. They may have different interests or have a different gender expression or sexual orientation from their foster care peers. They may be outliers even among the self-identified outcasts in the foster care system.
> (Perlmutter, 2017, p. 167)

Because of this, normalcy often excludes youth who do not meet traditional, middle-class images and norms (Perlmutter, 2017).

Barriers

In addition, even "traditional" foster youth face a number of barriers when trying to live normal lives. Pokempner et al. (2015) wrote that the safety oriented, risk averse nature of most CPS agencies makes implementing normalcy a difficult task. Because safety and fear of liability are their primary concerns, normalcy activities tend to be pushed aside (Pokempner et al., 2015).

In Grotenhuis and Behrer's (2016) survey of nearly 500 current and former foster youth, they found that foster youth reported exclusion from nearly every normal life activity. For example, nearly 47 percent had never ridden in a car with a friend, 30 percent never attended school field trips, 27 percent could not attend a church that they preferred and 18 percent reported not even being allowed to spend time by themselves. The restrictions were especially apparent for youth that were living or had lived in a congregate care placement. For some social activities, youth in congregate care settings were more than four times as likely to have restricted normalcy activities as those in foster of kinship homes. Nearly 60 percent of the youth identified the rules of the placement as the greatest barrier to them being allowed normal activities (Grotenhuis & Behrer, 2016).

This problem inherent in congregate care facilities was also identified by the Annie E. Casey Foundation (2015) that noted that not only do most group homes and RTCs not have a parent figure to make a human connection with the youth, they also serve youth who are placed there simply because state CPS agencies can find no other placement. The congregate care homes often operate on a point level system where youth are not allowed to participate in any activities until they earn points and for every infraction, points can be taken away and their activities further restricted (Annie E. Casey Foundation, 2015).

For my former clients in RTCs, this lack of normalcy problem continued on. For those lucky enough to attend a school off the RTC campus, they had to return directly after school via a bus operated by the placement. Perhaps on a weekend if my client's point level was sufficient, they would be allowed to attend a movie with the other RTC youth, but even then, they would be bused directly to the theater, supervised by RTC staff during the film and then bused directly back to the placement. Some of my clients spent months at a time within the confines of the RTC compound with no independent normal activities provided. Because the fear of liability was so ever present and the rules were so strict, the best option was simply to find my clients a foster or kinship home placement and get them out of congregate care.

The fear of liability drives much of the denial of normalcy, and I will discuss the topic at length in the next chapter. Simmons-Horton (2017) wrote that even with the adoption of the reasonable prudent parent standard as a shield against liability, many foster homes and congregate care facilities required written guarantees by CPS agencies that they would not be held liable if a foster child was injured while participating in normal activities. The state of Texas had even considered gathering data about the number of times that the reasonable prudent parent standard had been violated, so it could assuage fears by showing its contracted caregivers and facilities that the incident rate was low (Texas Children's Commission, 2019).

Another common barrier often identified is the simple lack of transportation and funding necessary for youth to have meaningful participation (Texas Children's Commission, 2019; Annie E. Casey Foundation, 2015; Pokempner et al., 2015). This was often an excuse used by caregivers for my clients. Some foster parents worked separate jobs and transportation was a problem. Some relied on foster care payments as their sole income, so any extra fees associated with a normalcy activity amounted to a reduction in their salary. Often a court order was necessary for CPS to arrange transportation and funding.

Finally, certain classes of foster youth, namely those with disabilities and those that identify as LGBTQ, have particular barriers to normalcy. The United

States Department of Health and Human Services (HHS) (2022) in its guidance to states reported that LGBTQ youth are overrepresented in foster care, are more likely to be placed in congregate care and have worse outcomes than their non-LGBTQ foster peers. They face systemic barriers to their participation in normal activities. HHS (2022) wrote that it was especially important for CPS agencies to ensure that LGBTQ youth are not excluded based on their sexual or gender identities. This includes allowing LGBTQ youth to participate in same-sex sleepovers, participating in LGBTQ organizations and going on dates (Capacity Building Center for States, 2016). Pokempner et al. (2015) wrote that a similar problem occurs for youth with disabilities as they are often denied normal activities for reasons of their disability. Normalcy for youth with disabilities then not only involves allowing them the opportunity, but also providing them with the necessary accommodations that allow them to meaningfully participate (Pokempner et al., 2015).

Research and Normalcy

Because normalcy is a somewhat recent foster care innovation, there are only a handful of studies to specifically look at its effect on foster youth. The most comprehensive thus far is the Texas Youth Permanency Study (TYPS), a 3-year longitudinal study that followed 197 foster youth between the ages of 14 and 20, as they experienced, aged out of and exited foster care (Ball et al., 2023a). The TYPS was the first study to specifically look at how normalcy affects foster youth relationships, life skills and overall well-being. It involved quarterly surveys with foster youth each year as well as a yearly in-depth survey and interview (Ball et al., 2023a).

The results were somewhat striking. Ball et al. (2023a) found that legal permanency, the often-quoted goal of all child welfare cases did not have a significant relationship with the youth's reported level of well-being. Instead, the authors found that normalcy along with relationship permanency were the measures most associated with well-being.

> A sense of normalcy contributed to a positive placement experience and a sense of wellbeing. From the youths ' perspective, normalcy was comprised of feeling part of a family, freedom to engage in age – appropriate social and extracurricular activities, and caregiver support for building life skills.
>
> (Ball et al., 2023a, p. 53)

For the youth in the study, normalcy that encompassed a sense of freedom actually was related to better relationships with their caretakers (Ball et al., 2023a). Foster youth placed in more restrictive settings like RTCs, reported having less trust with the caregivers and more feelings of stress and sadness. The youth that were denied normalcy activities also had the most difficult time with the transition out of foster care and to independent living. The restrictive nature of their foster care experience left them unable to meet the demands of young adulthood (Ball et al., 2023a).

Ball et al. (2023a) argued that normalcy is so important that it should be one of the key pillars for gauging success of a child welfare placement above that of legal permanence. In addition to increasing well-being and leading to stronger caregiver connections, normalcy had a significant impact on life skill development and peer relationships (Ball et al., 2023b). The researchers made a series of recommendations to promote better normalcy practices, including trauma informed training of caregivers that incorporates alternative views of what normal looks like for a youth, make sure that state agencies have appropriate funding to support transportation and extracurricular activities and adding a normalcy review as part of a child permanency review court hearing (Ball et al., 2023b).

The researchers developed the Framework for Normalcy in Child Welfare shown in Figure 3.1 to illustrate the relationship between normalcy activities and the benefits to children in care.

While the TYPS is the most comprehensive normalcy study to date, other researchers have examined more specific aspects of normalcy with implications for its implementation.

Kwak et al. (2018) examined longitudinal data from nearly 800 US foster youth and found that those that participated in organized school or sports clubs had more positive school engagement. They also found that youth who were part of academic clubs had fewer incidents of depression as compared to other foster youth (Kwak et al., 2018).

In a qualitative study of foster parent perceptions of normalcy, McRell et al. (2020) found that foster parents reported significant improvements following

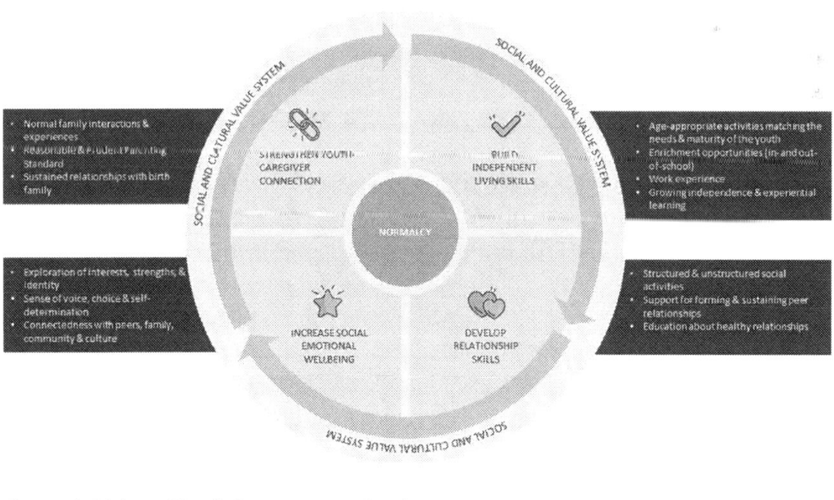

Figure 3.1 Texas Youth Permenency Study

Note: Ball, B., Belseth, T., & Faulkner, M. (2023b). *Normalcy: From concept to practice.* Texas Youth Permanency Study. Texas Institute for Child & Family Wellbeing

their jurisdictions adopting normalcy. Previously they encountered complex bureaucracy and the children in their care experienced negative social outcomes like being denied day trips across state lines. Following implementation, the foster parents reported a sense of empowerment in their decision-making which they believed had positive effects on the children in their care (McRell et al., 2020).

Alford et al. (2019) examined the use of cell phones for foster youth and caregiver attitudes. They reported that phones were a useful tool in promoting normalcy for foster youth, who used them in the same ways as their non-foster peers, to communicate with friends and browse the internet. However, they noted that cell phone use is still one of the normalcy aspects in which CPS agencies retain control due to fear that youth will contact family that they are forbidden to communicate with. The authors argued that his lack of full normalcy sets up conflict between the caregiver, the youth and the CPS agency (Alford et al., 2019).

In a related paper, Badillo-Urquiola et al. (2019) interviewed foster parents about internet use of the foster youth in their care and found that foster youth engage in higher risk internet activities, such as sexual communications with adults at more than four times the rate of their non-foster peers. Therefore, they recommended that normalcy for vulnerable youth would require specific policy guidance on how caregivers can allow and restrict internet access (Badillo-Urquiola et al., 2019).

Rutman and Hubberstey (2018) interviewed former foster youth about their educational experiences and normalcy and found that youth reported that the stability and predictability of their school routines were an important factor in promoting normalcy. The researchers noted that the routine of the school environment gave youth the opportunity to exert a measure of independence and control in their lives, thus highlighting the need to promote educational stability as a means towards normalcy (Rutman & Hubberstey, 2018).

In a study of dual status youth, adults that had experience both with the foster care and juvenile justice systems were interviewed to discuss their normalcy experiences (Simmons-Horton, 2021). Many of the youth reported being denied normalcy activities with some describing complicated bureaucracy just to see a friend or go out. Others reported lack of basic life skills, such as being taught about sexual health and menstruation (Simmons-Horton, 2021).

Driving is another aspect that has been studied and though most states include driving as an essential part of normalcy requirements, youth are often still not licensed at the same rate as their non-foster peers (Bornman & Johnston-Walsh, 2016). In their survey of more than 500 current and former foster youth, the authors found that only 17 percent had their learners permits and only 12 percent had a driver's license. Foster youth faced multiple barriers to operating a vehicle. Liability concerns for their potential adult instructors, the inability to acquire appropriate vehicle insurance and the costs associated all acted to deny foster youth the same normal access to driving (Bornman & Johnston-Walsh, 2016).

Sally was 16 and living in a locked down RTC surrounded by high chain link fence and an electric locked door that security would only open once a visitor showed their identification to the camera. Her school was onsite and the only activities were the occasional field trip to movies, which she often was unable to attend because she had a difficult time following the rules of the placement. She hated living there and along with several other girls at the facility planned and executed an elaborate escape involving distracting the adults and running out of the kitchen exit during a delivery. She was gone for a couple of days before CPS located her and took her back. She continued trying to run until the RTC asked that she be moved to another placement. She said she ran because she just wanted to meet some friends and hang out.

Participation

While a full discussion of child participation will be the focus of Chapter 6, it is useful to briefly look at the concept here as it relates to normalcy. One of the defining aspects of normalcy is that it allows foster youth a voice in their own lives, be that in the simple aspects of how they spend their free time to the more complicated matters of how they organize themselves. As Perlmutter (2017) discussed, organized foster youth telling their stories to legislators were one of the motivating forces behind the passage of Florida's normalcy law and then of the Preventing Sex Trafficking and Strengthening Families Act. An organization of foster youth known as Florida Youth Shine spent three years lobbying the Florida Legislature and in the final year sent 40 foster care youth members to the legislature and spent 12 weeks meeting with legislators and participating in session meetings prior to the passage of Florida's Let Kids be Kids (Funding Florida Legal Aid, 2013).

In their discussion of the creation of the NEYC Normalcy Bill of Rights, Augsberger et al. (2019) wrote that youth themselves perceived the NEYC organization as an opportunity for normalcy. The youth had the freedom to set agendas, call meetings and build a network of professional and social relationships. Because the Normalcy Bill of Rights was the joint efforts of foster youth from six states, the youth also reported feeling a sense of collective power and having their voices heard by CPS and government leaders (Augsberger et al., 2019).

The Youth Law Center (2020) argued that normalcy includes more than polite political participation, but also political and social protest. Given that a disproportionate number of foster youths are Black, the historical and current racial biases of the child protection system and the current climate of social justice activism, it is only natural that foster youth should be allowed to participate in protests and social justice movements. This participation can happen either in person or online and that caregivers need to allow foster youth space for this normal form of free expression (Youth Law Center, 2020).

International

Normalcy as a term almost exclusively appears in literature and statues of the United States. However, the concept or at least portions of it can be found in other parts of the world, though not always with the same understanding.

The UK's Foster Services National Minimum Standards (NMS) (2011) embraces many of the ideas inherent in normalcy. In its discussion of child safety, the NMS allows for child risk, stating

> Foster carers encourage children to take appropriate risks as a normal part of growing up. Children are helped to understand how to keep themselves safe, including when outside of the household or when using the internet or social media.
>
> The service implements a proportionate approach to any risk assessment.
>
> (NMS, 2011, para 4.4–4.5)

The NMS (2011) in its standard on leisure activities also makes clear that foster youth need age-appropriate leisure activities, such as visits with friends and school excursions for their development and that,

> Foster carers are supported to make reasonable and appropriate decisions within the authority delegated to them, without having to seek consent unnecessarily.
>
> (NMS, 2011, para 7.4)

The Canadian Standards for Foster Homes also has some overlap with normalcy. It states,

> Children are encouraged to participate in appropriate and available social and recreational activities according to their abilities and interests. These include school-related activities such as field trips, swimming lessons and other outings.
>
> (Ministry of Children and Family Development, 2023, p. 31)

It goes on to allow caregivers to sign permission forms for most extracurricular activities. The standards make clear that caregivers are not liable for good faith decisions made in this capacity. However, the Canadian authorities do make some limitations for high-risk activities such as snowmobiling (Ministry of Children and Family Development, 2023). This is in contrast with most US state views or normalcy that allow more types of high-risk participation.

Finally, the standards also mention that children in care have a right to maintain cultural practices and be free of discrimination based on religion, culture, disability, sexual and gender identity and race (Ministry of Children and Family Development, 2023).

In Australia, the State of Victoria, Department of Health and Human Services (2016) writes that caregivers can generally sign off on most day-to-day decisions but depending on the type and length of the placement, they require extra authorization agreements to make more impactful decisions, such as overnight stays or school activities. They also exclude a variety of high-risk activities as well as prohibiting travel out of the state without agency approval. Children in care also have several enumerated rights that coincide with normalcy, such as the right to participate,

- *to have fun and do activities that I enjoy*
- *to be able to take part in family traditions, and be able to learn about and be involved with cultural and religious groups that are important to me*
- *to be able to develop life skills and grow up to become the best person I can*

(State of Victoria, 2016, p. 15)

Likewise, New Zealand also shares some similar themes. Section 34 of the Oranga Tamariki National Care Standards and Related Matters Regulations (2018) acknowledges that children in care require support for "play, recreation and community needs". The New Zealand standards also include the need for funding to be made available for these activities. New Zealand also emphasizes allowing children cultural activities, language and expression (Oranga Tamariki, 2018).

In Norway, recent recommendations to the government regarding improvements to foster care involved making normalcy a larger part of children's lives and giving foster parent more ability to make these types of decisions (Skivenes, 2023).

At the EU level, the Council of the European Union (2021) in its establishment of the European Child Guarantee within the framework of promoting better education, also set forth the idea that children should be able to participate in extracurricular school activities and community and cultural events.

Finally, many aspects of normalcy can also be found within the CRC. Article 31 of the CRC (1989) states

1. *States Parties recognize the right of the child to rest and leisure, to engage in play and recreational activities appropriate to the age of the child and to participate freely in cultural life and the arts.*
2. *States Parties shall respect and promote the right of the child to participate fully in cultural and artistic life and shall encourage the provision of appropriate and equal opportunities for cultural, artistic, recreational and leisure activity.*

In the commentary on Article 31, the UN Committee of the Rights of the Child (2013) wrote in terms that mirror those of normalcy discussions in the US, including the notion that childhood comes with some measure of risk stating, "*some degree of risk and challenge is integral to play and recreational activities and is a necessary component of the benefits of these activities*" (para. 39, p. 12). The Committee also highlighted the special needs of children with disabilities and children from minority communities. It also emphasized that children that live in residential facilities should be guaranteed,

> both spaces and opportunities for children to associate with their peers in the community, to play and to participate in games, physical exercise, cultural and artistic life. Such measures should not be restricted to compulsory or organized activities; safe and stimulating environments are needed for children to engage in free play and recreation. Wherever possible, children should be afforded these opportunities within local communities.
>
> (para. 51, p. 12)

Lastly, the commentary laid out 13 necessary conditions for children to have the best environment Article 31 to be realized,

- *Freedom from stress;*
- *Freedom from social exclusion, prejudice or discrimination;*
- *An environment secure from social harm or violence;*
- *An environment sufficiently free from waste, pollution, traffic and other physical hazards to allow them to circulate freely and safely within their local neighbourhood;*
- *Availability of rest appropriate to their age and development;*
- *Availability of leisure time, free from other demands;*
- *Accessible space and time for play, free from adult control and management;*
- *Space and opportunities to play outdoors unaccompanied in a diverse and challenging physical environment, with easy access to supportive adults, when necessary;*
- *Opportunities to experience, interact with and play in natural environments and the animal world;*
- *Opportunities to invest in their own space and time so as to create and transform their world, using their imagination and languages;*
- *Opportunities to explore and understand the cultural and artistic heritage of their community, participate in, create and shape it;*
- *Opportunities to participate with other children in games, sports and other recreational activities, supported, where necessary, by trained facilitators or coaches;*
- *Recognition by parents, teachers and society as a whole of the value and legitimacy of the rights provided for in article 31.*

(para. 32, p. 10–11)

So, in many ways, aspects of normalcy have already been embraced by the international community. However, none of the nation specific standards go into quite as much detail as the US and none quite match the breadth of the concept at least not as articulated in their foster care standards. While play and recreation are important components, normalcy is also about youth making their own decisions, acquiring life skills, making mistakes and directing their own path in life.

The UN commentary on Article 31 probably gets the closest to normalcy. Interestingly it was being created at about the same time as US lawmakers were creating normalcy statutes and just prior to the passage of the PSTSFA, though neither document references the other. Importantly, Article 31 acknowledges risk, but it does lack the life skills and milestone emphasis that is found in other normalcy statutes.

Arguably, the CRC in its totality with the rights to play, participate, free expression and association encompass all the primary aspects of normalcy all be it in a more complex form. It is also relevant to recall that the CRC and Article 31are general rights that are supposed to be applied to all children. Though the commentary mentions children in care, it does not contain provisions specifically for them.

What Is Normal

Unlike best interest, there are not libraries worth of critiques on normalcy. In fact, there is near unanimous consensus that children in care require and are entitled to a normal childhood and youth and that denying them normal activities is actually emotionally, developmentally and mentally damaging them.

In their study of normalcy laws and foster parents, McRell et al. (2020) found that the two primary problems associated with normalcy across the US was its uneven application from jurisdiction to jurisdiction and the lack of funding set aside by the states to make sure that foster youth could participate.

Still, a good faith argument can be made that normal is potentially as subjective a standard as best interest. This is essentially Perlmutter's (2017) argument that normalcy standards do not go far enough to consider a definition beyond middle class, White America. There are also rich criticisms of the use of the word normal by doctors, social scientists and psychologists when it is used to impose normality from the outside and implies a judgment on any behavior that does not comply with outside standards (Rost, 2021).

This is a valid critique that requires us to expand our definition of normal and take special care that activities beyond the mainstream are not automatically labeled abnormal. However, normalcy in the foster care context is not about imposing outside ideas of normal onto a youth, though admittedly that does occur in the child welfare system in general.

Most normalcy statues include specific provisions regarding culture and identity and the associated activities. It is also telling that NEYC's Normalcy Bill of Rights, again designed by foster youth themselves, specifically calls out for protections of

- *Youth in secure facilities,*
- *Youth from varying ethnic, religious, and cultural backgrounds – including Native youth,*

- *Youth with non-conforming gender identification and sexual orientations, and,*
- *Youth with physical and mental disabilities (IEP, learning disabilities, physical handicaps).*

(NEYC, 2016b, p. 1)

While there will always be subjectivity in human decision-making and majority community standards will obviously guide decisions about normality, at the heart of normalcy is a universality that is less subjective. The freedom to visit with family, to spend time with friends, to learn and practice adult skills, to have romantic relationships and to take risks are part of almost every life regardless of background or culture.

Ultimately, it is this universal aspect of normalcy that takes into account the desires and voice of the foster youth themselves that makes it a better standard for us to make decisions.

References

Alford, K. A., Denby, R. W., & Gomez, E. (2019). Use of smartphone technology in foster care to build relational competence: Voices of caregivers and implications for prudent parenting. *Journal of Family Social Work*, *22*(3), 209–230. https://doi.org/10.1080/10522158.2018.1558428

The Annie E. Casey Foundation. (2015). *What young people need to thrive: Leveraging the strengthening families act to promote normalcy*. Retrieved March 8, 2024, from https://assets.aecf.org/m/resourcedoc/aecf-whatyoungpeopleneedtothrive-2015.pdf

Arizona Department of Children and Families. (2022). *The "got to guide": A guide for foster and kinship caregivers*. Retrieved March 7, 2024, from https://dcs.az.gov/sites/default/files/DCS-Forms/CSO-2143-kinship-foster-go-to-guide.pdf

Augsberger, A., Springwater, J. S., Hilliard-Koshinsky, G., Barber, K., & Martinez, L. S. (2019). Youth participation in policy advocacy: Examination of a multi-state former and current foster care youth coalition. *Children and Youth Services Review*, *107*, 104491. https://doi.org/10.1016/j.childyouth.2019.104491

Badillo-Urquiola, K., Page, X., & Wisniewski, P. J. (2019). *Risk vs. restriction: The tension between providing a sense of normalcy and keeping foster teens safe online* [Conference session]. Proceedings of the 2019 CHI Conference on Human Factors in Computing Systems. https://doi.org/10.1145/3290605.3300497

Ball, B., Belseth, T., & Faulkner, M. (2023b). *Normalcy: From concept to practice*. Texas Youth Permanency Study, Texas Institute for Child & Family Wellbeing. Retrieved March 20, 2024, from https://txicfw.socialwork.utexas.edu/wp-content/uploads/2023/01/The-Concept-of-Normalcy-in-Child-Welfare_January-2023.pdf

Ball, B., Marra, L., Bellseth, T., & Faulkner, M. (2023a). *Final report: The Texas Youth permanency study*. Texas Institute for Child and Family Well Being. Retrieved March 20, 2024, from https://txicfw.socialwork.utexas.edu/research/project/texas-youth-permanency-study/

Blackshere, R. (2013). Florida and California work towards promoting normalcy in the foster care system. *The Imprint Youth and Family News*. Retrieved March 4, 2024, from https://imprintnews.org/featured/florida-and-california-work-towards-promoting-normalcy-in-the-foster-care-system/3538

Bornman, B., & Johnston-Walsh, L. (2016). *Keys to independence: driving for foster youth*. Pennsylvania Children and Youth Administrators Association & Penn State

Dickinson Law's Children's Advocacy Clinic. Retrieved March 21, 2024, from https://dickinsonlaw.psu.edu/sites/default/files/2020-02/Keys-to-Independence-White-Paper.pdf

Capacity Building Center for States. (2016). *Considerations for LGBTQ children and youth in foster care: Exploring normalcy as it relates to P.L. 113–183.* Children's Bureau, Administration for Children and Families, U.S. Department of Health and Human Services.

Council of the European Union. (2021). *Council Recommendation (EU) 2021/1004 of 14 June 2021 establishing a European Child Guarantee.* Retrieved March 25, 2024, from https://EUR-Lex – 32021H1004 – EN – EUR-Lex (europa.eu)

Fla. Stat. § 39.4091. https://www.flcourts.gov/content/download/868075/file/Chapter%2039%202022-10-24.pdf

Florida GAL. (2014). *A voice heard: Let kids be kids.* Florida Guardian Ad Litem Survey Report. Retrieved March 4, 2024, from https://guardianadlitem.org/wp-content/uploads/2014/08/Let-Kids-Be-Kids-2014.pdf

Foster Services National Minimum Standards (NMS). (2011). *Department of Education.* Retrieved March 22, 2024, from https://www.gov.uk/government/publications/fostering-services-national-minimum-standards

Funding Florida Legal Aid. (2013). *Florida foster youth shine at the Capitol.* Children's Legal Services. Retrieved March 22, 2024, from https://fundingfla.org/florida-foster-youth-shine-at-the-capitol/

Grotenhuis, C., & Behrer, C. (2016). *Foster care: When normal ain't normal.* Issue Brief. Youth Policy Institute of Iowa. Retrieved March 19, 2024, from https://iowaaftercare.org/PDF%20files/IssueBrief_Normalcy.pdf

Hawaii Department of Human Services. (2016). *Don't say "No" until you "Know" a guide for caregivers to promote normalcy and well-being for children and young people in foster care.* Retrieved March 7, 2024, from https://humanservices.hawaii.gov/wp-content/uploads/2017/10/Dont-Say-No-Until-You-Know-Handout-revised-6-2017.pdf

Huggins, B. (2019). Former foster youth, advocate shares why normalcy is necessary. *The Imprint, Youth and Family News.* Retrieved March 18, 2024, from https://imprintnews.org/youth-voice/former-foster-youth-advocate-shares-why-normalcy-is-necessary/34097

The Illinois Department of Children and Family Services. (n.d.). *Normalcy policy lets foster parents make normal decisions.* Retrieved March 7, 2024, from https://dcfs.illinois.gov/content/dam/soi/en/web/dcfs/documents/loving-homes/normalcy/documents/normalcy_chart.1.0.pdf

Jacobson, P. (2016). Promoting "normalcy" for foster children: The preventing sex trafficking and strengthening families act. *Missouri Law Review*, *81*, 21.

Jim Casey Youth Opportunities Initiative. (2011). *The adolescent brain: New research and its implications for youth people transitioning from foster care.* Retrieved March 18, 2024, from https://assets.aecf.org/m/resourcedoc/AECF-theAdolescentBrain-2011.pdf

Juvenile Law Center. (2013). *Teen success agreement.* Youth Fostering Change. Retrieved March 22, 2024, from https://jlc.org/resources/teen-success-agreement

Kwak, Y., Mihalec-Adkins, B., Mishra, A. A., & Christ, S. L. (2018). Differential impacts of participation in organized activities and maltreatment types on adolescent academic and socioemotional development. *Child Abuse & Neglect*, *78*, 107–117. https://doi.org/10.1016/j.chiabu.2017.09.026

McRell, A. S., Holmes, C. E., Singh, A., Levkoff, S. E., Schooley, B., Hikmet, N., & Seay, K. D. (2020). Youth in foster care and the reasonable and prudent parenting standard. *Child Maltreatment*, *26*(3), 302–312. https://doi.org/10.1177/1077559520957748

Ministry of Children and Family Development. (2023). Standards for foster homes. *British Columbia*. Retrieved March 24, 2024, from https://www2.gov.bc.ca/assets/gov/family-and-social-supports/foster-parenting/standards_foster_homes.pdf

National Foster Care Youth & Alumni Policy Council. (2013). *Improving well-being by addressing normalcy for foster youth*. Retrieved March 18, 2024, from https://www.nationalpolicycouncil.org/sites/default/files/docs/landingpage/Normalcy%20Priorities.pdf

New England Youth Coalition. (2016a). *Normalcy definition*. Retrieved March 18, 2024, from https://img1.wsimg.com/blobby/go/aa733825-dec1-4c7c-8186-9d77c28f0de9/downloads/Approved_NormalcyDefinition_FINAL_highres_bann.pdf?ver=1574808219079

New England Youth Coalition. (2016b). *Normalcy bill of rights*. Retrieved March 18, 2024, from https://img1.wsimg.com/blobby/go/aa733825-dec1-4c7c-8186-9d77c28f0de9/downloads/Approved_NormalcyBillofRights_FINAL_high-res_ba.pdf?ver=1574808032340

North Carolina Division of Social Services. (2015). *Reasonable and prudent parent activities guide*. https://policies.ncdhhs.gov/divisional/social-services/child-welfare/policy-manuals/reasonable_prudent_parenting_activities_guide.pdf

Oranga Tamariki (National Care Standards and Related Matters) Regulations 2018 (LI 2018/111). https://www.legislation.govt.nz/regulation/public/2018/0111/latest/lms56030.html

Pennsylvania Youth Advisory Board. (2016). *Developmentally appropriate freedoms and normalcy recommendations*. Center for the Study of Social Policy. Retrieved March 22, 2024, from https://cssp.org/resource/2016-dafguidereader/

Perlmutter, B. (2017). "Letting kids be kids": Youth voice and activism to reform foster care and promote "normalcy". *Studies in Law, Politics, and Society, 72*. Retrieved March 5, 2024, from https://repository.law.miami.edu/cgi/viewcontent.cgi?article=1210&context=fac_books

Pokempner, J. (2016). *The role of the court in implementing the older youth provisions of the strengthening families act*. ABA Center on Children and the Law Youth Engagement Project. Retrieved March 8, 2024, from https://jlc.org/sites/default/files/publication_pdfs/ABAIssueBrief-SFAforCourts-Feb2016_0.pdf

Pokempner, J., Mordecai, K., Rosado, L., & Subrahmanyam, D. (2015). Promoting normalcy for children and youth in foster care. *Juvenile Law Center*. Retrieved March 18, 2024, from https://jlc.org/sites/default/files/publication_pdfs/JLC-NormalcyGuide-2015FINAL.pdf

Preventing Sex Trafficking and Strengthening Families Act of 2014 (H.R. 4980). *Congress.gov*. Retrieved March 7, 2024, from https://www.congress.gov/bill/113th-congress/house-bill/4980/text

Rost, M. (2021). To normalize is to impose a requirement on an existence: Why health professionals should think twice before using the term "normal" with patients. *Journal of Bioethical Inquiry, 18*(3), 389–394. https://doi.org/10.1007/s11673-021-10122-2

Rutman, D., & Hubberstey, C. (2018). Fostering educational success of children and youth in care: Perspectives of youth with experience living in care. *Children and Youth Services Review, 94*, 257–264. https://doi.org/10.1016/j.childyouth.2018.10.022

Simmons-Horton, S. Y. (2017). Providing age-appropriate activities for youth in foster care: Policy implementation process in three states. *Children and Youth Services Review, 82*, 383–391. https://doi.org/10.1016/j.childyouth.2017.10.007

Simmons-Horton, S. Y. (2021). "A bad combination": Lived experiences of youth involved in the foster care and juvenile justice systems. *Child and Adolescent Social Work Journal, 38*(6), 583–597. https://doi.org/10.1007/s10560-020-00693-1

Skivenes, M. (2023). *Improving foster care in Norway*. Center for Research of Discretion and Paternalism. Blogpost. Retrieved March 25, 2024, from uib.no

State of Victoria, Department of Health and Human Services. (2016). *Victorian handbook for foster carers*. Victorian Government. Retrieved March 24, 2024, from https://services.dffh.vic.gov.au/sites/default/files/2021-07/Victorian%20Foster%20carer%20handbook%202%20copy.pdf

Texas Children's Commission. (2019). *Normalcy for children and youth in foster care roundtable report*. University of Texas at Austin. Retrieved March 20, 2024, from https://www.texaschildrenscommission.gov/media/c5odg54d/normalcy-report-final-print.pdf

UN Committee on the Rights of the Child, General Comment No. 17. (2013). *On the right of the child to rest, leisure, play, recreational activities, cultural life and the arts (art. 31)*. Retrieved March 25, 2024, from https://digitallibrary.un.org/record/778539?v=pdf

United Nations Convention on the Rights of the Child (CRC). (1989). https://www.ohchr.org/en/instruments-mechanisms/instruments/convention-rights-child

U.S. Department of Health & Human Services, Administration for Children and Families, Administration on Children, Youth and Families, Children's Bureau. (2022). *Guidance for title IV-B and IV-E agencies when serving LGBTQI+ children and youth*. Retrieved March 20, 2024, from https://www.acf.hhs.gov/cb/policy-guidance/im-22-01

Youth Law Center. (2018). *Providing normalcy for California foster youth*. Retrieved March 8, 2024, from https://www.ylc.org/wp-content/uploads/2018/12/Providing-Normalcy-for-California-Foster-Youth-053118.pdf

Youth Law Center. (2020). *Social justice activism and normalcy*. Retrieved March 8, 2024, from https://www.ylc.org/resource/social-justice-activism-and-normalcy/

4 Risk, Normalcy and Best Interest

On the surface both best interest and normalcy seem like they have the same goal, the stability and well-being of a child in care. This is true in a broad fashion. Best interest is supposedly about keeping a child safe from harm and meeting their physical, emotional and mental needs, whereas normalcy is about allowing them freedom to make choices about their everyday life. Certainly, so long as youth are in danger from immediate violence or severe neglect, a normal life might be impossible.

Still, as described in Chapter 2, best interest is a deeply flawed legal standard that promotes bias, inequality and despite 200 years of use, has no universally understood definition. In addition, best interest fosters a conservative, risk averse decision-making standard. This risk aversion is inherent part of the child welfare system. It leads to the elevation of safety beyond all other concerns and thusly with the goal of keeping kids safe, best interest denies foster youth their participation and freedom and ultimately is detrimental to their overall well-being.

Despite the push for normalcy, as a legal standard it remains subservient to best interest as best interest language was inserted into normalcy statues and discussions. This language ultimately clouds the purpose of normalcy and dilutes its positive effects.

Reasonable Prudent Parent Standard

As discussed in the prior chapter, one of the hallmarks of normalcy is that it allows caregivers to make normalcy decisions on behalf of the children in their care without seeking complicated approval from CPS agencies and courts. The decisions themselves are governed by the reasonable prudent parent standard (RPP).

Like normalcy in general, the RPP has its roots in the early state laws, such as the ones from California and Florida that established the normalcy doctrine (Jacobson, 2016). The standard then made its way into the Preventing Sex Trafficking and Strengthening Families Act with almost no changes (Jacobson, 2016). The PSTSFA defines it thusly as,

> the standard characterized by careful and sensible parental decisions that maintain the health, safety, and best interests of a child while at the same

DOI: 10.4324/9781003510253-4

> time encouraging the emotional and developmental growth of the child, that a caregiver shall use when determining whether to allow a child in foster care under the responsibility of the State to participate in extracurricular, enrichment, cultural, and social activities.
>
> (Title 1 Subtitle B § 111(a)(10)(A)

As can be seen in the definition above, the words "best interest" are baked into the definition of a reasonable prudent parent as are mentions of health and safety. However, the purpose of the reasonable prudent parent standard is not about transforming normalcy decisions into best interest decisions. It is ultimately about caregiver liability.

This is made clear in Title 1 Subtitle B § 111(b)(C) that mandates that states include liability waivers as part of their adoption of the RPP. This waiver of liability for caregivers is then explicitly made to them during trainings. For instance, the Tennessee Department of Children's Services (2016) policy guidance states that so long as caregivers exercise their judgment under RPP they will not be held liable for any injuries to a child who is participating in a normalcy activity so long as they were not grossly negligent or committed an intentional act of harm. The Kentucky statute states

> A caregiver shall not be liable as a result of the caregiver's approval of the participation of a child who is in the custody of the cabinet in an age or developmentally appropriate activity, so long as the caregiver acts in accordance with the reasonable and prudent parent standard.
>
> Ky. Rev. Stat. § 605.102(3)

Likewise, Arizona law reads,

> The state shall indemnify and hold harmless the agency or foster parents for liability that may be incurred or alleged as a result of giving permission pursuant to subsection A if it is reasonably and prudently given. The state shall provide the defense of any action alleging such liability.
>
> Ariz. Rev. Stat. § 8–513 (B)

CPS agencies generally also provide guidance to caregivers on how to implement the standard. The New York City Administration for Children's Services (2018) suggests that caregivers answer a series of 17 questions before making a RPP decision, such as

> Does this activity promote the child's cognitive, social, emotional, physical, and/or educational development?
>
> Has the child shown maturity in decision-making and exhibited responsible behavior that is appropriate for their age/ability?
>
> Have I reviewed any medical or other history in considering whether the activity is in the child's best interests?

> Does the child have the necessary and appropriate safety equipment, such as bicycle helmet, shin guards, etc.?
>
> (NYCAC, 2018, p. 20)

The Philadelphia Department of Human Services (2018) asks caregivers to consider nine factors, such as,

> The potential risk factors and appropriateness of the extracurricular, enrichment, cultural or social activity or experience.
>
> The best interest of the child, based on information known by the caregiver. Providing the child with the most family-like living experience possible.
>
> (PDHS, 2018, p. 1)

Similar language is found throughout US jurisdictions and their purpose is to provide liability protection to caregivers for injuries to children in care. Still because best interest is part of RPP and it is part of the much of the guidance to foster parents, all normalcy decisions are embedded within a greater best interest decision-making framework.

Briefly, from an international perspective, the UN Committee of the Rights of the Child (2013) wrote that the CRC's Article 31 does not conflict with best interest as having the right to play, rest and leisure is fundamentally in a child's best interest. The Committee also linked Article 31 with a child's right to be heard, right to participation and right to association. Still even the Article 31 commentary highlights that best interest should be considered when determining the appropriate amount of risk for children (UN Committee of the Rights of the Child, 2013).

Jack, a 15-year-old male, had been in care since he was a toddler, but he never found early permanency. As he got older, his behavior worsened, and he would curse caregivers, break items and fight with other kids in the home. This led him to being placed in a series of RTCs across the state. He picked up a juvenile charge when he spit on a school resource officer trying to break up a fight between him and another student. In his free time, he loved video games and anything to do with robots. Except for a few excursions and the occasional video game if his placement had one, he was denied real normalcy for almost a decade and spent years in a locked down facility. When a foster home that specialized in older boys had an open spot, CPS did not want to place him there for fear of his past behavior. They wanted him to demonstrate he could be good enough for a foster home placement. The judge ordered the placement over CPS objections. Jack began to flourish in his new home. His school attendance and his grades improved. His bad behaviors ceased entirely. He joined a school club.

Risk Aversion

A natural enemy to normalcy and childhood well-being, risk aversion in child protection is part of larger societal trends that regards childhood as a time of existential risk and judges parents and caretakers for all failures to prevent injury to children. Numerous researchers and commentators have pointed out this growing risk aversion and the negative consequences for youth that follow (Gill, 2007; Cooke et al., 2021; Vigdal & Brønnick, 2022; Gray et al., 2023).

Gill (2007) wrote that in the past children were thought of as having capabilities and independence that we do not conceive of today. As an example, as recently as the 1970s, 80 percent of parents allowed 7-year-old children to go to school on their own or walk to a store, but by the '90s most parents reported that this activity was only appropriate for 10-year-olds. Some primary reasons for the increased risk aversion come from the changing physical landscape of communities that discouraged walkable neighborhoods, the increasingly online nature of relationships that fails to build ties with neighbors and community, and the spread and amplification of rare but tragic events involving children by the media and the internet. Because parents became more risk averse, this in turn pushed institutions like schools and CPS agencies into more risk aversion (Gill, 2007).

Brussoni (2024) argued that a parental trend that began in the 1980s emphasized a highly structure parenting style of intensive interaction with their children. Parents are bombarded with information about the need to keep children safe. This fear has led parents to prioritize screens over, riskier independent play time resulting in UK children spending nearly 30 percent less time outside in 2015 than then 1975 peers (Brussoni, 2024).

In a survey of US state laws regarding independence, Redleaf (2020) wrote that the many criminal and child protection laws and policies have unreasonable limits on normal childhood independence. Most states' child protection statutes were so broad that failure to supervise regardless of age or duration could be considered neglect. Some states, like Maryland, make it a crime for any child under 8 years old to be unsupervised for any amount of time. In Connecticut that age is 12 years old. Additionally, many states criminalize leaving a child alone in a car for any amount of time. The overall effect of these laws and policies is that childhood independence can be punished and parents are held accountable for activities they themselves might have grown up doing (Redleaf, 2020).

Research has shown that these risk averse beliefs come with negative con sequences for all children. Gray et al. (2023) in their metanalysis review of the effects of mental health effects of the lack of childhood independence also noted consistent reports that children today have fewer independent freedoms than those before. They wrote,

> Beginning in the 1960s and accelerating in the 1980s, the implicit understanding shifted from that of children as competent, responsible, and resilient to the opposite, as advice focused increasingly on children's needs for supervision and protection . . . What has declined specifically is children's freedom to engage in activities that involve some degree of risk and personal responsibility away from adults.
>
> (Gray et al., 2023, p. 2)

The researchers noted that at the same time, mental illness rates in children rose. Using the same scales, children reported more incidents of anxiety and depression. Even more tellingly, suicide rates increased by 3.5 times from 1950 through 2005 and then increased another 2.4 times through 2020 (Gray et al., 2023).

Relatedly other research has found correlational links between risk averse helicopter parents and increased incidents of anxiety and depression in their children (Vigdal & Brønnick, 2022); that the children of risk averse parents engaged in less physical activity (Jerebine et al., 2024); and that children who experience unstructured times scored better on self-directed executive functioning tasks than those who do not (Barker et al., 2014).

Meanwhile, the positive effects of independence, play and risk tolerance in childhood is equally well established by research. Sando et al. (2021) observed that risky play was associated with childhood measures of well-being and physical activity. Children learn better, have better memories and have better life trajectories when allowed opportunities for more independent play (Yogman et al., 2018). Kvalnes and Sandseter (2023) wrote that risky play promotes physical motor coordination and reduces anxiety.

In a major longitudinal study, Weikart (1998) found that preschoolers who were given free play time had significantly better outcomes in school at age 15, than those who were denied free play time. Then again as 23-year-old adults, the free play cohort were more likely to be married and less likely to have been fired from their job or arrested (Weikart, 1998).

Gray et al. (2023) wrote that the denial of childhood independence and poor mental health have an evolutionary link. Indigenous communities, whose daily lives are closer to those of our ancestors allow even toddlers considerably more freedom than parents in modernized states. Young children take part in many more community activities and are given greater responsibilities as they age. Evolution would have favored children with a biological drive for independence and risk taking and this drive is being denied in modern communities (Gray et al., 2023).

Independence and risky play are so important for childhood physical, mental and emotional development that the Canadian Pediatric Society recently issued a position statement encouraging doctors, parents and communities to adopt practices to encourage this behavior (Beaulieu & Beno, 2024). Brussoni et al. (2012) argued that the standard to promote child well-being it was important to keep, "*children as safe as necessary, not as safe as possible*" (p. 3142).

Childhood Well-being

Central to the idea that a healthy life involves more than just protection from danger is well-being. Numerous researchers and governmental entities have proposed various definitions of childhood well-being (O'Hare, 2022). Early attempts at defining and tracking well-being often focused on socioeconomic and demographic factors, such as poverty rates, teen pregnancies, education, death rates and drug use (Moore, 2020). Positive factors and the subjective experiences of children were generally absent from any early measurements (Moore, 2020).

As research and data collection improved, the concept of well-being was widened to include mental and emotional health, behavior and the child's environment (Moore, 2020). Researchers began to conceptualize that well-being was more than just the physical health of the child and it needed to include the idea of the "whole child". Well-being also began to be considered over the life course of the child with the idea that one stage of childhood could affect the next and that could go on to affect adulthood. Childhood itself began to be seen as its own stage of life rather than simply the prelude to adulthood (Moore, 2020).

Life course studies also led to the distinction between childhood well-being and well-becoming (O'Hare, 2022). Well-becoming looks primarily at indicators such as education that point towards measures of future adult success, whereas well-being looks at more immediate concerns, such as if a child is currently sick or hungry. Both perspectives are needed for a more comprehensive understanding of overall childhood well-being (O'Hare, 2022).

The newest models of comprehensive childhood well-being emphasize five broad categories, "*cognitive and academic development; mental and emotional well-being; social behavior; and physical health and functioning, [and] relationships*" (Moore, 2020, p. 734). O'Hare (2022) wrote that in addition researchers have been increasingly adding children's subjective experiences in their measures of well-being. While more difficult to obtain than some simpler demographic information, subjective measurements are important because how children feel about their lives, their relationships and their emotional states are a valuable piece of overall well-being (O'Hare, 2022).

All of these notions are reflected in UNICEF's (2007) six primary measurements of well-being; "*material well-being, health and safety, education, peer and family relationships, behaviours and risks, and young people's own subjective sense of well-being*" (p. 2). UNICEF in turn wrote that its own concept of child well-being is closely aligned with the rights of children found within the CRC (UNICEF, 2007).

The CRC is routinely cited as a legal document that encompasses a holistic view of childhood well-being (O'Hare, 2022; Land & Lamb, 2014; Prada & Sanchez-Fernandez, 2021). Dock (2014) wrote that the totality of children's rights found within the CRC ultimately lead to well-being. "*Child's well-being can be defined as the realization of the child's rights and the fulfillment of the opportunity for the child to be all he or she can be in light of the child's abilities, potential, and skills*" (Dock, 2014, p. 205). The right to be protected from abuse and neglect found within CRC Article 19 is certainly fundamental to the well-being of children, but it is only one right among many.

It is also important to recall here that US normalcy statutes also have used the language of well-being, such as Florida's Let Kids Be Kids law. The National Foster Care Youth and Alumni Policy Council (2013) also endorsed normalcy as a path to well-being. Lastly, it was also one of the primary measurements in the Texas Youth Permanency Study that found strong correlations between normalcy and foster youth well-being, with the study authors arguing that well-being should be a primary metric by which we measure the success of the child welfare system (Ball et al., 2023).

Child Protection vs Child Welfare

Perhaps the most fundamental argument in the field is about the purpose of the child welfare system. Is it about the child protection, which promotes child safety and family removals or abut child welfare, which promotes child well-being and family preservation? In everyday practice around the world, it is obviously a little bit of both, but CPS agencies in different countries and jurisdictions work under laws and policies that favor one or the other depending on the circumstances of the case, the work culture and the local community. This in turn has large implications for how CPS workers and foster parents interpret best interest and normalcy.

Berger and Slack (2014) found that overall while every jurisdiction has some hybrid elements, countries that spend more of their GDP on social welfare programs in general tend to be closer in alignment with child welfare practices, whereas those that spend less in total GDP tend to favor child safety related measures. Australia, Canada and the United States were in the child safety group, while countries like Belgium, Denmark and Sweden leaned towards child welfare (Berger & Slack, 2014).

Nations with the child welfare leaning also tended to have lower rates of childhood poverty and with some outliers tended to rate higher on global childhood well-being. However, differences in how the countries report and classify their data makes direct comparisons complicated. Interestingly though, there appeared to be no correlation between rates of child deaths regardless of the CPS alignment (Berger & Slack, 2014).

In the US some researchers have attributed the cultural shift from child welfare to child protection partially as a result of the creation of mandatory reporting laws which increased the number of child welfare complaints to CPS agencies, but did not translate into greater resources (Jones et al., 2015; Lindsey, 2004).

However, in the UK, which does not have mandatory reporting, multiple researchers reported that despite a governmental push towards and a desire for a child welfare orientation, most workers still approached their cases from a child protection perspective (Spratt, 2001; Hayes & Spratt, 2012; Munro, 2011).

The Child Welfare System and Risk Aversion

Set against the larger societal trend of risk aversion for childhood activities discussed before, is the specific risk aversion found throughout CPS agencies around the globe. This specific risk aversion inherent in child welfare practices leads CPS workers to prioritize safety above well-being, limits foster children's ability to lead a more normal life and actually endangers families and children by bringing more children into care than would otherwise be warranted.

Some studies have looked at how internal beliefs drive risk decisions by CPS workers. Keddell's (2017) study of New Zealand caseworkers found that risk averse and risk tolerant workers both perceived the same risk and safety factors in a vignette case, but the risk averse group placed more emphasis on safety focusing on the child's past trauma and the potential for future maltreatment. The risk averse group also expressed more confidence in their decisions than the risk tolerant workers (Keddell, 2017).

In a US study, Fluke et al. (2016) reported that CPS workers with less experience and more cases were more likely to prefer a child safety orientation. They also found that workers who perceived their CPS agency to have a shared vision also tended to favor child safety (Fluke et al., 2016).

As mentioned above, one of the most common traits for a CPS agency is an embedded sense of risk aversion. In a report presented to the UK parliament, Munro (2011) criticized the practice writing,

> Those involved in child protection must be "risk sensible". There is no option of being risk averse since there is no absolutely safe option. In reality, risk averse practice usually entails displacing the risk onto someone else. Even if every child who was considered or suspected to be suffering harm was removed from their birth family, that would only incur different risks.
>
> (Munro, 2011, p. 60)

In a second UK report a decade later, MacAlister (2020) also identified risk aversion as an ongoing structural barrier to improving child welfare services and noted that the bureaucracy of the system, along with notions of safeguarding children encouraged risk averse behavior that was ultimately bad for families and children.

In two studies directly related to normalcy, Milligan (2011) reported that risk averse practices by residential home caretakers in Scotland meant that children were not provided recreational opportunities with one caretaker describing approaching the activities for children as if they were wrapped in cotton. Another study of Scottish residential centers reported that caretakers' fear and risk aversion prevented them from providing even necessary nurturing physical contact to the children in need of emotional security and attachment (Grant, 2011).

This risk aversion also bleeds into how foster parents care for children (Berridge et al., 2014). Foster parent surveys showed that some were also fearful of providing normal activities and normal care.

> Blanket policies or guidance (or their interpretation by social workers and their managers) can inhibit normal life in the foster home to the

> extent that children can miss out on ordinary physical affection and the reassurance of touch that is so important for healthy development.
>
> (p. 114)

Foster parents also reported experiencing blame from CPS workers with threats of punishment when they themselves made mistakes (Berridge et al., 2014).

The UK is not the only nation where CPS agencies have been criticized for risk averse practices. Blumhardt et al. (2017) wrote that the New Zealand system's risk aversion was related to CPS being unwilling to relinquish any control of an open case or investigation. This coupled with time pressures to make quick decisions led to an environment where CPS workers favor risk avoidance. They wrote, "*control-heavy systems frequently impose processes and interventions on families rather than handing families power to shape the support they receive*" (Blumhardt et al., 2017, p. 25).

In Australia, an independent inquiry into foster care services also wrote that a risk averse culture was hinderance reported by caregivers (Arney et al., 2022). The report noted that CPS staff approached cases and families with a rigidity that reflected internal performance measurements more than the child's actual needs (Arney et al., 2022).

A Council of Europe report from the Committee on Social Affairs, Health and Sustainable Development (2018) also identified risk aversion as an ongoing problem in European child services.

Of course, CPS in the US also has its own risk aversion problems. In one study of initial intake decision-making, Kearney et al. (2023) found that a culture of risk aversion leads to a higher rate of false positives, that is, families investigated when no maltreatment occurred. They noted that since investigations alone can be damaging for families and the mental health of children, "*not only do high rates of investigations potentially harm and alienate children and families, they limit the resources available to the CPS agency*" (Kearney et al., 2023, p. 6).

CPS Errors and Culture of Fear

Because risk in child welfare can sometimes mean the death or serious injury of a child, it is completely reasonable that child welfare workers might lean towards risk aversion. However, what might naturally be slight risk averse orientation has been expanded by a fear of making any mistakes.

Berrick and Chambers (2020) wrote that false positive errors in in decision-making can have particularly negative effects on disadvantaged communities.

> An injustice against a single family is grave. Yet when violations such as erroneous family break- up occur or are perceived to occur disproportionately within a single neighbourhood or community, the damage reverberates.
>
> (Berrick & Chambers, 2020, p. 238)

Because these types of errors are often made against marginalized communities, they do not receive widespread media attention, whereas false negative errors that do result in injury or death to child are likely to make the news and receive public scrutiny. These false negative errors often lead to public outrage and call into question the trust and work of the CPS agency (Berrick & Chambers, 2020).

Camasso and Jagannathan (2013) wrote that publicized instances of horrific child abuse fuels,

> the "routinization of outrage," i.e., the process by which social outrage over child fatalities and other horrific instances of child maltreatment penetrate deeply into CPS information, service delivery, and decision-making flows.
>
> (Camasso & Jagannathan, 2013, p. 1644)

The result is generally that CPS adopts a more zero tolerance risk averse stance towards families that changes the workplace culture to one where CPS workers are encouraged to fall into line. This finally leads to more employee turnover, with new hires replacing more experienced workers, which again leads to a calcification of risk aversion (Camasso & Jagannathan, 2013).

Stoddart (2017) argued that these moral panic events often lead to consequences that are not commiserate with the actual risks involved. With a focus on blame and accountability, moral panics can lead to changes in CPS rules and policies that force the agency to investigate more families with more scrutiny. These panics also induce CPS agencies to focus on risk to themselves, which subsequently causes them to shift to more bureaucratic accountability. This conversely lessens the time workers have to actually spend with children and families (Stoddart, 2017)

In their research of how child abuse and child welfare are reported by US news agencies Han et al. (2019) found that nearly 60 percent of the news coverage was about a specific instance of child maltreatment and again nearly 60 percent of those were about the death of a child. They also found that the media tended to portray CPS as a struggling agency beset by problems. In more than half the stories, after the fact solutions, such as policy changes or the termination and resignation of staff were mentioned, while less than 1 percent mentioned any of the societal and structural problems associated with child abuse (Han et al., 2019).

Casey Family Programs (2023) reported that workforce retention has been an ongoing problem for CPS agencies for several decades. One of the solutions Casey Family (2023) recommended was to shift CPS organizational culture away from a model of blame. This culture of blame and fear not only has negative consequences for families who are falsely investigated, but it also has led to a series workforce turnover crisis, where nearly 50 percent of CPS workers leave the job within two years (Cull & Lindsey, 2023).

In a study of how risk aversion affects CPS workers individually, Fenton and Kelly (2017) found workers reported more ethical stress when forced to routinely make risk averse decisions. The fear of making the wrong decision, led them to make "safer" decisions, but also contributed to their stress as they were prevented from making decisions based on their own values and training. The researchers argued that the workers suffered from a minor, but sustained form of moral injury as a result (Fenton & Kelly, 2017).

In the UK where CPS workers faced similar organizational pressures Munro (2011) coined the term "defensive practices" to describe how workers react. Munro wrote,

> Concern with managing uncertainty has been affected by the level of public outcry when mistakes are made, so that there has been a shift towards defensive practice where a concern with protecting oneself or one's agency has competed, and sometimes overridden, a concern with protecting children. In this respect, the focus on process and recording needed by the audit system has offered a tempting solution. As identified in the first review report, if it is generally agreed that "good" practice equals following procedures and keeping records well, then these are all tasks within the control of managers. From a management perspective, a concentration on auditing increasingly prescribed procedures offers a way of defending the organisation and fending off criticism. But the availability of the "correct procedures were followed" defence is a siren call. It seems to hold out security but actually creates a feedback loop that reinforces the defensive routine based on a procedural perspective which hampers professional learning. From the perspective of the front line, this has contributed to many feeling that they are working in a compliance culture where meeting performance management demands becomes the dominant focus rather than meeting the needs of children and their families. When these conflict, even the most dedicated child-centred professionals can feel pressured to prioritise the performance demand over the child's needs.
>
> (Munro, 2011, p. 20)

In Whittaker and Havard's (2016) study, social work students reported that defensive practices were essentially rooted in fear and a culture of blame. The students reported that defenses practices led to risk averse decisions that followed a narrow procedural formula to reduce the chance that blame could be assigned to the decision-maker and that ultimately the defensive practice decisions were subjective (Whittaker & Havard, 2016).

MacAlister (2020) reported the same defensive practices that Munro found a decade prior. The culture of blame and rigidity led to CPS workers to feel under supported and led to poorer decision-making (MacAlister, 2020).

Sicora (2017) argued that child welfare decision-making inherently involves risk and the possibility of error and mistakes. They are ultimately ethical decisions as an error of either kind could result in harm to a child or family. However, blame culture with public displays of punishment is one of the greatest obstacles to change within child welfare agencies (Sicora, 2017).

Risk aversion and blame also only allow CPS workers to focus on a narrow category of risk that emphasizes only the biological family (Gambrill, 2017). In actuality, there are risks associated with almost every step of a child welfare case and CPS agencies can actively encourage ignorance of those other risks. Gambrill (2017) wrote that CPS workers are often not aware of the quality of community services they offer, what outcomes they produce, whether the risk assessments and expertise they rely on are valid, if there is fraud involved in any program claims, if government directives have set unreasonable standards and even if their own biases might hamper their decision-making. All of these areas represent potential risks to children and families, but these are never factored into CPS risk analysis.

Some researchers have also linked CPS risk aversion with the rise of neoliberalism (Stoddart, 2017; Pollack, 2008; Stanford, 2009). Neoliberal policies emphasize risk as an empirically measurable phenomenon and assign failures of risk to individuals (Stanford, 2009). This market centered ideology of services reflects a "*reduction in the welfare state through measures which include decentralizing, downsizing, privatization, and other pro-market practices to social care, along with an increase in public accountability*" (Stoddart, 2017, p. 23). Bureaucracy and standardized practices are used to provide a superficial excuse for controlling risks with the idea of individual accountability (Stoddart, 2017). Pollack (2008) wrote "*Audit forms the visible track record of social worker's attempts to assess and reduce risk – therefore, the social worker's job is less about the 'right' decision and more about a 'defensible' decision*" (p. 1274).

Families on the receiving end of a risk averse CPS policies report a host of negative experiences (Gupta & Blumhardt, 2016). Families told researchers that they instead of being supported with resources, they felt policed and punished by CPS. Families said that they were viewed only as source of risk for their children and that their lived experiences of structural poverty were often dismissed and only their individual choices were judged. Finally, families also expressed frustration that any resistance on their part to CPS demands was treated as proof of bad intention rather than as defense of their family unit (Gupta & Blumhardt, 2016).

In my own practice, I observed this culture of fear among caseworkers routinely. Caseworkers would tell me in private that they supported a decision regarding a child or family, but their supervisor would not allow them to take the action. This would often entail forcing the parties into a contested court hearing and wasting resources on all sides. A careful observer could often tell when a caseworker was being forced to take a position as their testimony would change from "I think this is a good idea for the child because" to "CPS believes this is best for the child".

This also made working with even the best caseworkers a challenge, as I knew that even if the caseworker and I were in alignment about the needs of a child, it was actually the supervisor or the regional manager that I had to convince. In my experience, supervisors and managers were the most risk averse and the most inflexible. State level directors could sometimes be reasoned with, but mid-management always required a court order.

Risk Assessments

One of the primary ways that CPS agencies around the world have attempted to manage risk is through the use of risk assessment instruments (Mickelson et al., 2017). Before their creation, most decisions were left to the individual judgment of the caseworker, but instruments began to appear in the 1980s as a way to bring more consistency and objectivity to CPS decision-making as there was a push by agencies for more scientific methods. The risk assessments are used to attempt to measure the probability of a harm occurring or the magnitude of the potential harm generally related to the likelihood of or reoccurrence of child maltreatment (Mickelson et al., 2017).

The instruments themselves tend to be either actuarial tools or ones based on consensus building (Mickelson et al., 2017). Actuarial tools rely on statistical weights and measures based on identified risk factors that have been associated with child abuse or neglect. The consensus-based tools, which have been found to be less accurate at prediction, tend to be more flexible and allow practitioners more leeway in how the define risk and sometimes even allow caseworker to overrule the tool's score. Both types of tools essentially have workers answering questions or checklists about a case or family (Mickelson et al., 2017).

All of the tools have come under criticism, Hardy (2017) wrote

> their results lack specificity when applied to a person or family rather than to a population, raising questions about the extent they are useful in working with individuals. Nor do they provide indicators regarding intervention or risk management because they are not based upon dynamic associations. There is also a suggestion that they encourage an inflated sense of expertise among practitioners.
>
> (Hardy, 2017, p. 397)

Researchers have also criticized the actuarial tools for not considering family protective factors, for being used incorrectly and having limited predictability, whereas the consensus-based tools have problems with their reliability, are not often tested in multiple jurisdictions and are subject to bias (Mickelson et al., 2017). In my practice it was not uncommon to hear workers fill out a risk assessment multiple times until they got the results that they wanted.

In a scoping review of the literature surrounding risk assessment tools used in the US, McNellan et al. (2022) reported that the various tools effectiveness are not supported by the most robust scientific evidence and that validation of the tools carried out by CPS agencies has been ad hoc and subject to the particular whims of each jurisdiction. The tools' interrater reliability is often only judged using vignettes, so real-world applicability is still questioned. The tools generally are also not tested on subgroups, so racial and class biases can still seep through (McNellan et al., 2022). This disproportionality concern has also been raised about Australian tools used on Indigenous people (Mickelson et al., 2017) and New Zealand tools used on the native Māori population (Keddell, 2022).

In recent years, CPS agencies have also turned to the use of algorithmic based predictive models that harness large amounts of data to help make better risk related decisions (McNellan et al., 2022). However, these too have drawn criticism for potential biases embedded in the models as they are built using historical data that has had a disproportionate effect on poor and minority communities (Samant et al., 2021).

After years of unstable placements, Destiny, a 15-year-old, female had developed emotional and behavioral issues that made it difficult for her to be placed in a home. Even worse for her, Destiny's younger sister had been returned to their biological mother. CPS allowed Destiny weekend visits, but she was always returned back to her RTC. Because of their volatile history, the visits with her family often went poorly, and her own mother told CPS that she was unwilling to take Destiny back home. CPS had no real plan for Destiny to successfully age out of care. She was doing poorly in school and became withdrawn. Because Destiny scored high enough on a community risk and needs assessment, CPS was able to enroll her and her mother in a home-based mental health wraparound service. A few points difference in her score, though, and she would have been ineligible.

Best Interest as Risk Aversion

So altogether we have a societal trend that has pushed hypervigilance and risk aversion as a parenting style. This has led to a marked decrease in independence for children over the last few decades. This risk averse culture prioritizes safety above all else and many states even have laws that punish parents for allowing their children the sort of independence that would have been normal during their own childhoods.

This risk aversion has negative real-world consequences for all children as it deprives them of not only their rights, but also metal and emotional resilience as well as the life skills necessary to function in the world. Children that are allowed independence tend to have better outcomes than those that have more of their freedoms restricted.

Added to this societal risk aversion trend is a specific risk aversion embedded in neoliberal child welfare practices that focus on individual accountability. CPS agencies tend to overreact to public media stories of children being injured or killed. This leads them to investigate more families and to create a work culture that focuses on blame and mistakes. This toxic work environment drives out good CPS workers and is one of the reasons that CPS agencies have struggled for so long to retain quality workers.

In an effort to reduce errors and mitigate risk, CPS agencies have embraced complex bureaucracy and risk assessment tools. However, these tools only have limited success and have major critiques of their general use.

It sometimes gets obscured by the complexity of the child welfare system, but this CPS risk aversion is the sum result of millions of child welfare decisions that favor safety, or at least the illusion of safety couched in the bureaucratic language that protocols and procedures have been followed.

Getting a child out of an RTC into a home is riskier because the staff say the child's behavior issues have not be extinguished. Returning a child to their family home is risky because mom still has not completed all her mandatory family therapy sessions. Allowing a youth to stay over with the grandmother is risky because the grandmother has a previous arrest for drug possession. Allowing a youth to transfer to a regular school is risky because there is a possibility, they could leave campus. The list could go on.

These decisions are all made under a best interest framework. It is in a child's best interest to stay at the RTC. It is in the child's best interest to delay reunification because of problems with mom. It is in the child's best interest to not visit the grandmother because of her criminal history. It is in the child's best interest to stay in the alternative school where the child can be more closely monitored.

Because best interest has no agreed upon definition, because it allows such wide discretion and subjectivity, because it does not require consistency in its usage from case to case, because it allows internal bias and value judgments, best interest is the perfect decision-making framework for a risk averse CPS culture that lives in fear of media attention and blame. From the right perspective, CPS can argue almost anything is either for or against a child's best interest. Best interest allows CPS agencies and workers the professional cover to claim to be working in a child's interests when really, they are working in their own.

To be clear this is not to say that most caseworkers are not conscientious, ethical practitioners trying to do their best for a child within the system in which they work. It was extremely rare in my experience to find an actually bad caseworker. They were generally overworked with too many cases, too many administrative requirements and too little power on their level to make any big changes. Many requests to caseworkers made on behalf of my clients elicited the same response, "I need to check with my supervisor".

Certainly, the best interest standard did not create on its own the current culture of risk aversion and fear of blame and error. However, the imprecision and discretion of best interest does allow this sort of risk averse culture to flourish. Procedure and then safety become the only benchmarks for which best interest are judged.

Contrast that with normalcy, which encourages a more holistic view of children and their well-being. Normalcy is inherently risk tolerant. It recognizes that risk is a part of every life and that children and youth have the right to take risks. Well-being in children is more than just keeping them safe.

These two trends risk averse best interest and risk tolerant normalcy are now operating simultaneously with the child welfare system and pull it in different directions However, since normalcy has best interest language built into the RPP liability standard and within the CRC's rights of the child, the risk aversion found in best interest still dominates the overall legal decision-making framework.

I acknowledge the potential criticism here that best interest and normalcy are used for different types of decisions. Best interest decisions are part of removals, reunification, placement and adoption, whereas normalcy are day-to-day child well-being decisions. Under US law this is true. However, I will discuss this critique at length in Chapter 8 and why I think it does not apply.

References

Ariz. Rev. Stat. § 8–513 (B). https://www.azleg.gov/arsDetail/?title=8

Arney, F., Schutz, C., Hawkes, M., Bevan, K., & Barnes, M. (2022). *Report of the independent inquiry into foster and kinship care.* Minister for Child Protection, South Australian Government. https://www.sa.gov.au/__data/assets/pdf_file/0004/816547/Report-of-the-Independent-Inquiry-into-Foster-and-Kinship-Care.pdf

Ball, B., Marra, L., Bellseth, T., & Faulkner, M. (2023). *Final report: The Texas Youth Permanency Study.* Texas Institute for Child and Family Well Being. Retrieved March 20, 2024, from https://txicfw.socialwork.utexas.edu/research/project/texas-youth-permanency-study/

Barker, J. E., Semenov, A. D., Michaelson, L., Provan, L. S., Snyder, H. R., & Munakata, Y. (2014). Less-structured time in children's daily lives predicts self-directed executive functioning. *Frontiers in Psychology, 5.* https://doi.org/10.3389/fpsyg.2014.00593

Beaulieu, E., & Beno, S. (2024). *Healthy childhood development through outdoor risky play: Navigating the balance with injury prevention.* Canadian Pediatric Society. Retrieved April 2, 2024, from https://cps.ca/en/documents/position/outdoor-risky-play

Berger, L. M., & Slack, K. S. (2014). Child protection and child well-being. In A. Ben-Arieh, F. Casas, I. Frønes, & J. E. Korbin (Eds.), *Handbook of child well-being: Theories, methods and policies in global perspective* (pp. 2965–2992). Springer Netherlands. https://doi.org/10.1007/978-90-481-9063-8_120

Berrick, J. D., & Chambers, J. (2020). Preventing and responding to errors in us child protection. In K. Biesel, J. Masson, N. Parton, & T. Pösö (Eds.), *Errors and mistakes in child protection: International discourses, approaches and strategies* (pp. 235–254). Bristol University Press. https://doi.org/10.46692/9781447350927.013

Berridge, D., Biehal, N., Hendry, E., Slade, J., & Tapsfield, R. (2014). Refocusing our approach to safeguarding looked after children in placements. In T. Rahilly & E. Hendry (Eds.), *Promoting the wellbeing of children in care, messages from research* (pp. 104–124). NSPCC UK. Retrieved April 8, 2024, from https://clok.uclan.ac.uk/14634/1/promoting-wellbeing-children-in-care-messages-from-research.pdf

Blumhardt, H., Uk, A. T. D., & Gupta, A. (2017). Radical practice in a risk-averse environment: Learning from ATD Fourth World UK. *Aotearoa New Zealand Social Work, 29*, 19. https://doi.org/10.11157/anzswj-vol29iss2id288

Brussoni, M. (2024). Why children need risk, fear, and excitement in play. *After Babel.* Retrieved April 1, 2024, from https://www.afterbabel.com/p/why-children-need-risk-fear-and-excitement

Brussoni, M., Olsen, L. L., Pike, I., & Sleet, D. A. (2012). Risky play and children's safety: Balancing priorities for optimal child development. *International Journal of Environmental Research and Public Health, 9*(9), 3134–3148. https://doi.org/10.3390/ijerph9093134

Camasso, M. J., & Jagannathan, R. (2013). Decision making in child protective services: A risky business? *Risk Analysis*, *33*(9), 1636–1649. https://doi.org/10.1111/j.1539-6924.2012.01931.x

Casey Family Programs. (2023). How are child protection agencies navigating and addressing workforce challenges? *Strategy Brief: Healthy Organizations*. Retrieved April 4, 2024, from https://www.casey.org/media/23.07-QFF-HO-Workforce-Challenges-1.pdf

Committee on Social Affairs, Health and Sustainable Development. (2018). *Striking a balance between the best interest of the child and the need to keep families together*. Council of Europe. Doc. 14568. Retrieved April 4, 2024, from https://assembly.coe.int/nw/xml/XRef/Xref-XML2HTML-en.asp?fileid=24770&lang=en

Cooke, M., Wong, S., & Press, F. (2021). Towards a re-conceptualisation of risk in early childhood education. *Contemporary Issues in Early Childhood*, *22*(1), 5–19. https://doi.org/10.1177/1463949119840740

Cull, M., & Lindsey, T. (2023). Addressing the CT child welfare workforce crisis and shifting focus from blame to change. *Hartford Courant*. Retrieved April 4, 2024, from https://portal.ct.gov/DCF/Press-Room/Press-Releases-Latest-News/Addressing-the-CT-child-welfare-workforce-crisis-and-shifting-focus-from-blame-to-change

Doek, J. E. (2014). Child well-being: Children's rights perspective. In A. Ben-Arieh, F. Casas, I. Frønes, & J. E. Korbin (Eds.), *Handbook of child well-being: Theories, methods and policies in global perspective* (pp. 187–217). Springer Netherlands. https://doi.org/10.1007/978-90-481-9063-8_9

Fenton, J., & Kelly, T. B. (2017). 'Risk is king and needs to take a backseat!' Can social workers' experiences of moral injury strengthen practice? *Journal of Social Work Practice*, *31*(4), 461–475. https://doi.org/10.1080/02650533.2017.1394827

Fluke, J. D., Corwin, T. W., Hollinshead, D. M., & Maher, E. J. (2016). Family preservation or child safety? Associations between child welfare workers' experience, position, and perspectives. *Children and Youth Services Review*, *69*, 210–218. https://doi.org/10.1016/j.childyouth.2016.08.012

Gambrill, E. (2017). Avoidable ignorance and the ethics of risk in child welfare. *Journal of Social Work Practice*, *31*(4), 379–393. https://doi.org/10.1080/02650533.2017.1394824

Gill, T. (2007). *No fear: Growing up in a risk averse society*. Calouste Gulbenkian Foundation. Retrieved April 1, 2024, from https://timrgill.files.wordpress.com/2010/10/no-fear-19-12-07.pdf

Grant, K. (2011). The importance of understanding attachment and resilience in residential child care: An argument against risk-averse practice. *Scottish Journal of Residential Child Care*, *10*(1). Retrieved April 4, 2024, from https://strathprints.strath.ac.uk/87857/1/Grant-SJRCC-2011-The-importance-of-understanding-attachment-and-resilience.pdf

Gray, P., Lancy, D. F., & Bjorklund, D. F. (2023). Decline in independent activity as a cause of decline in children's mental well-being: Summary of the evidence. *Journal of Pediatrics*, *260*, 113352. https://doi.org/10.1016/j.jpeds.2023.02.004

Gupta, A., & Blumhardt, H. (2016). Giving poverty a voice: Families experiences of social work practice in a risk-averse child protection system. *Families, Relationships and Societies*, *5*, 163–172. https://doi.org/10.1332/204674316X14540714620166

Han, S., Nixon, L., Mejia, P., Marvel, D., & Dorfman, L. (2019). *The child welfare system in U.S. news: What is missing*. Berkley Media Studies Group. Retrieved April 4, 2024, from https://www.bmsg.org/wp-content/uploads/2019/04/bmsg_child_welfare_domestic_violence_news_analysis2019.pdf

Hardy, M. (2017). In defence of actuarialism: Interrogating the logic of risk in social work practice. *Journal of Social Work Practice*, *31*(4), 395–410. https://doi.org/10.1080/02650533.2017.1394828

Hayes, D., & Spratt, T. (2012). Child welfare as child protection then and now: What social workers did and continue to do. *The British Journal of Social Work*, *44*(3), 615–635. https://doi.org/10.1093/bjsw/bcs161

Jacobson, P. (2016). Promoting "normalcy" for foster children: The preventing sex trafficking and strengthening families act. *Missouri Law Review*, *81*, 21.

Jerebine, A. G., Mohebbi, M., Lander, N., Eyre, E., Duncan, M., & Barnett, L. M. (2024). Playing it safe: The relationship between parent attitudes to risk and injury, and children's adventurous play and physical activity. *Psychology of Sport and Exercise*, *70*, Article 102536. https://doi.org/10.1016/j.psychsport.2023.102536

Jones, A. S., LaLiberte, T., & Piescher, K. N. (2015). Defining and strengthening child well-being in child protection. *Children and Youth Services Review*, *54*, 57–70. https://doi.org/10.1016/j.childyouth.2015.05.001

Kearney, A. D., Wilson, E. S., Hollinshead, D. M., Poletika, M., Kestian, H. H., Stigdon, T. J., Miller, E. A., & Fluke, J. D. (2023). Child welfare triage: Use of screening threshold analysis to evaluate intake decision-making. *Children and Youth Services Review*, *144*, 106710. https://doi.org/10.1016/j.childyouth.2022.106710

Keddell, E. (2017). Comparing risk-averse and risk-friendly practitioners in child welfare decision-making: A mixed methods study. *Journal of Social Work Practice*, *31*(4), 411–429. https://doi.org/10.1080/02650533.2017.1394822

Keddell, E. (2022). Mechanisms of inequity: The impact of instrumental biases in the child protection system. *Societies*, *12*(3), 83. https://www.mdpi.com/2075-4698/12/3/83

Kvalnes, Ø., & Hansen Sandseter, E. B. (2023). Experiences, mastery, and development through risk. In *Risky play: An ethical challenge* (pp. 31–45). Springer International Publishing. https://doi.org/10.1007/978-3-031-25552-6_3

Ky. Rev. Stat. § 605.102(3). https://apps.legislature.ky.gov/law/statutes/statute.aspx?id=45711

Lamb, V. L., & Land, K. C. (2014). Methodologies used in the construction of composite child well-being indices. In A. Ben-Arieh, F. Casas, I. Frønes, & J. E. Korbin (Eds.), *Handbook of child well-being: Theories, methods and policies in global perspective* (pp. 2739–2755). Springer Netherlands. https://doi.org/10.1007/978-90-481-9063-8_163

Lindsey, D. (2004). *The welfare of children*. Oxford University Press, USA.

MacAlister, J. (2020). *The case for change: The independent review of children's social care*. Retrieved April 3, 2024, from https://fdac.org.uk/wp-content/uploads/2021/06/case-for-change.pdf

McNellan, C. R., Gibbs, D. J., Knobel, A. S., & Putnam-Hornstein, E. (2022). The evidence base for risk assessment tools used in U.S. child protection investigations: A systematic scoping review. *Child Abuse & Neglect*, *134*, 105887. https://doi.org/10.1016/j.chiabu.2022.105887

Mickelson, N., LaLiberte, T., & Piescher, K. (2017). *Assessing risk: A comparison of tools for child welfare practice with indigenous families*. Center for Advanced Studies in Child Welfare, University of Minnesota. Retrieved April 5, 2024, from https://cascw.umn.edu/wp-content/uploads/2018/01/Risk-Assessment_FinalReport.pdf

Milligan, I. (2011). Resisting risk-averse practice: The contribution of social pedagogy. *Children Australia*, *36*(4), 207–213. https://doi.org/10.1375/jcas.36.4.207

Moore, K. A. (2020). Developing an indicator system to measure child well-being: Lessons learned over time. *Child Indicators Research*, *13*(2), 729–739. https://doi.org/10.1007/s12187-019-09644-4

Munro, E. (2011). *The Munro review of child protection: Final report, a child-centred system*. CM (8062). Stationery Office. Retrieved April 3, 2024, from https://assets.publishing.service.gov.uk/media/5a7b455ee5274a34770ea939/Munro-Review.pdf

National Foster Care Youth & Alumni Policy Council. (2013). *Improving well-being by addressing normalcy for foster youth.* Retrieved March 18, 2024, from https://www.nationalpolicycouncil.org/sites/default/files/docs/landingpage/Normalcy%20Priorities.pdf

New York City Administration for Children's Services. (2018). *Applying the reasonable prudent parent standard: Supporting normative experience for children, youth and adults in foster care.* Retrieved March 29, 2024, from https://www.nyc.gov/assets/acs/pdf/covid19/ReasonableandPrudentParenting.pdf

O'Hare, W. (2022). Analytic frameworks and perspectives for measuring child well-being. In *A practitioner's guide to using child indicators* (pp. 19–29). Springer International Publishing. https://doi.org/10.1007/978-3-030-90291-9_2

Philadelphia Department of Human Services. (2018). *What about reasonable and prudent parenting? What foster parents should know.* Retrieved March 29, 2024, from https://www.phila.gov/media/20181219154625/What-About-Reasonable-Prudent-Parenting.pdf

Pollack, S. (2008). Labelling clients 'risky': Social work and the neo-liberal welfare state. *The British Journal of Social Work*, *40*(4), 1263–1278. https://doi.org/10.1093/bjsw/bcn079

Prada, A., & Sanchez-Fernandez, P. (2021). World child well-being index: A multidimensional perspective. *Child Indicators Research*, *14*(6), 2119–2144. https://doi.org/10.1007/s12187-021-09848-7

Preventing Sex Trafficking and Strengthening Families Act. *Congress.gov*. Retrieved March 7, 2024, from https://www.congress.gov/bill/113th-congress/house-bill/4980/text

Redleaf, D. L. (2020). *Where is it safe and legal to give children reasonable independence?* American Bar Association: Children's Rights Legal Committee. Retrieved April 1, 2024, from https://www.americanbar.org/groups/litigation/resources/newsletters/childrens-rights/where-it-safe-legal-give-children-reasonable-independence/?login

Samant, A., Horowitz, A., Xu, K., & Beiers, S. (2021). *Family surveillance by algorithm: The rapidly spreading tools few have heard of.* American Civil Liberties Union. https://www.aclu.org/sites/default/files/field_document/aclu_family_surveillance_by_algorithm.pdf

Sando, O. J., Kleppe, R., & Sandseter, E. B. H. (2021). Risky play and children's well-being, involvement and physical activity. *Child Indicators Research*, *14*(4), 1435–1451. https://doi.org/10.1007/s12187-021-09804-5

Sicora, A. (2017). Reflective practice, risk and mistakes in social work. *Journal of Social Work Practice*, *31*(4), 491–502. https://doi.org/10.1080/02650533.2017.1394823

Spratt, T. (2001). The influence of child protection orientation on child welfare practice. *The British Journal of Social Work*, *31*(6), 933–954. http://www.jstor.org/stable/23716471

Stanford, S. (2009). 'Speaking back' to fear: Responding to the moral dilemmas of risk in social work practice. *The British Journal of Social Work*, *40*(4), 1065–1080. https://doi.org/10.1093/bjsw/bcp156

Stoddart, J. (2017). *The risk of risk: An exploration of the impact of "risk" on child welfare decision-making* [Theses and Dissertations (Comprehensive), 1906]. https://scholars.wlu.ca/etd/1906

Tennessee Department of Children's Services. (2016). *Protocol for reasonable and prudent parenting supplemental to DCS policy: 16.3, desired characteristics of foster parents and 16.8, responsibilities of approved foster homes.* Retrieved March 29, 2024, from https://files.dcs.tn.gov/policies/chap16/ProtocolReasonablePrudentParenting.pdf

UN Committee on the Rights of the Child (CRC), General Comment No. 17. (2013). *On the right of the child to rest, leisure, play, recreational activities, cultural life and the arts (art. 31)*. Retrieved March 25, 2024, from https://digitallibrary.un.org/record/778539?v=pdf

UNICEF. (2007). *Child poverty in perspective: An overview of child well-being in rich countries*. Report Card 7. Innocenti Research Centre. Retrieved April 7, 2024, from https://www.unicef-irc.org/publications/pdf/rc7_eng.pdf

Vigdal, J. S., & Brønnick, K. K. (2022). A systematic review of "helicopter parenting" and its relationship with anxiety and depression. *Frontiers in Psychology*, *13*, 872981. https://doi.org/10.3389/fpsyg.2022.872981

Weikart, D. P. (1998). Changing early childhood development through educational intervention. *Preventive Medicine*, *27*(2), 233–237. https://doi.org/10.1006/pmed.1998.0280

Whittaker, A., & Havard, T. (2016). Defensive practice as 'fear-based' practice: Social work's open secret? *The British Journal of Social Work*, *46*(5), 1158–1174. https://doi.org/10.1093/bjsw/bcv048

Yogman, M., Garner, A., Hutchinson, J., Hirsh-Pasek, K., Golinkoff, R. M., Baum, R., Gambon, T., Lavin, A., Mattson, G., Wissow, L., Hill, D. L., Ameenuddin, N., Chassiakos, Y. R., Cross, C., Boyd, R.,. Mendelson, R., Moreno, M. A., Radesky, J., Swanson, W. S., . . . Smith, J. (2018). The power of play: A pediatric role in enhancing development in young children. *Pediatrics*, *142*(3). https://doi.org/10.1542/peds.2018-2058

5 Decision-Making

From a simple legal perspective, the child welfare system is almost entirely about decision-making. Back in the Harris County Juvenile Court, judges are asked to approve, modify, or overrule hundreds of CPS agency decisions every day. Some like removal, reunification, permanency and adoption are on their face, life altering decisions for the family and children involved. Even simpler decisions like placement or services can have long-term and lasting consequences. Most decisions in the US come to the court from CPS caseworkers asking the judge to approve an internal agency decision, though judges are also called upon by parents, foster parents, kinship family, CASA volunteers and even foster children themselves.

Because of the importance of decision-making, researchers around the world have focused a great deal of effort to understand how child welfare decisions are made with multiple theories being put forth to describe the decision-making process at each stage of a child welfare case. Like the discussion on best interest, there is so much material that entire books on decision-making have been written. Still the sections that follow should provide a reasonable overview of what we have learned about the process, the broad types of decisions and the factors that influence decision-making. Since every decision is made under a best interest legal structure, all of the following research ultimately describes best interest decision-making, though it is not described with those words.

Before delving into the specifics though, it is important to understand the context of child welfare decision-making. Benbenishty and Fluke (2020) wrote that uncertainty governs every aspect. Caseworkers rarely have a complete set of information and they do not know the probabilities of positive outcomes for their choices, such as removal or reunification. They also do not know if their choices will bring about any negative outcomes (Benbenishty & Fluke, 2020).

Added on to this uncertainty, is idea that the utility of each outcome is often subjective (Benbenishty & Fluke, 2020). There is no agreed upon value for the most child welfare decisions. This is compounded by the fact that the decisions are often not binary. For instance, a child with behavioral issues, could be placed in a regular foster home with services, a kinship home, a therapeutic foster home or an RTC. Each of these carries unknown probabilities for both positive and negative outcomes (Benbenishty & Fluke, 2020).

DOI: 10.4324/9781003510253-5

Investigation

The initial set of decisions that CPS workers must make regarding child maltreatment concerns intake and then investigation. The United States Department of Health and Human Services (HHS) (2023) reported that in 2022 more than 4,270,000 referrals were made to intake screeners, which represented reports on more than 7,500,000 children. The national average is that a little over 50 percent are screened out. However, there is a lot of variation within the states, with some like Alabama reporting screen in rates of nearly 99 percent compared to Vermont with a screen in rate of less than 17 percent (HHS, 2023).

In a recent study of Indiana CPS' screen in decisions, Kearney et al. (2023) found that the screen in decisions were not terribly accurate. Of the 252,000 reports that the researchers collected during a six-month window, they found that only about 41 percent of screened in calls were true positive cases of child maltreatment. The false positive rate by contrast was more than 50 percent and a true negative rate where CPS correctly screened out non-abuse cases was less than 5 percent (Kearney et al., 2023).

In a meta-analysis of 18 studies, Damman et al. (2020) tried to extract what factors lead to a CPS decision to investigate a referral of child maltreatment. They reported that referrals by professionals, such as doctors and teachers, referrals involving injury and those involving a known perpetrator were all more likely to result in a CPS investigation. If more than one child was referred and if the children referred were younger, that also corresponded with an increased probability of investigation, whereas children with a known history of behavioral disorders were less likely to have an investigation. Caregiver and family factors, such as a parent with a disability or one with a history of substance abuse led to higher rates of investigation. Finally, CPS agency and worker related factors, such as worker beliefs about their duty to investigate and office specific managerial practices also led to an increase in investigations (Damman et al., 2020).

Substantiation

Following the investigation, the next major decision is the one to substantiate findings of child maltreatment.

Font et al. (2020) wrote that the substantiation decision was important not only as it could lead to the removal of children in danger, but also because substantiation generally leads to a child and family receiving some sort of family support services. The substantiation decision also is what fuels the creation of child abuse offender databases, which are used for later enforcement actions. However, the decision is still simply that of an individual case worker on a particular case and does not always mean that child abuse or neglect has actually occurred and conversely unsubstantiated cases could still involve child abuse and neglect (Font et al., 2020).

Using data from the National Survey of Child and Adolescent Well- Being (NSCAW II), Font et al. (2020) looked at approximately five thousand cases from across the country to try to determine what factors influenced decision-making. They found that when workers had the ability to collaborate with other agencies and could offer community services even without a finding of substantiation, then substantiation rates declined. Additionally, though the effect was small, the more standardized assessments that were used, the more likely that a case would be substantiated (Font et al., 2020).

While the researchers did not find any evidence that race and age played a part in substantiation decisions, they did find evidence that an increase in the Hispanic population of the county resulted in an increased number of substantiations (Font et al., 2020). This is similar to Drake et al. (2023) that also looked at US national data and again found no evidence of racial bias in substantiations either for Black or Hispanic families. However, the racial findings are disputed as other researchers have found evidence of racial bias (Dettlaff et al., 2011; Henry et al., 2020; Kahn & Hansen, 2017)

Dettlaff et al. (2011) examined more than 180,000 Texas child protection records from 2003–2005 and found firstly that that income was a significant predictor of substantiation decisions, with low-income families being more likely to have findings of child abuse or neglect substantiated. This finding obscures the effect of race, which they argue leads some policy experts to assume that poverty is the only significant factor. However, they note that when poverty is controlled in their model, then Black and Hispanic families are once again more likely to receive a substantiation finding than White families. The researchers argued that income is an important factor for caseworkers when making substantiation decisions, but it is not the deciding factor. Caseworkers seem to have a lower decision-making threshold for Black families than for White families when making a substantiation case (Dettlaff et al., 2011)

In a study that looked at failure to protect substantiation decisions, Henry et al. (2020) also found evidence that Black families were substantiated at a higher rate. Kahn and Hansen (2017) argued that while the rate of higher substantiation was low, over the course of thousands of cases it did result in disproportionality for Black families.

In their study of what demographic and geographic factors affect substantiation and removal decisions, Maguire-Jack et al. (2020) noted that minority children are disproportionately represented in foster care overall, but the local data showed large differences. The researchers found that for substantiation decisions, minority children with the exception of Asian children all had higher rates than those of White children. They also found that rural counties and counties where there were more single heads of households also correlated with increased substantiation. However, counties with high poverty, higher juvenile arrest rates and with a larger percentage of Black population all had a decreased rate of substantiation (Maguire-Jack et al., 2020).

In the Dettlaff et al. (2011) study out of all of the factors, the type of reported abuse and who made the initial complaint were the most predictive of substantiation. The researchers reported that allegations of maltreatment coming from police, doctors, teachers and identifiable third parties were more likely than those of a family member or an anonymous reporter to be substantiated. Additionally, allegations of abandonment and ongoing abuse were more likely to be substantiated as compared to allegations of neglect (Dettlaff et al., 2011).

In the Font et al. (2020) study, individual case factors related to the family such as the presence of domestic violence or substance abuse were the most likely to increase substantiations. The researchers noted that overall, these factors led to a great deal of variability between substantiation decisions between counties and different child welfare agencies (Font et al., 2020).

Similarly in a Canadian study, Stoddart et al. (2018) found that the type of abuse resulted in different substantiation rates with neglect being substantiated more often than physical abuse except in cases where evidence of physical abuse was found. Again, cases where the caregiver had issues with domestic violence or substance abuse also had higher rates. However, the researchers found that the highest predictor was the caseworker's internal prediction of future maltreatment (Stoddart et al., 2018).

It is not surprising that substantiation decisions can be affected by cultural as well as individual caseworker and case factors. In a vignette study of more than eight hundred caseworkers in Israel, Northern Ireland, Spain and the Netherlands, Benbenishty et al. (2015) attempted to identify commonalities and differences in how social workers from different countries make substantiation and risk assessment decisions when given the same facts. In all of the countries, participants did not consider mother's wishes to be a factor in deciding on substantiation; however, other factors diverged by country and system, though there was substantial variation inside countries as well (Benbenishty et al., 2015).

Overall, caseworkers from the Netherlands were less likely than their counterparts in other countries to decide on substantiation, with Israel and Northern Ireland caseworkers the most likely to substantiate a maltreatment case. Spanish caseworkers were more likely to believe that removing the child from the home was necessary whereas Dutch and Israeli caseworkers favored family preservation more often (Benbenishty et al., 2015).

Removal

Following substantiation, caseworkers are then asked to make a decision about removing a child from the home or in the alternative to provide some type of home-based family support often known as differential response.

In a study pulling again from the National Data Archive on Child Abuse and Neglect database, Bhatti-Sinclair and Sutcliffe (2012) found that child specific factors, such as the child having emotional, behavioral and medical problems was highly predictive of a child being removed as was the age of the child, with infants being the most likely to be removed. These factors were actually more important than the abuse or neglect itself and those of the child's household or caregiver (Bhatti-Sinclair & Sutcliffe, 2012).

Graham et al. (2021) examined factors leading to the removal of children from their homes by child protection workers in Texas. They surveyed more than a thousand CPS workers and identified five factors that they believed played a part in a removal decision. Factors, such as their sense of risk to the child and the income of the investigated family increased the chance of removal, whereas having more Hispanic families in their caseload and having more cases and less organizational support decreased the likelihood that a child would be removed. Individual factors about the caseworker did not seem to make any difference in removal decisions. The researchers also noted that the most important variable for individual caseworkers was their perception of worry about their own personal liability and that caseworkers that reported more worry were more likely to support removal decisions and that those caseworkers that reported more worry also tended to report less support from their supervisors (Graham et al., 2020). This finding of course harks back to the last chapter's discussion of risk aversion.

As for racial bias in removal decisions, minority children with the exception of Asian children were removed at higher rates than White children at percentages higher than even the racial differences within the substantiation decisions (Maguire-Jack et al., 2020). Similarly, counties with more single head households were more likely to have children removed, but children in rural counties were actually less likely to be removed. The researchers wrote that geographic and demographic factors cannot explain the disproportionality of minority children, but the differences between urban and rural, poor and wealthy and percentage of minority population suggest that county level features are part of the decision-making matrix of caseworkers (Maguire-Jack et al., 2020).

Britner and Mossler (2002) studied the difference in removal decision-making among different professions within the child welfare system. In a vignette study of judges, caseworkers, mental health workers and Court Appointed Special Advocates (CASA) volunteers, the researchers found that the different professions used different information to make their removal decisions. Social workers and mental health workers centered their decisions based more on family factors, and the services available to the families and their ability to access those services. Judges and CASA volunteers on the other hand were more likely to weigh factors related to the child and the possibility of the abuse being repeated (Britner & Mossler, 2002). In my own experiment, which I discuss at length in Chapter 7, I made some similar findings that different roles within child welfare tend to responded to questions differently.

In a recent study of which factors influence removal decision-making, researchers analyzed caseworker survey data along with case files (Hollinshead et al., 2021). They found that infants and small children were more likely to be removed than children over 10 years of age and that allegations of maltreatment that were coupled with parental substance abuse were more likely to result in removal than allegations of just physical abuse. Additionally, cases where abuse had been previously reported also led to more removal decisions (Hollinshead et al., 2021).

The researchers also looked at external agency and location factors that might influence removal decisions and found that regions where caseworkers perceived that community services were better had fewer removals (Hollinshead et al., 2021). Similar to the findings of (Graham et al., 2020), the authors stated that caseworkers who believed that they had the support of their agency and supervisor were less likely to order removal. Interestingly, caseworkers who reported having a shared vision of child protection among their coworkers were more likely to order removal, which the authors theorize might be due to worker group conformity (Hollinshead et al., 2021).

Outside of the US, researcher have also found numerous overlapping reasons for removal decisions. In a vignette study of Dutch caseworkers and judges, researchers looked at the psychological reasons that individual caseworkers use to either support or deny a decision to remove a child (de Haan et al., 2019). They found that the professional backgrounds and experience of individual caseworkers and judges did not play a significant role in decisions to remove a child. Beliefs about whether parents could change their behavior and beliefs about the negative consequences of removal were more likely to lead to decisions to keep a child with the parents. A strong belief that parents could not change was the most likely internal factor for a caseworker or judge to support a removal decision (de Haan et al., 2019).

In a second vignette study of caseworkers in the Netherlands, researchers tested how caseworker attitudes and beliefs influence removal decisions (Bartelink et al., 2018). They found, like the results of de Haan et al., (2019), that caseworkers who had internal beliefs that removal would result in harm were less likely to order children to be removed (Bartelink et al., 2018).

In an earlier Israeli vignette study Shapira and Benbenishty (1993) also found a distinction between decision-making among two types of caseworkers, which they identified as those more interested in family relationships and those that were more focused on abuse. They found that the two groups focused on different case factors when making their removal decisions and were consistent across vignettes in the factors they identified as import and, in the decision, to remove or not (Shapira & Benbenishty, 1993).

Chateauneuf et al. (2021) conducted structured interviews with Canadian caseworkers looking for reasons why they made removal decisions. Through the interviews they identified four themes of consensus decision-making with their coworkers, the legal and regulatory framework that governed their work, their individual judgment regarding the risk to the child and the individual values and beliefs about child welfare work that the caseworkers brought to their jobs. The researchers explained that removal decision-making is actually a complex process that begins with caseworker's own subjective opinion and beliefs and that then is molded both by the mandatory legal framework and by the opinions of others in the agency (Chateauneuf et al., 2021).

Jonas was 10-years-old with a diagnosis of nonverbal autism that led him to have serious behavioral outburst. He lived at home with his single mother, who had mild intellectual impairments and lived via disability payments. When Jonas came to school multiple days in a row with dog feces stains on his clothes and smelling of urine, the teacher called in a CPS report. CPS began their investigation and quickly substantiated that Jonas was being neglected. His mother said she struggled to care for him, and she herself has several bruises from where he had hit her. He was removed from the home. CASA hoped he would be placed in therapeutic home, but his mother did not approve of the removal, and through her attorney she fought to have him returned. CPS ultimately provided him community services and the family were reunited.

Termination

Unlike the other decisions discussed thus far, the termination of parental rights at least in a US context is purely a legal judicial decision. While CPS workers might make the initial decision to seek termination, the ultimate judgment rest with the court. Termination is sometimes referred to as the death penalty of child welfare because the final decision means that parents can lose their legal rights forever.

Because termination is a legal decision, it is important to consider briefly the laws that govern it in the US. The Adoption and Safe Families Act of 1997 is widely seen as increasing the speed and number of removals nationwide as a desire to protect children led and promote permanency led to an expedited 15-month timeline following removal by which CPS agencies should file in court the notice to seek termination (Desir, 2021; Philip et al., 2023; Raz & Edwards, 2023).

States have varying statutes that list the factors that judges must consider for termination, but there is substantial overlap. For instance, both Michigan Code § 712A.19b (2023) and Georgia Code § 15–11-311 (2022) frame the decision as one to be made in the child's best interests and they consider the type and severity of the abuse or neglect as well as the possibility for it to reoccur in the future. Both codes also ask courts to consider the efforts made by the parents to maintain a proper relationship with their children and their efforts to comply with CPS family safety plans.

Prior to initiating termination, CPS must make reasonable efforts to attempt to reunify the family; however, the term reasonable efforts do not have a uniform meaning and both states and courts have interpreted it in a different way (Desir, 2021). Though appellate courts have on occasion struck down a parental termination for failure to provide reasonable efforts, this is unusual (Desir, 2021).

It should be noted that both the Adoption and Safe Families Act and the use of reasonable efforts are ongoing controversies within the US child welfare community that are tied to federal funding and disproportionality (Roberts, 2022; Desir, 2021; Edwards, 2018). They are beyond the scope of this chapter and this book, but worth further reading for a deeper understanding of parental termination.

Back to the termination decision itself, using national data, Noonan and Burke (2005) found a number of factors that correlated with higher rates of termination. Regarding the child themselves, Black and Hispanic children were actually less likely to be terminated, but also less likely to be reunified than White children. Older children were also less likely to be terminated, whereas children with disabilities were more likely (Noonan & Burke, 2005). However, when Wildeman et al. (2020) did an updated analysis of 16 years' worth of federal data, they did find evidence of a racial bias in terminations with Native American and Black children especially affected. They noted, though, that individual states had drastically different termination rates for their populations with some states having rates nearly seven times higher than their neighbor (Wildeman et al., 2020).

Noonan and Burke (2005) also found that while children who were brought into care for physical abuse were less likely to be reunified than those brought in for neglect, neither group had significant differences in termination rates. Children with single mothers also had higher termination rates. Usurpingly, children who had adoption as a case goal were also terminated at higher rates, which the researchers argued means that CPS does not generally pursue termination until the agency believes it has located a potential adoptive placement (Noonan & Burke, 2005).

As to consideration from the judges themselves, there are only a few studies that look at judicial termination decision-making. In a vignette study of 133 child welfare judges, Summers et al. (2012) divided judges into two categories, low experience and high experience. For both groups, the perceived risk of returning a child to their parental home was the most significant factor in deciding to terminate. However, high experienced judges perceived less risk than their less experienced counterparts and were more likely to focus on case factors that did not support termination. Less experienced judges were more likely to rely on personal beliefs and to cite the possibility of future adoption as a deciding factor. They wrote,

> Although there was no statistical difference in risk perception overall, the process by which judges reached this information appears to be very different. This has serious implications for juvenile court judges. Low experience judges may not be adequately equipped to recognize important case factors, which may ultimately lead to incorrect decisions.
>
> (Summers et al., 2012, p. 109)

In another study, Vesneski (2013) examined 100 North Carolina court termination decisions and found that judges often included more than double the factors than what were found in federal and state statutes. Judges were particularly interested in the parents' compliance with CPS ordered services, such as mental health counseling and substance abuse. The judges also made multiple reference to the economic instability of the parents despite poverty not being a statutory reason for termination. With the addition of non-statutory factors and a focus on case compliance, Veneski (2013) argued that judges actually engage in termination policy change.

Other studies that examined termination cases found mental health, substance abuse and incarceration as significant factors in termination decisions (Olmstead et al., 2011; Meyer et al., 2010).

Finally, from a practical perspective, while termination is considered permanent, there are legal ways for which parents can have their rights reinstated. Also, for older children and youth that wish to remain in contact with a parent, termination is often only in letter as cell phones and social media make prohibiting contact almost impossible. It is not unusual for a court to bring a terminated parent back into a permanency plan once it is clear the child wants contact, the parent is not a danger to the child and the child has yet to find permanency elsewhere.

Reunification and Permanency

If termination is the death penalty, then, permanency and reunification would be considered the happy endings of a CPS case. Like the prior decisions, researchers have found that reunification decisions are complex and can be affected by multiple external and internal factors.

In the U.S., Cheng (2010) conducted a longitudinal analysis of national data and linked reunification likelihood with improved caseworker engagement with the family that allowed the family to access the necessary services. This result seems to be confirmed by Phillips (2023) who also found that increased communication between the worker and the family led to higher rates of reunification. Other researchers identified family therapy and the use of special education services for the child as factors towards a successful reunification, whereas parents use of substance abuse services as a negative correlation (Miller et al., 2006). Finally, Wittenstrom et al. (2015) demonstrated that race also seems to be an issue, as they found that Black children were reunified at much slower rates than White children; however, this rate varied considerably based on case factors so that infant Black children were reunified nearly 80 percent slower than their White counterparts. That race affects reunification rates and speed in generally found throughout the literature (Carnochan et al., 2013).

In their literature review, Carnochan et al. (2013) wrote that several factors had been identified as preventing reunification. Children placed in a kinship home with a relative and children who had been in care longer and in less stable placements were both less likely to be reunified. Families with ongoing instability related to poverty or substance abuse were also less likely to reunify as were children with disabilities and those removed as infants (Carnochan et al., 2013).

As to how the actual decisions are made, Edwards (2024) questioned 26 judges and hearing officers about reunification. The majority of the judges reported that the most significant factors for reunification were that the parent completed substance abuse programs, received positive mental health supports and the caseworker's positive assessment of the parent's visits with the child and their perception that the parent was ready for the child's return.

Outside of the US, researchers have also identified multiple factors related to reunification. In Spain, Martin et al. (2020) found that children who stayed in care longer and those whose parents had substance abuse problems were less likely to reunify. Lopez et al. (2013) found that contrary to US studies, children placed in kinship care were more likely to be returned; however, like other studies they also found that reunification was more likely when the parents were cooperative with CPS and for children who had not been in care very long.

In the UK context, positive reunification factors include the caseworker's assessment of decreased risk and parental improvement (Biehal et al., 2015). Farmer (1996) found that for children with emotional and social problems, the introduction of special education services was linked to successful reunification.

In the Netherlands, like the US and Spain, children were more likely to return if they had been in care for shorter times and if the parents had maintained consistent contact throughout the case (Goemans et al., 2016). When Dutch caseworkers and judges were questioned, they identified the parents' functioning and use of case supports as well as the child's development and wants as primary decision-making factors (Teunissen et al., 2021).

An Australian study also looked at the speed of reunifications and found that children tended to be reunified just past the three-month case mark, but once past that date, reunifications slowed down (Fernandez & Lee, 2011). Older children reunified faster than infants, while children removed for parental substance abuse were reunified at the slowest rate (Fernandez & Lee, 2011).

Finally, in a Norwegian study, Quartey (2024) wrote that caseworkers emphasized the voice of the child and their desire to return home as a primary consideration. Like in other countries, they also identified the parents' cooperation and willingness to change as important factors when the recommended reunification (Quartey, 2024).

Though there is variation among the country specific findings, the repeated ideas that communication and cooperation with CPS and shorter time in care lead to reunifications seems to be a consistent finding. This is consistent with the legal advice that parent attorneys often give, which is simply do whatever CPS tells you to. The faster you comply with all of their demands, the faster the case will end and you will be reunified.

Caseworker and Agency

Thus far, I have tried to briefly describe some of the types of decisions inherent in a CPS case and the surrounding factors that might influence those decision especially related to the case type, family and child. However, different studies have found various individual factors and agency factors for child welfare decision-making, including, outside influences unrelated to the case (Britner & Mossler, 2002), perceptions of race, ethnicity and poverty (Lindsey, 2004) and personal beliefs about parenting, politics and cultural background (Arad-Davidzon & Benbenishty, 2008).

In Britner and Mossler's (2002) removal vignette study of judges, CASA, social workers and guardian ad litems, they found that while all groups rated the seriousness and nature of the abuse, the groups relied on different information within the same vignette and came to different conclusions regarding removal and services. Out of 18 factors identified by the researchers, half had significant differences among the professional groups (Britner & Mossler, 2002). A similar result was found by McCafferty et al. (2021) who in a vignette study found that even though caseworkers gave similar reasons based on the case fact pattern, there was ultimately no consistency in the decisions made. Again, in another vignette study, Mosteiro et al. (2018) found the same with different child welfare practitioners coming to opposing conclusions and recommendations. The differences came about as a result of individual beliefs about the importance of family preservation (Mosteiro et al., 2018).

In one study, Vanderloo (2017) wrote that more experienced caseworkers were more likely to approval of removals. However, most studies show that older and more experienced workers tend to favor keeping families together (Fluke et al., 2016; Strolin-Goltzmann & Holbrook, 2023; Clark et al., 2021). Using the Dalgleish Scale that measures caseworkers on a spectrum from family preservation to child safety orientation, researchers found that caseworkers that had been in the field longer tended to cluster towards the family preservation side of the scale (Fluke et al., 2016).

Other researchers using the Dalgleish Scale have also found that CPS worker orientation towards safety or family preservation have an influence on child welfare decision-making. Middel et al. (2024) found that workers with higher internal beliefs about child safety also rated parents as less moral and were thusly more likely to approve or removal. Hollinshead et al. (2021) reported a similar finding where caseworkers with stronger internal beliefs about family preservation were more likely to keep children with their family.

In a Portuguese vignette study of caseworker decision-making, Rodrigues et al. (2015) also found that worker perceptions about the benefits of removal had significant effects on their removal decisions as did their perception of whether their colleagues would approve of their decision. They went on to note that workers who believed the removal decision would make them subjectively happier were, not surprisingly, also more likely to support removal. The researchers explained that the anticipatory positive emotion was likely the result of past experiences where a child removal decision had been perceived as correct. Workers who had more favorable beliefs about child protection were more likely to support removal than workers that placed more value on family preservation (Rodrigues et al., 2015).

In addition to individual caseworker factors, other researchers have identified several CPS agency related factors that can influence decision-making. Hollinshead et al. (2021) reported that CPS workers that perceived high levels of agency support were more likely to approve of removals. Font and Maguire-Jack (2015) examined agency factors related to substantiations and found that substantiation rates were higher in places where CPS agencies lacked the proper resources and had fewer community partnerships for providing services to unsubstantiated cases. Finally, in an international comparative study, CPS workers in England, Finland, Norway and the US all expressed frustration with internal pressure that did not provide them with enough time to make the best decisions (Berrick et al., 2016).

Bias and Heuristics

In addition to the reasons and factors that researchers have linked to case, caseworker and agency decision-making, there have also been numerous studies that examined the types of biases and heuristics that caseworkers use. Gambrill (2008) wrote that child welfare practitioners are subject to the same constraints on decision-making as the rest of us. Confirmation bias, overconfidence, selective perception, poor memory and selective memory can all come into play when making child welfare decisions. Also, institutional and individual barriers in how caseworkers can access and process information can also lead to decision-making errors (Gambrill, 2008).

As with many other portions of the child welfare field, an outcome that supports racial bias against Black families in decision-making has been found in both the hotline intake and the investigation stage (Baron et al., 2024), substation, removal (Maguire-Jack et al., 2020), termination (Wildeman et al., 2020) and reunification (Carnochan et al., 2013).

As for internal biases, Spratt et al. (2015) conducted a study on confirmation bias in Northern Ireland social workers and found that the workers often stuck with their first assumptions. They noted that social workers often have to make quick decisions involving lots of information under pressure, but confirmation bias can lead to them ignoring information and avenues of support for children that could be beneficial (Spratt et al., 2015).

Nyathi (2018) reported that caseworkers used both individual heuristics and analytic judgment when making decisions, but they tended to use analytics only when it suited them. Pressures for consensus building by both the agency and the families often influenced final decisions (Nyathi, 2018).

Munro (1999) examined data from England for a 20-year period looking for records from 45 official inquiries where it was obvious in hindsight that child protection workers made a mistake and a child was killed and several common themes emerged. Social workers rarely revised their initial risk assessments even when new information was presented and failed to consult other experts that had different information than them. Many of the cases also had failure of communication issues, where information was not properly conveyed within the child protection system (Munro, 1999).

In a Netherlands vignette and think aloud study of how caseworkers make decisions matching children with foster families, researchers tested how heuristic thinking would affect outcomes (Zeijlmans et al., 2019). Three possible heuristics were identified by the researchers. Caseworkers had some tendency to rate the first foster family mentioned as the best match indicating a possible recognition heuristic. Additionally, caseworkers rejected families based on one criterion even though other facts about the family might have been a good match for the child, which the researcher saw as evidence of a one reason heuristic. Finally, the caseworkers demonstrated some elements of the tradeoff heuristic, though the researchers cautioned that this result could also be from confirmation bias (Zeijlmans et al., 2019).

McCafferty et al. (2021) conducted a vignette and interview study of UK caseworkers and found that caseworkers had very little consistency with their colleagues regarding what action they would take when presented with the same vignette. Though most agreed on the risk factors and the general reasoning behind their decision, some favored foster care, others adoption and a few others kinship placement. The researchers argued that most of the caseworkers picked a more aggressive placement strategy because that represented a safer option for themselves even though other options might have been better for the child. This inconsistency along with a risk aversion heuristic and a bias towards more aggressive placements could mean that many children are inappropriately placed throughout the child welfare system (McCafferty et al., 2021).

Despite the inconsistency, errors and biases that seem to be inseparable from child welfare decision-making, Munro (2019) argued that it is because of the complexity of the work and the changing information over the course of the case, that child protection agencies should adopt an organizational policy that allows for errors. Munro (2019) argued that child welfare agencies tend to be especially risk averse to their own organization where failures are punished and no one takes responsibility and this not only hinders decision-making, but also innovation. Munro (2019) suggested that decisions under pressure with changing information should be judged by the quality of the decision-making at the time and not the final outcome.

Behavioral Science

It is worth separating this from the above section on bias found specifically in child welfare research. Though there are obvious overlaps, there has been little research specifically linking the findings of behavioral science directly to the child welfare decision-making. Though the science has been applied to related aspects of child welfare and the foster care system such as early child hood interventions (Gennetian et al., 2017), to recruit foster families and adoptive families (Kirkman, 2020; Kantar Publik UK, 2022), and domestic violence (Barry et al., 2022) to name a few.

In their seminal paper, Jolls et al. (1998) describe the ways people actually interact with the law. They wrote that that human decision-making is limited by bounded rationality, bounded will power and bounded self-interest. These bounds interact with decision-making whenever humans have to guess about probable events and their outcomes, when decisions have long-term consequences and when we have the power to punish others (Jolls et al., 1998). Though their paper did not cover any aspect of foster care of child welfare, the applications of these three ideas should be self-evident.

In one of the few papers to attempt to apply direct behavioral science findings to the child welfare field, Daminger et al. (2015) highlighted the effects on scarcity on poor families. They argued that scarcity forced parents to spend so much of their internal bandwidth on meeting daily needs that parents must have a narrow focus on whatever the current demand is that they are unable to make more insightful and longer-term decisions to the betterment of their families (Daminger et al., 2015).

In response to this paper, Casey Family Programs discussed scarcity on the CPS services side (Moore et al., 2022). They wrote that time scarcity is one of the biggest factors for CPS staff. Given little time to make decisions along with a heavy workload can mean that workers make screen in, investigation and removal decisions that they otherwise might not, especially those that are seen as safer decisions. Because of these time constraints, workers might fall back on implicit biases that include beliefs about poverty, race, class and neighborhood to make their decisions under pressure. This is one of the reasons that CPS agencies need to cut the workloads for their staff and give workers more time to do their jobs (Moore et al., 2022).

Judicial Decision-Making

Though judges are mentioned in a few of the above studies, they are unsurprisingly not as represented in research as caseworkers, especially in the child welfare context. However, given their importance in the final case decisions, it is valuable to discuss the bit of research that currently exists.

Firstly, research has shown for some time that judges in general use biases such as anchoring and hindsight when reaching their opinions (Guthrie et al., 2007). Fraidin (2013) argued that dependency judges might be particularly susceptible to some biases because of the nature of child welfare cases. Dependency cases have time pressures that force judges to make sometimes quick life altering decisions. They also involved hearing the same parties over multiple hearings, sometimes even over the course of years subjecting them to possibility of anchoring. Because of the unique nature of child welfare hearings that are nonpublic and generally have the same set of attorneys, caseworkers and CASA, dependency judges might be subject to groupthink biases (Fraidin, 2013).

In an analysis of the available literature, Summers et al. (2024) ultimately concluded that there is insufficient research on child welfare judicial decision-making to make any real conclusions though.

Group Decision-Making

A trend in recent decades has been to encourage the use of group decision-making in child welfare with the goal of making the process more participatory for families, build consensus among the parties and hopefully improve outcomes for the affected children. Though CPS decisions have always generally had multiple levels of supervisors and management, group decision-making involves a distinct group decision-making framework.

One of the most popular models is known as Team Decision-Making (TDM) and is a creation of the Annie E. Casey Foundation (2014). TDM consist of a collaborative meeting where families, parties, community partners and CPS discuss any change of placement, removal or permanency change. The meetings are led by social workers whose sole duty is to facilitate these meetings (Annie E. Casey, 2014).

Investigation reports from pilot studies showed promising result for TDM when the model was adhered to with fidelity, with some sites reducing child placement changes by 40 percent and by others showing a 70 reduction in removals (Annie E. Casey, 2014). In a recent randomized controlled trial Rushovich et al. (2021) demonstrated a similar result with families that participated in TDM being less likely to experience removal. They also found that participants from all sides rated the TDM process favorably and caseworker reported that the meetings allowed them to have a better understanding of the family (Rushovich et al., 2021).

A second widely used model is known as Family Group Decision-Making (FGDM) also incorporates family involvement and allows family to developed their own plan and participate in a family group conference led by a facilitator (Berzin et al., 2008). However, unlike TDM, researchers have found mostly mixed results on outcomes, such as removal, reunification and permanency (Hollinshead et al., 2017; Frost et al., 2014).

In a meta-analysis of FGDM studies, McGinn et al. (2020) went so far as to claim that despite decades of research there was no good evidence that the group meetings led to any improved outcomes for the families or children involved. This was in line with the negative results of prior studies (Hollinshead et al., 2017; Berzin et al., 2008). Though there are significant differences in when and how CPS agencies implement FGDM meetings, so some of the mixed results could be from poor implementation (Frost et al., 2014; Allan et al., 2017). Still other researchers have argued that the value of these meetings might not translate directly into easily measured case goal outcomes, it

> may have had benefits related to bringing family and community members together, providing a mechanism for information sharing, providing families with additional services, and giving the family a role in making child welfare decisions.
>
> (Berzin et al., 2008, p. 51)

My experience as an attorney going to family group conferences was that they provided a good outlet for all of the parties to come together and discuss the family and child needs. They were useful for facilitating service referrals, which while helpful to my client would not necessarily show up on a case outcome measurement.

Carlos and Juan were identical 5-year-old twins being raised by their single mother with her live-in boyfriend. Mom worked third shift and on two occasions within a week when she was alone, she fell asleep, and the boys got out of the house and onto a nearby busy road. The first time, police returned the children home, but the second time, CPS intervened and removed them from care. Mom's boyfriend was willing to watch the children in the future, but he had an arrest record and an old criminal drug possession conviction, so CPS believed he was not a safe option. The boys were moved to a foster home where their behaviors quickly deteriorated. There was suspicion that Juan might have a disability, so reunification was further delayed while CPS attempted to have him tested and given therapy. Both boys were clear from the beginning that they wanted to return home, and mom followed all of CPS's requests, including extensive drug screening even though she had no history of any substance abuse. Finally, when mom was able to move to a second shift at work, CPS allowed them both of the boys to come home with Juan set up to receive early childhood intervention services.

Decision-Making Ecology

In an effort to better understand how child welfare decisions are actually made, researchers have also developed a number of decision-making frameworks to explain the process. Perhaps the most widely used framework for understanding these decisions is the Decision-Making Ecology (DME) developed by Baumann et al. (2011). It has been used in multiple studies to help explain decision-making in predicting reoccurring maltreatment (Maguire-Jack & Font, 2014), placement (Strolin-Goltzman & Holbrook, 2023; Graham et al., 2020; Dettlaff et al., 2015), substantiation (Font & Maguire-Jack, 2015), reunification (Wittenstrom et al., 2015), matching children and foster homes (Zeijlmans et al., 2017) and networked decisions (Keddell & Hyslop, 2019) just to name a few.

The model starts with the premise that humans are prone to mistakes and that all decisions must be understood within their larger context (Fluke et al., 2022). Figure 5.1 below describes the basic structure of the model. Decision-making in the center diamond is influenced by case factors, organizational factors, external factors and individual decision-maker factors. This ultimately produces an outcome in the case, the results of which feed back into the four influence factors (Fluke et al., 2022).

Fluke et al. (2022) describe the factors and process thusly,

> Case information regarding an incident of maltreatment is necessary for a caseworker to make informed assessments and decisions, yet some of the assessments and decisions depend on external factors, such as law translated into policies that govern what constitutes an appropriate response. Furthermore, the translation of such standards by organizational management, and their use by staff, will vary as a function of individual decision-maker factors, such as knowledge and skill, as well as the

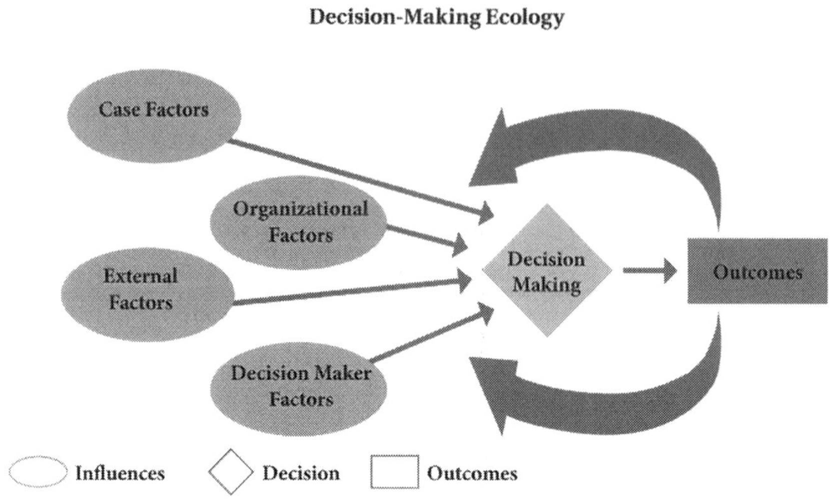

Figure 5.1 Decision-Making Ecology

> actual and perceived costs and benefits (outcomes) of the decision to the decision maker, the client and/or the agency.
>
> (Fluke et al., 2022, p. 615)

The DME process is not a one-time decision, but is present throughout each decision in the case and begins with the initial intake decision all the way through the end of the case with each type of decision having a different decision-making threshold based on the where it occurs during the case. An internal psychological part of the DME, is the General Assessment and Decision-Making Model (GADM) which itself has three parts (Fluke et al., 2022).

Firstly, GADM underscores the difference between a judgment about the evidence needed to make a decision and the decision itself. The second part of the model is the threshold for making decisions, essentially how much evidence is required for a decision to be made. This is a personal subjective threshold based on the individual experiences and beliefs of the caseworker. Third is the standard required to shift the initial threshold. This is the amount of new evidence needed to change the decision. For instance, organization policy could dictate decisions that would not be made by the individual normally, or from an individual perspective, experience in the field might change a worker's initial beliefs (Fluke et al., 2022).

From an outcome perspective, the end result of a decisions will have different effects for the caseworker, the agency and for the other parties involved and that each of these will have different levels of utility from the decision. As noted earlier, all of the child welfare decisions are full of uncertainty and therefore contain the risk of error (Fluke et al., 2022).

Fluke et al. (2022) describe an example of a removal decision that contains four outcomes and two possibilities for error. A correct decision to remove a child prevents future harm whereas a false positive removal inflicts unwarranted trauma on the child and family. A correct decision to leave a child in their home prevents an unneeded government intrusion and family trauma, but a false negative risks allowing the child to be subsequently mistreated (Fluke et al., 2022).

> Different caseworkers will value these consequences differently. A way to demonstrate this and roughly identify threshold placement is for a decision maker to answer this question: Given that you can't avoid the possibility of error, which one do you want to avoid the most? At one level it is nearly as simple as that. However, it might be difficult to articulate why you have a preference to avoid one error and not the other. One reason for this is that there are a number of stakeholders on the decision. In child protection these include: The child, the family, the caseworker themselves, their work unit, their supervisor, their agency, other professionals, the courts, and society in general. There are sets of consequences for each of these stakeholders for each outcome.
>
> (Fluke et al., 2022, p. 621)

As noted earlier, even though few researchers have asked directly about best interest in their decision-making studies, investigation, removal, placement, reunification and termination are all ultimately best interest decisions, so it is appropriate still to try to understand them through a DME framework. Under the DME, best interest comes into decision-making as part of the outside influences.

Firstly, best interest is a legal requirement imposed on the case by the legislature and courts, thus it comes in as an external factor. It also is part of the organizational factors as internal policy, trainings and organizational culture will create a shared understanding as to how best interest is interpreted at different stages of the case. Finally, best interest with its eternally broad, vague and subjective definition will be filtered through the individual beliefs, preferences and biases of the individual worker.

Going further, Fluke et al. (2022) noted that the various stakeholders each have a preferred outcome and that each decision holds the possibility of multiple modes of error. Best interests for the child, family, court, CPS, foster parents, CASA, kinship family, community services and society at large all can have different meanings throughout different portions of the case leading to widely different outcomes. A correct decision by the family might be perceived as an error by the foster parents. CPS might disagree with a court's judgment.

Under the DME framework, best interest decisions be they removals, placements or reunifications are constantly being pressured from multiple sources with their own external, organizational and internal factors and their own thresholds for decision-making. A senior judge, an attorney for CASA and rookie CPS investigator might have vastly different thresholds and tolerances for error. Again, they might even perceive error differently.

The final result is an extremely complex web of overlapping decisions made by numerous people throughout the child welfare system. It is no surprise the that best interest, which can morph itself into whatever shape the community, the organization or the individual need it to be, has become the default in decision-making. In the US system, all of these big case decisions are ultimately decided by a judge, but how judicial rulings fit within a DME framework has yet to be fully determined. Future research to expand the DME to better include legal and judicial decision-makers would be valuable to the field. Certainly, judges have their own sets of influential factors. Judges hear arguments from attorneys, hear testimony from witnesses, read evidentiary reports prepared by experts and have oversight from appellate courts. Each of these in turn have their own set of influential decision-making factors and thresholds.

This again is just for the big case decisions made by judges, with outcomes that are easier for researchers and governments to measure. In between each of the significant case decisions that reach the court are hundreds of lesser decisions that shape the lives of the families and the children involved. Which evaluation does the child need? Would individual or family therapy be better? Will the foster parent advocate for school issues or does an educational representative need to be determined? Does the parent qualify for the in-treatment substance abuse program? Can the agency find another worker to facilitate more sibling visits? Does the judge have space on the docket for a last-minute addition? Did the CASA volunteer have the training to actually judge the interaction between the parent and child during their visit at the CPS office?

Each of these decisions made by dozens of people at different points on the case have ripple effect outcomes on those larger case questions. A poor evaluation means a misdiagnosed child not receiving help and having a placement breakdown, which then makes CPS more reluctant to reunify because the child is not stable. A parent whose case was not accepted for a specialized drug court program, never gets the intensive treatment and case management and eventually has their rights terminated.

The DME does a good job of explaining how particular decisions come about in child welfare, but no decision is an island. This is a churning decision river with multiple forks and tributaries that quite frankly might be impossible to model completely. Unfortunately, no research has ever directly applied the DME to a normalcy decision, but like the other decisions discussed, they would undoubtedly have multiple influences and take place as part of this decision-making river.

Conclusion

In the end we know that decision-making is complex and depends on multiple case factors, such as type of abuse, age of the child, race of the family and the cooperation of the parents. These case factors are then filtered through organizational factors, such as a particular CPS office's tolerance for risk. These themselves might be the result of external factors like the presence or lack of community resources for families in need or whether the location is urban or rural. Finally, individual factors, such as a belief in the purpose of child welfare and an individual's own risk tolerance and decision thresholds come into play. Onto this complexity, all of the factors shift and change throughout different phases of the case.

As discussed earlier in the best interest chapter, what this means for families being investigated is that the same family under the same circumstances could be drastically affected by different decisions made for them depending on the caseworker assigned to their case, that caseworker's supervisor's experience and beliefs and the community in which the family lives.

One of the frustrating things about representing foster youth was not knowing what CPS would do with any particular case. The stated early goal was always reunification, but depending on the temperament of the worker, whether CASA was involved, which court it was assigned and what attorney the parents got appointed from the rotating wheel, the end result was never very predictable.

So, what do we know about decision-making for foster children? It depends on hundreds of factors, most of which are out of control of the family or even the caseworker.

References

Allan, H., Harlaar, N., Hollinshead, D., Drury, I., & Merkel-Holguin, L. (2017). The impact of worker and agency characteristics on FGC referrals in child welfare. *Children and Youth Services Review*, *81*, 229–237. https://doi.org/10.1016/j.childyouth.2017.08.013

Annie E. Cassey Foundation. (2014). *Team decision making: Engaging families in placement decisions*. Retrieved May 16, 2024, from https://assets.aecf.org/m/resourcedoc/AECF-TeamDecisionMakingCaseStudy-2014.pdf

Arad-Davidzon, B., & Benbenishty, R. (2008). The role of workers' attitudes and parent and child wishes in child protection workers' assessments and recommendation regarding removal and reunification. *Children and Youth Services Review*, *30*(1), 107–121. https://doi.org/10.1016/j.childyouth.2007.07.003

Baron, E. J., Doyle, J. J., Jr., Emanuel, N., Hull, P., & Ryan, J. (2024). Discrimination in multiphase systems: Evidence from child protection*. *The Quarterly Journal of Economics*. Advance online publication. https://doi.org/10.1093/qje/qjae007

Barry, B., Morales, L., & Carthy, A. (2022). *An evidence review of behavioural economics in the justice sector*. https://doi.org/10.13140/RG.2.2.19104.87042

Bartelink, C., Knorth, E. J., López López, M., Koopmans, C., Ten Berge, I. J., Witteman, C., & van Yperen, T. A. (2018). Reasons for placement decisions in a case of suspected child abuse: The role of reasoning, work experience and attitudes in decision-making. *Child Abuse & Neglect*, *83*, 129–141. https://doi.org/10.1016/j.chiabu.2018.06.013

Baumann, D. J., Dalgleish, L., Fluke, J., & Kern, H. (2011). *The decision-making ecology*. American Humane Association. Retrieved May 1, 2024, from https://www.researchgate.net/profile/John-Fluke/publication/240245616_The_Decision-Making_Ecology/links/0deec51c4af8feb30e000000/The-Decision-Making-Ecology.pdf

Benbenishty, R., Davidson-Arad, B., López, M., Devaney, J., Spratt, T., Koopmans, C., Knorth, E. J., Witteman, C. L. M., Del Valle, J. F., & Hayes, D. (2015). Decision making in child protection: An international comparative study on maltreatment substantiation, risk assessment and interventions recommendations, and the role of professionals' child welfare attitudes. *Child Abuse & Neglect*, *49*, 63–75. https://doi.org/10.1016/j.chiabu.2015.03.015

Benbenishty, R., & Fluke, J. D. (2020). Frameworks and models in decision-making and judgment in child welfare and protection. In J. D. Fluke, M. L. López, R. Benbenishty, E. J. Knorth, & D. J. Baumann (Eds.), *Decision-making and judgment in child welfare and protection: Theory, research, and practice*. Oxford University Press. https://doi.org/10.1093/oso/9780190059538.003.0001

Berrick, J., Dickens, J., Pösö, T., & Skivenes, M. (2016). Time, institutional support, and quality of decision making in child protection: A cross-country analysis. *Human Service Organizations: Management, Leadership & Governance*, *40*(5), 451–468. https://doi.org/10.1080/23303131.2016.1159637

Berzin, S. C., Cohen, E., Thomas, K., & Dawson, W. C. (2008). Does family group decision making affect child welfare outcomes? Findings from a randomized control study. *Child Welfare*, *87*(4), 35–54.

Bhatti-Sinclair, K., & Sutcliffe, C. (2012). What determines the out-of-home placement of children in the USA? *Children and Youth Services Review*, *34*(9), 1749–1755. https://doi.org/10.1016/j.childyouth.2012.05.004

Biehal, N., Sinclair, I., & Wade, J. (2015). Reunifying abused or neglected children: Decision-making and outcomes. *Child Abuse & Neglect*, *49*, 107–118. https://doi.org/10.1016/j.chiabu.2015.04.014

Britner, P. A., & Mossler, D. G. (2002). Professionals' decision-making about out-of-home placements following instances of child abuse. *Child Abuse & Neglect*, *26*(4), 317–332. https://doi.org/10.1016/S0145-2134(02)00311-3

Carnochan, S., Lee, C., & Austin, M. J. (2013). Achieving timely reunification. *Journal of Evidence-Based Social Work*, *10*(3), 179–195. https://doi.org/10.1080/15433714.2013.788948

Chateauneuf, D., Poirier, M.-A., & Pagé, G. (2021). Decision-making in foster care: A view on the dynamic and collective nature of the process. *Journal of Social Work*, *21*(4), 730–752. https://doi.org/10.1177/1468017320928825

Cheng, T. C. (2010). Factors associated with reunification: A longitudinal analysis of long-term foster care. *Children and Youth Services Review*, *32*(10), 1311–1316. https://doi.org/10.1016/j.childyouth.2010.04.023

Clark, S., Byers, K., Akin, B. A., Dunkerley, S., Wright, K., & McCall, S. (2021). *Child safety and family preservation: Investigating the relationships between tenure, type of employment, and values influencing decision making among child welfare professionals* [Conference session]. 25th Annual Society for Social Work and Research Annual Conference, Social Work Science for Social Change. Retrieved October 25, 2023, from https://socwel.ku.edu/child-safety-and-family-preservation-investigating-relationships-between-tenure-type-employment-and

Daminger, A., Hayes, J., Barrows, A., & Wright, J. (2015). Poverty interrupted applying behavioral science to the context of chronic scarcity. *Ideas*, *42*. Retrieved May 20, 2024, from http://www.ideas42.org/wp-content/uploads/2015/05/I42_PovertyWhitePaper_Digital_FINAL-1.pdf

Damman, J. L., Johnson-Motoyama, M., Wells, S. J., & Harrington, K. (2020). Factors associated with the decision to investigate child protective services referrals: A systematic review. *Child & Family Social Work*, *25*(4), 785–804. https://doi.org/10.1111/cfs.12755

de Haan, W. D., van Berkel, S. R., van der Asdonk, S., Finkenauer, C., Forder, C. J., van IJzendoorn, M. H., Schuengel, C., & Alink, L. R. A. (2019). Out-of-home placement decisions: How individual characteristics of professionals are reflected in deciding about child protection cases. *Developmental Child Welfare*, *1*(4), 312–326. https://doi.org/10.1177/2516103219887974

Desir, K. (2021). The turtle & the hare in a race against the clock: Defining "reasonable efforts" to prevent termination of parental rights under the adoption and safe families act of 1997 (2021). *Student Works*, *1159*. https://scholarship.shu.edu/student_scholarship/1159

Dettlaff, A. J., Christopher Graham, J., Holzman, J., Baumann, D. J., & Fluke, J. D. (2015). Development of an instrument to understand the child protective services decision-making process, with a focus on placement decisions. *Child Abuse & Neglect*, *49*, 24–34. https://doi.org/10.1016/j.chiabu.2015.04.007

Dettlaff, A. J., Rivaux, S. L., Baumann, D. J., Fluke, J. D., Rycraft, J. R., & James, J. (2011). Disentangling substantiation: The influence of race, income, and risk on the substantiation decision in child welfare. *Children and Youth Services Review*, *33*(9), 1630–1637. https://doi.org/10.1016/j.childyouth.2011.04.005

Drake, B., Jones, D., Kim, H., Gyourko, J., Garcia, A., Barth, R. P., Font, S. A., Putnam-Hornstein, E., Duerr Berrick, J., Greeson, J. K. P., Cook, V., Kohl, P. L., & Jonson-Reid, M. (2023). Racial/ethnic differences in child protective services reporting, substantiation and placement, with comparison to non-CPS risks and outcomes: 2005–2019. *Child Maltreatment*, *28*(4), 683–699. https://doi.org/10.1177/10775595231167320

Edwards, L. (2018). Ignoring reasonable efforts: How courts fail to promote prevention. *The Imprint: Youth and Family News.* Retrieved May 9, 2024, from https://imprintnews.org/top-stories/ignoring-reasonable-efforts-why-court-system-fail-promote-prevention/32974

Edwards, N. M. (2024). Court-level stakeholders' reunification decisions and perceived role in parents' readiness to support early emotional development post-abuse and/or neglect. *Journal of Public Child Welfare*, 1–25. https://doi.org/10.1080/15548732.2024.2315119

Farmer, E. (1996). Family reunification with high risk children: Lessons from research. *Children and Youth Services Review*, *18*(4), 403–424. https://doi.org/10.1016/0190-7409(96)00012-6

Fernandez, E., & Lee, J.-S. (2011). Returning children in care to their families: Factors associated with the speed of reunification. *Child Indicators Research*, *4*(4), 749–765. https://doi.org/10.1007/s12187-011-9121-7

Fluke, J. D., Bauman, D. J., Dalgleish, L. I., & Kern, H. D. (2022). Decisions to protect children: A decision-making ecology. In R. D. Krugman & J. E. Korbin (Eds.), *Handbook of child maltreatment* (pp. 611–626). Springer International Publishing. https://doi.org/10.1007/978-3-030-82479-2_31

Fluke, J. D., Corwin, T. W., Hollinshead, D. M., & Maher, E. J. (2016). Family preservation or child safety? Associations between child welfare workers' experience, position, and perspectives. *Children and Youth Services Review*, *69*, 210–218. https://doi.org/10.1016/j.childyouth.2016.08.012

Font, S. A., & Maguire-Jack, K. (2015). Decision-making in child protective services: Influences at multiple levels of the social ecology. *Child Abuse & Neglect*, *47*, 70–82. https://doi.org/10.1016/j.chiabu.2015.02.005

Font, S. A., Maguire-Jack, K., & Dillard, R. (2020). The decision to substantiate allegations of child maltreatment. In *Decision making and judgement in child welfare and protection: Theory, research, and practice* (pp. 173–193). Oxford University Press. http://dx.doi.org/10.1093/oso/9780190059538.003.0008

Fraidin, M. (2013). Decision-making in dependency court: Heuristics, cognitive biases, and accountability. *Cleveland State Law Review*, *60*, 913. https://ssrn.com/abstract=2358602

Frost, N., Abram, F., & Burgess, H. (2014). Family group conferences: Evidence, outcomes and future research. *Child & Family Social Work*, *19*(4), 501–507. https://doi.org/10.1111/cfs.12049

Gambrill, E. (2008). Decision making in child welfare: Constraints and potentials. In D. Lindsey & A. Shlonsky (Eds.), *Child welfare research: Advances for practice and policy* (pp. 175–193). Oxford University Press. https://doi.org/10.1093/acprof:oso/9780195304961.003.0010

Gennetian, L., Darling, M., & Aber, L. (2017). Behavioral economics and developmental science: A new framework to support early childhood interventions. *Journal of Applied Research on Children: Informing Policy for Children at Risk*, *7*. https://doi.org/10.58464/2155-5834.1298

Georgia Code § 15–11-311. (2022). Retrieved May 9, 2024, from https://law.justia.com/codes/georgia/2022/title-15/chapter-11/article-4/part-5/section-15-11-311/

Goemans, A., Vanderfaeillie, J., Damen, H., Pijnenburg, H., & Van Holen, F. (2016). Reunification of foster children: Factors associated with reunification outcomes in Flanders and the Netherlands. *Children and Youth Services Review*, *70*, 284–292. https://doi.org/10.1016/j.childyouth.2016.09.023

Graham, J. C., Dettlaff, A. J., Baumann, D. J., & Fluke, J. D. (2020). The decision-making ecology of placing a child into foster care: A structural equation model. In J. D. Fluke, M. L. López, R. Benbenishty, E. J. Knorth, & D. J. Baumann (Eds.), *Decision-making and judgment in child welfare and protection: Theory, research, and practice* (p. 111). Oxford University Press. https://doi.org/10.1093/oso/9780190059538.003.0005

Guthrie, C., Rachlinski, J. J., & Wistrich, A. J. (2007). Blinking on the bench: How judges decide cases. *Cornell Law Review*, *93*(1), 1–44.

Henry, C., Victor, B. G., Ryan, J. P., & Perron, B. E. (2020). Substantiated allegations of failure to protect in the child welfare system: Against whom, in what context, and with what justification? *Children and Youth Services Review*, *116*, 105091. https://doi.org/10.1016/j.childyouth.2020.105091

Hollinshead, D., Currie, D., Kroll, K., Feldman, S. W., Monahan-Price, K., & Fluke, J. (2021). Associations between case, staff, and agency characteristics and the decision to place a child in out-of-home care. *International Journal on Child Maltreatment: Research, Policy and Practice*, *4*, 325–347. https://doi.org/10.1007/s42448-021-00083-9

Hollinshead, D. M., Corwin, T. W., Maher, E. J., Merkel-Holguin, L., Allan, H., & Fluke, J. D. (2017). Effectiveness of family group conferencing in preventing repeat referrals to child protective services and out-of-home placements. *Child Abuse & Neglect*, *69*, 285–294. https://doi.org/10.1016/j.chiabu.2017.04.022

Jolls, C., Sunstein, C., & Thaler, R. (1998). *A behavioral approach to law and economics.* Harvard Law School John M. Olin Center for Law, Economics and Business Discussion Paper Series, 50. https://doi.org/10.2307/1229304

Kahn, N. E., & Hansen, M. E. (2017). Measuring racial disparities in foster care placement: A case study of Texas. *Children and Youth Services Review*, *76*, 213–226. https://doi.org/10.1016/j.childyouth.2017.03.009

Kantar Public UK. (2022). *Applying behavioural insights to fostering and adoption in England Research report.* UK Department of Education. Retrieved May 20, 2024, from https://www.gov.uk/government/publications/applying-behavioural-insights-to-fostering-and-adoption-in-england

Kearney, A. D., Wilson, E. S., Hollinshead, D. M., Poletika, M., Kestian, H. H., Stigdon, T. J., Miller, E. A., & Fluke, J. D. (2023). Child welfare triage: Use of screening threshold analysis to evaluate intake decision-making. *Children and Youth Services Review*, *144*, 106710. https://doi.org/10.1016/j.childyouth.2022.106710

Keddell, E., & Hyslop, I. (2019). Networked decisions: Decision-making thresholds in child protection. *The British Journal of Social Work*, *50*(7), 1961–1980. https://doi.org/10.1093/bjsw/bcz131

Kirkman, E. (2020). *How can behavioral science be used to recruit foster and adoptive families? Lessons from the field*. Casey Family Programs. Retrieved May 20, 2024, from https://www.casey.org/behavioral-insight-recruitment/

Lindsey, D. (2004). *The welfare of children* (2nd ed.). Oxford University Press.

López, M., del Valle, J. F., Montserrat, C., & Bravo, A. (2013). Factors associated with family reunification for children in foster care. *Child & Family Social Work*, *18*(2), 226–236. https://doi.org/10.1111/j.1365-2206.2012.00847.x

Maguire-Jack, K., & Font, S. A. (2014). Predicting recurrent maltreatment among high-risk families: Applying the decision-making ecology framework. *Children and Youth Services Review*, *43*, 29–39. https://doi.org/10.1016/j.childyouth.2014.04.014

Maguire-Jack, K., Font, S. A., & Dillard, R. (2020). Child protective services decision-making: The role of children's race and county factors. *American Journal of Orthopsychiatry*, *90*(1), 48–62. https://doi.org/10.1037/ort0000388

Martín, E., González-Navasa, P., & Betancort, M. (2020). Who will go back home? Factors associated with decisions to address family reunification from residential care. *Children and Youth Services Review*, *109*, 104729. https://doi.org/10.1016/j.childyouth.2019.104729

McCafferty, P., Duffy, J., & Hayes, D. (2021). Permanency decisions in child welfare: A qualitative study. *British Journal of Social Work*, *51*(6), 2134–2154. https://doi.org/10.1093/bjsw/bcab095

McGinn, T., Best, P., Wilson, J., Chereni, A., Kamndaya, M., & Shlonsky, A. (2020). Family group decision-making for children at risk of abuse or neglect: A systematic review. *Campbell Systematic Reviews*, *16*(3), e1088. https://doi.org/10.1002/cl2.1088

Meyer, A. S., McWey, L. M., McKendrick, W., & Henderson, T. L. (2010). Substance using parents, foster care, and termination of parental rights: The importance of risk factors for legal outcomes. *Children and Youth Services Review*, *32*(5), 639–649. https://doi.org/10.1016/j.childyouth.2009.12.011

Michigan Code § 712A.19b. (2023). Retrieved May 9, 2024, from https://law.justia.com/codes/michigan/chapters-701-713/statute-act-288-of-1939/division-288-1939-xiia/section-712a-19b/

Middel, F., Fluke, J., & Hahn, A. (2024). *The effect of child protection attitudes on child protection decision-making: The mediating role of stereotypes* [Unpublished Manuscript].

Miller, K. A., Fisher, P. A., Fetrow, B., & Jordan, K. (2006). Trouble on the journey home: Reunification failures in foster care. *Children and Youth Services Review*, *28*(3), 260–274. https://doi.org/10.1016/j.childyouth.2005.03.010

Moore, K., Frishberg, E., Barrows, A., Yates-Berg, A., & ideas42 (2022). *How could behavioral design improve frontline child welfare practice? Lessons from the field*. Casey Family Programs. Retrieved May 20, 2024, from https://www.casey.org/ideas42-reduce-staff-stressors/

Mosteiro, A., Beloki, U., Sobremonte, E., & Rodríguez, A. (2018). Dimensions for argument and variability in child protection decision-making. *Journal of Social Work Practice*, *32*(2), 169–187. https://doi.org/10.1080/02650533.2018.1439459

Munro, E. (1999). Common errors of reasoning in child protection work. *Child Abuse & Neglect*, *23*(8), 745–758. https://doi.org/10.1016/s0145-2134(99)00053-8

Munro, E. (2019). Decision-making under uncertainty in child protection: Creating a just and learning culture. *Child & Family Social Work*, *24*, 123–130. https://doi.org/10.1111/cfs.12589

Noonan, K., & Burke, K. (2005). Termination of parental rights: Which foster care children are affected? *The Social Science Journal*, *42*(2), 241–256. https://doi.org/10.1016/j.soscij.2005.03.012

Nyathi, N. (2018). Child protection decision-making: Social workers' perceptions. *Journal of Social Work Practice*, *32*(2), 189–203. https://doi.org/10.1080/02650533.2018.1448768

Olmstead, S. B., McWey, L. M., & Henderson, T. (2011). In the child's best interest: Terminating the rights of fathers with children in foster care. *Journal of Family Issues*, *32*(1), 31–54. https://doi.org/10.1177/0192513x10375411

Philip, A., Hager, E., ProPublica, & Khimm, S. (2023). The 'death penalty' of child welfare: In six months or less, some parents lose their kids forever. *ProPublica*. Retrieved May 8, 2024, from https://www.propublica.org/article/six-months-or-less-parents-lose-kids-forever

Phillips, J. D. (2023). A mixed methods study of how interprofessional communication relates to timely reunification in the U.S. child welfare system. *Journal of Public Child Welfare*, *17*(3), 543–568. https://doi.org/10.1080/15548732.2022.2069201

Quartey, D. S. (2024). Child welfare practitioners' perspectives on factors that promote, and hinder family reunification after out-of-home placement in Norway: A micro-meso systems analysis. *Nordic Social Work Research*, 1–14. https://doi.org/10.1080/2156857X.2024.2313617

Raz, M., & Edwards, F. (2023). Termination of parental rights is common and should not be seen as a proxy for child abuse. *Social Work*, *69*(1), 109–112. https://doi.org/10.1093/sw/swad047

Roberts, D. (2022). The Clinton-era adoption law that still devastates black families today. *Slate*. Retrieved May 9, 2024, from https://slate.com/news-and-politics/2022/11/racial-justice-bad-clinton-adoption-law.html

Rodrigues, L., Calheiros, M., & Pereira, C. (2015). The decision of out-of-home placement in residential care after parental neglect: Empirically testing a psychosocial model. *Child Abuse & Neglect*, *49*, 35–49. https://doi.org/10.1016/j.chiabu.2015.03.014

Rushovich, B., Hebert, A., Crampton, D., & Malm, K. (2021). Results from a randomized controlled trial of team decision-making. *Children and Youth Services Review*, *131*, 106263. https://doi.org/10.1016/j.childyouth.2021.106263

Shapira, M., & Benbenishty, R. (1993). Modeling judgments and decisions in cases of alleged child abuse and neglect. *Social Work Research & Abstracts*, *29*, 14–19. https://doi.org/10.1093/swra/29.2.14

Spratt, T., Devaney, J., & Hayes, D. (2015). In and out of home care decisions: The influence of confirmation bias in developing decision supportive reasoning. *Child Abuse & Neglect*, *49*, 76–85. https://doi.org/10.1016/j.chiabu.2015.01.015

Stoddart, J. K., Fallon, B., Trocmé, N., & Fluke, J. (2018). Substantiated child maltreatment: Which factors do workers focus on when making this critical decision? *Children and Youth Services Review*, *87*, 1–8. https://doi.org/10.1016/j.childyouth.2018.01.018

Strolin-Goltzman, J., & Holbrook, H. (2023). The influence of decision-making ecology on placement into foster care. *Children and Youth Services Review*, *148*, 106882. https://doi.org/10.1016/j.childyouth.2023.106882

Summers, A., Gatowski, S., & Dobbin, S. (2012). Terminating parental rights: The relation of judicial experience and expectancy-related factors to risk perceptions in child protection cases. *Psychology, Crime & Law*, *18*(1), 95–112. https://doi.org/10.1080/1068316X.2011.589388

Summers, A., Marsh, S. C., & Burke, J. L. (2024). Judicial decision-making in juvenile dependency and juvenile justice cases. In M. K. Miller, L. A. Yelderman, M. T. Huss, & J. A. Cantone (Eds.), *The Cambridge handbook of psychology and legal decision-making* (pp. 582–598). Cambridge University Press. https://doi.org/10.1017/9781009119375.038

Teunissen, M. S. L., Goemans, A., van Holen, F., Vanderfaeillie, J., Nefs, H. T., Pijnenburg, H. M., Damen, H., & Vedder, P. H. (2021). Family reunification decision-making in Dutch family foster care: A dual perspective approach. *Child & Youth Care Forum*, *50*(2), 199–228. https://doi.org/10.1007/s10566-020-09569-y

U.S. Department of Health & Human Services, Administration for Children and Families, Administration on Children, Youth and Families, Children's Bureau. (2023). *Child maltreatment 2021*. https://www.acf.hhs.gov/cb/data-research/child-maltreatment.

Vanderloo, M. J. (2017). *Caseworker factors that influence removal decisions in child welfare investigations* [Doctoral Dissertation, University of Utah, College of Social Work]. Retrieved October 20, 2023, from https://collections.lib.utah.edu/dl_files/55/fa/55fac9934240bcc8502002f6a5fb8d411856aea9.pdf

Vesneski, W. (2013). *Judging parents: Courts, child welfare, and criteria for terminating parental rights* [Doctoral Dissertation, University of Washington]. http://hdl.handle.net/1773/22572

Wildeman, C., Edwards, F. R., & Wakefield, S. (2020). The cumulative prevalence of termination of parental rights for U.S. children, 2000–2016. *Child Maltreatment*, *25*(1), 32–42. https://doi.org/10.1177/1077559519848499

Wittenstrom, K., Baumann, D. J., Fluke, J., Graham, J. C., & James, J. (2015). The impact of drugs, infants, single mothers, and relatives on reunification: A decision-making ecology approach. *Child Abuse & Neglect*, *49*, 86–96. https://doi.org/10.1016/j.chiabu.2015.06.010

Zeijlmans, K., López, M., Grietens, H., & Knorth, E. J. (2017). Matching children with foster carers: A literature review. *Children and Youth Services Review*, *73*, 257–265. https://doi.org/10.1016/j.childyouth.2016.12.017

Zeijlmans, K., López, M., Grietens, H., & Knorth, E. J. (2019). Heuristic decision-making in foster care matching: Evidence from a think-aloud study. *Child Abuse & Neglect*, *88*, 400–411. https://doi.org/10.1016/j.chiabu.2018.12.007

6 Children's Rights and Participation

The specialty court in Houston has a special child waiting room away from the busy hallway that court staff have decorated with couches, a TV with Netflix and filled with games, toys and books. Because sometimes kids might have to wait several hours before their case is heard, the court wanted a place where the kids could be more comfortable. Though child participation occurs in family courts as well, in the specialty court, it is strongly encouraged. When the youth request or the judge thinks it might be helpful, they meet alone in chambers before then taking their testimony during the hearing. The practice means that court days are long and case hearings take more time, but the children are always heard even when the court cannot order what they want.

The right for foster children to be heard and participate in their own case is just one of many rights of children in general. However, children's rights and participation are a complicated and controversial tangle of interrelated issues. Do all children have the same rights from birth or are some rights acquired as they age? How do these rights interact with the rights of parents? What is the obligation of adults to protect children's rights versus their obligation to protect the children themselves?

Again, this is a topic that could already fill a small library and continues to inspire new legal, philosophical and scientific scholarship each year. In the sections that follow, I will attempt to synthesize some of this literature and what it all means for children in the welfare system.

Philosophy

To help understand why children's rights remain controversial, we need to first understand the legal philosophical framework from which they are conceived. Archard (2023) first notes that the concept of childhood is fluid across time and cultural and by definition means that children are by their nature different than adults. Cowden (2012) wrote that under the CRC anyone below 18 is a child, but 17-year-olds and infants are hardly the same. The unifying concept tying them together is that they are not adults. Herring (2023) wrote that childhood is often defined by listing traits that adults possess, but children do not, such as the ability to care for themselves or experience. Childhood then

DOI: 10.4324/9781003510253-6

is an approximation of both biology and culture where generally a person has not developed their full mental and physical capabilities (Cowden, 2012). Although even this definition is somewhat reductive as it does not properly incorporate people with disabilities.

Arguably the law itself does not really provide a consistent definition of a child or minor or even particularly an adult with different states and different ages allowing or prohibiting certain acts. Cramer (2020) wrote that young people in the US are prohibited from buying alcohol or tobacco until they are 21 years old even though the age of majority is generally 18. Likewise, 18-year-olds can purchase a rifle, but only 21-year-olds can buy a handgun (ATF, 2022). This is perhaps made odder by the fact that 17-year-olds can enlist in active duty in the military (usa.gov., n.d.).

The U.S. Department of Labor (n.d.) allows 14-year-olds to work and allows children of any ages to work on their family farm. As one state example, Virginia allows 15-year-olds to sign a contract for life insurance (Prebeck, 2023). There is no minimum age requirement for minors to obtain a federal student loan, though they are required to show that they are eligible for college admission (U.S. Department of Education, n.d.). The US Supreme Court in *Reno v. Flores* even allowed 16-year-olds in immigration proceeding to waive deportation rights writing, *"It has not been shown that all of them are too young or too ignorant to exercise that right when the form asking them to assert or waive it is presented* " 507 US 292, 309 (1993).

US states also set widely different age of sexual consent laws, with most states allowing 16-year-olds to consent, but some even allow children as young as 12 or 13 to consent so long as their partner is no more than two to four years older (HHS, 2004). European Union Agency for Fundamental Rights (2017) reports that Europe has similar laws related to sexual consent with most nations allowing 14- to 15-year-olds to consent to sex and most applying a three-year age gap to sex between youths. In the US minors are often allowed to marry at 16 years old, with some states requiring parental or judicial consent and once married the statutory rape age of consent laws are no longer applied (Reiss, 2021).

Likewise, criminal liability can vary greatly by state. The Interstate Commission for Juveniles (2024) reported that all of the states allow youth 16 and older to be charged as adults in criminal trials. Most states limit this to serious felonies, but many allow for prosecutions of youth as young as 14 and a few states even 12. The Child Rights International Network (n.d.) reports similar polices across Europe with most nations setting criminal responsibility at 14 years old, though many European countries do not allow adult prosecution for youth.

One of the core ways that children differ is in their capacity, which Cowden (2012) writes is different not only among adults and children, but between children of different ages. Children are often denied rights because they lack their full capacities,

> To hold a right one must have certain capacities, such as the capacity to feel pain, make choices or to think rationally. Children are in a state

> of developing those capacities and acquiring competency and therefore cannot hold the rights, unlike adults whose physical and cognitive competencies are fully developed.
>
> (Cowden, 2012, p. 365)

This notion of capacity is often tied to will theory, which posits that humans have rights because they are able to make autonomous choices (Noogle, 2018). Because will theory is generally incompatible with young children, some disabled people and people in a coma, it is often rejected by philosophers looking to find a basis for children's rights (Archard, 2023). Instead, children's rights are generally grounded in interest theory, which frames rights as being interest protecting rather than choice. "*A person has a right to X because having X serves that person's vital interest*" (Noogle, 2018, p. 104).

Because a pure interpretation of interest theory does not allow for a special moral status for humans, some scholars have suggested a hybrid will and interest model for children's rights (Noogle, 2018). Essentially, children begin life under an interest theory model, but as they gain more capacity and development, they transition to a will theory model that is more protective of their decisions (Noogle, 2018).

In addition to the will and interest frameworks, children's rights also tend to divided by scholars into liberationist and protectionist camps (Noogle, 2018). Protectionist acknowledge that adults owe a host of duties to children to protect them and encourage their upbringing, but that does not mean that children automatically have rights. The adult protection is sufficient for their interests until they reach adulthood and not having rights does not equate not having moral status (Archard, 2023). Historically, protectionist ideas provided the motivation behind the ending of child labor, the creation of juvenile courts and the child welfare system (Noogle, 2018).

One of the most common used ideas to justify the exclusion of children's rights is that they are more vulnerable than adults (Herring, 2023). This protectionist idea leans into a child's weakness and inexperience in relation to adults and is the legal basis for many laws that grant children special status, such as prohibitions against the sale of alcohol or cigarettes (Herring, 2023). Keddell (2018) argued that this idea of vulnerability has been used historically to justify state interventions into families especially targeting minority and poor communities. "*In this formulation, the child is an exposed victim in need of rescuing. By far the majority of families in contact with child protection systems do not fit this stereotype*" (Keddell, 2018, p. 9).

Liberationist argue that children should be granted the same rights as adults, with strict liberationist even going so far as to believe that children should have the right to leave their home (Noogle, 2018). One liberationist argument is that the denial of rights to children is actually one of the culturally enforced elements that maintains their childhood status or stated otherwise "*they cannot have rights because they are incapable but they are incapable only because they do not have these rights*" (Archard, 2023, para. 37). Noogle (2018) noted that the liberationist ideas have had some impact in courts now listening to children's testimony and in the medical professions' obtaining children's consent when possible.

Though most liberationist philosophers take a more nuanced, middle ground approach that acknowledges the differences in childhood and their changing needs and capabilities, (Noogle, 2018) a common liberationist critique of the denial of rights to children is that the decision is arbitrary (Archard, 2023). The difference between a middle-aged adult and a toddler might be significant, but the difference between a 17 and an 18-year-old might be minimal, thus the line between them is arbitrary. Of course, some arbitrary division somewhere must be made if society is to make any division at all (Archard, 2023).

Herring (2023) wrote that the focus on vulnerability of childhood is also fundamentally misplaced. Though the focus of the law positions individuals as the agents of harm towards children, it is more likely that both adults and children will be harmed by government interventions and policies that create or ignore economic, environmental or societal dangers. More importantly, adults share all of the same vulnerabilities as children in that individuals cannot alone guarantee their own personal safety nor their rights.

> The point here is that our nature is to be vulnerable . . . We might like to think we are self-sufficient and independent, but society has built up a wide range of structures and forms of assistance which disguise our vulnerability. We are profoundly dependent on others and social provision for survival.
>
> (Herring, 2023, p. 1516)

Another criticism of protectionist ideas is that they treat children as if they are not true human beings (Vissing, 2023). This is often framed as human beings versus human becomings. Children are thought of as human beings in progress, which emphasizes their future selves as opposed to who they are in the present moment.

> Children from a rights-perspective have value not because of what they do or might become in the future but because of who they are in this moment. Children matter merely because they exist. Their worlds of today matter; the future hasn't happened yet and what will happen tomorrow is dependent upon what happens today.
>
> (Vissing, 2023, p. 21)

Vissing (2023) argued that viewing children not quite fully formed humans from a rights standpoint is a particularly dangerous as historically people considered not quite human have suffered greatly from others. Keddell (2018) extended this argument to children in the child welfare system and wrote that not only are they not considered beings in their current present state, but the system perceives them to be "damaged becomings" (p.11).

Herring (2023) noted that from a legal perspective there are essentially three ways of looking at children's rights. Firstly, children and adults share the same rights, but adults have additional rights than children. The second and most commonly adopted strategy, is that adults and children have different rights and some of those rights overlap such as the right to life, but others such as the right to education are exclusively to children. Finally, the third perspective is the liberationist one where adults and children share all of the same rights (Herring, 2023).

Another way to think about children's rights come from, Feinberg (1980) who argued that children have a right to an open future, which essentially entails that their rights are held in trust by adults so that important decisions are not made for them. Once the child develops the autonomy to make an informed decision, that right becomes theirs and it is no longer the duty of adults to hold that right (Feinberg, 1980). This is generally interpreted by scholars to imply that children be given reasonable opportunities for a healthy adult life and not that every childhood needs to be maximized to allow as many as possible options (Noogle, 2018).

As with most philosophy, a hybrid of many of these ideas seems the most applicable to real-world children in the care system. I do not believe there is a serious argument that children have no rights, but what those rights are and how they come into being is debatable. Best interest as a concept generally seems to run counter to those rights especially in a child welfare setting as even under a rights in trust model, it takes life altering decisions away from foster youth.

The day-to-day practice of the child welfare world leaves little time for a philosophical discussion of the origin of children's rights. Foster homes need to be found. Parents need to be served. Therapy needs to be scheduled. Mediation needs to commence. Family visits need to be monitored. Yet, this daily whack-a-mole approach to child welfare prevents CPS, courts and others from seriously considering the rights of children in care and ultimately denies their rights.

No one in the real world would argue that an infant and a 17-year-old have the same capabilities, vulnerabilities and needs, yet they are lumped together by the law. No one could likewise can argue that an infant or toddler can really give informed decisions about their child welfare cases. For each year of age though, the question becomes murkier, but certainly there is a point where a child or youth can meaningfully make choices about their own lives and where their rights truly emerge.

International Children's Rights

Beyond the philosophical, there are multiple legal texts and documents that have granted rights to children around the world both internationally, regionally and nationally.

The 1923 Geneva Declaration of the Rights of the Child is widely seen as the first international attempt to articulate special rights for children (Sacotte et al., 2023). The Geneva Declaration (1923) is a simple six paragraphs, but it includes provisions that children be fed, sheltered, provided medical care, be first to receive services, be free from exploitation and be provided the means and opportunity to earn a living and contribute to society. Interestingly in what could be thought of as an early precursor to normalcy, the Geneva Declaration (1923) also states, "*The child must be given the means requisite for its normal development, both materially and spiritually*" (para. 2).

Sacotte et al. (2023) wrote that the next international child rights document came from the United Nations 1959 Declaration of the Rights of the Child, which adopted the rights of the Geneva Declaration as well as additional rights, such as the right to education, the right to disability services and protection from neglect and discrimination. Though ambitious in time, the Geneva Declaration and 1959 Declaration continued to view children from a protectionist perspective that placed their rights as something that adults must guarantee through services and laws and not as individual right holders of their own (Kosher et al., 2016).

The first binding international instruments to grant children rights were the International Covenant on Civil and Political Rights and the International Covenant on Economic, Social and Cultural Rights (Sacotte et al., 2023). These were not specifically for children's rights, but did include broad provisions against slavery, inhumane punishment and rights to the family (Sacotte et al., 2023).

Of course, as discussed in prior chapters, the most important and comprehensive children's rights document is the 1989 Convention on the Rights of the Child (CRC). The 54 articles within the treaty lay out a number of substantive rights that scholars have generally divided into three categories, provision, participation and protection known as the "three Ps" (Vissing, 2023).

Provision lays out rights that are owed to children like education, healthcare, housing, food, social services and love and nurturing (Vissing, 2023). Participation incorporates the right to play and have free time that are important for normalcy as well as the rights to assemble, privacy, free expression and self-guided decision-making. Vissing (2023) noted that of the three Ps, this one is the most likely to cause conflict with adult interests. Lastly, protection, like the name implies, are rights to prevent harm, abuse, trafficking and exploitation of children (Vissing, 2023).

The CRC is considered one of the most successful international treaties in history as it has near universal support and went into law faster than any other treaty (Kosher et al., 2016). Though the United States helped draft and promulgate the CRC, it has signed but never ratified the convention, making it a global outlier (Sacotte et al., 2023).

Though foster children are the beneficiaries of all of the CRC rights, there are several that directly apply. The most on point is of course Article 20: Protection of Children Without Families, which specifically addresses the situation of children who are temporarily or permanently deprived of their family environment and must be looked after by the state properly by people who respect their religion, culture and language (CRC, 1989).

Article 21 Adoption, Article 9 Separation from Parents, Article 25 Review of Treatment, Article 19 Protection from Abuse and Neglect, Article 18 Parental Responsibilities and State Assistance and of course Article 3 Best Interests of the Child, also all have direct connection for children in care (CRC, 1989).

Finally, in an effort to clarify the CRC's relations to child welfare, the United Nations (2010) has issued Guidelines for the Alternative Care of Children. The guidelines emphasize the importance of the family structure and keeping children with their families when possible. They also ensure the provision of suitable alternative care when necessary, prioritizing options that promote the child's development and well-being. Governments are encouraged to fulfill their responsibilities and obligations regarding child welfare, considering the specific economic, social and cultural contexts of each country (UN, 2010).

The UN (2010) also highlighted the importance of prioritizing the best interests of the child in all decisions regarding their care, ensuring their safety, well-being and development. Decisions should be made on a case-by-case basis, taking into account the child's specific needs, background and preferences, ensuring that all children are treated equally regardless of their background or circumstances. The guidelines note that children should be consulted and their views considered in all decisions affecting them, according to their age and maturity. In addition, the decision to place a child in alternative care should involve judicial, administrative, or other recognized procedures with legal safeguards (UN, 2010).

Finally, in addition to the CRC, there are also regional international instruments, such as the African Charter on the Rights and Welfare of the Child, the European Convention on the Exercise of Children's Rights, the Inter-American Convention on the Rights of the Child, the ASEAN Declaration on the Rights of Children in the Context of Migration, and the Arab Charter on Human Rights that impact the rights of children in the signatory nations.

Children's Rights in the USA

Because this book has a special focus on normalcy and normalcy is inherently a creation of US jurisprudence, it is useful to discuss children's rights specifically as they are found in the US.

Vissing (2023) wrote that early rights of children came about because of the Progressive Movement at the beginning of the 20th Century. While not truly rights in legal sense, early progressives did establish protections for children for child labor, education and maltreatment. Though it is important to acknowledge that these early protections did not apply to Black and other minority children (Vissing, 2023).

At the US Supreme Court level, Chilton (2022) noted that children rights have had mixed results. Though the Court has found that children are entitled to constitutional rights since the 1932 *Powell v. Alabama*, the exact nature of these rights is still uncertain. Over the last century, the Court has found that children have equal protection, juvenile due process rights and rights to free speech, the Court has generally been unwilling to infringe too deeply into the rights of parents, which it has routinely upheld.

> The prevailing fear remains that if the Court granted children too many individual, fundamental rights, children's rights would come into frequent conflict with parental rights, undermining the integrity of the family structure so adamantly protected by the Court.
>
> (Chilton, 2022, p. 402)

The law gets especially complicated regarding sexual reproductive health, abortion and the conflict between parental control and a youth's bodily autonomy (Chilton, 2022).

In the US, the picture is of course complicated by rights granted by the state. For instance, every state's constitution includes a mandate for an education system, but the right to an education has been interpreted differently in different states (Dallman & Nath, 2020). As the organization, Human Rights Watch (2022) reported because children's rights are often left to the states to regulate, children in different states can have fewer rights then their neighbor across the state border.

Though the US is not bound by the CRC, Human Rights Watch (2022) still monitors and rates its compliance with CRC rights. Using only four measures rated A to F, child marriage, corporal punishment, juvenile justice and child labor, the organization found that not a single state even received an overall B score and only seven received C scores. Most states were ranked a D and 16 received a failing grade (Human Rights Watch, 2022). The poor scores on corporal punishment and juvenile justice as especially relevant for children in the care system given the overlaps with the juvenile justice system. Many states allow children to be tried as adults and sentenced to life imprisonment, while some still allow for juvenile prisons and even alternative care centers to use corporal punishment (Human Rights Watch, 2022).

As for the rights of foster children specifically, Chilton (2022) wrote that courts have often found a duty on behalf of the state CPS agency to provide education, healthcare and the adequate necessities, such as safety, food and housing. For instance, federal courts have written

> We now hold that when the state places a child in state-regulated foster care, the state has entered into a special relationship with that child which imposes upon it certain affirmative duties. The failure to perform such duties can give rise, under sufficiently culpable circumstances, to liability under section 1983.
>
> *Nicini v. Morra*, 212 F.3d 798, 808 (3d Cir. 2000)

See also The Wisconsin Court of Appeals that wrote,

> We hold that those entrusted with the task of ensuring that children are placed in a safe and secure foster home owe a constitutional duty that is determined by a professional judgment standard.
>
> *Kara B. v. Dane County*, 205 Wis. 2d 140, 158 (Wis. 1996)

Of course, while HHS (2023) list nearly 50 federal laws with connection to child welfare and protection passed just since 1980, the laws are generally not connected with a substantive right for children in care. As described in Chapter 2, federal law does require that foster children have representation, but this is not uniformly interpreted as a right to counsel in every state (Malempati, 2014). Another example is the Preventing Sex Trafficking and Strengthening Families Act (2014) which,

> Gives children age 14 and older authority to participate in: (1) the development of their own case plans, in consultation with up to two members of the case planning team; as well as (2) transitional planning for a successful adulthood. Specifies additional requirements for a case plan, including specification of a child's rights with respect to education, health, visitation, and court participation, the right to be provided with certain documents (indicated in Sec. 114), and the right to stay safe and avoid exploitation.
>
> (Sec. 113)

Foster Care Bill of Rights

In a push to recognize the unique lived experience and challenges of foster care, the federal government tied some federal dollars for states to create their own foster care bill of rights (Reyes, 2012). The National Conference of State Legislatures (2019) reported that 15 states and the territory of Puerto Rico have passed Foster Children's Bill of Rights.

On first glance the rights embedded in these documents are substantial. For instance, Pennsylvania's Children in Foster Care Act (2010) provides that a foster youth should be able to live in the least restrictive environment, the ability to consent to medical and mental health treatment, to have education stability, to have as frequent visits as possible with family, to develop job skills and attend court. Additionally foster youth have the right to be informed of their rights upon entering care and can file grievances with their CPS agency if their rights have been violated (Pennsylvania Statute Title 11 Chapter 35, 2010).

Arizona has Ariz. Rev. Stat. § 8–529 (2023) governing foster care and kinship care rights. It includes 26 rights for a child, such as to know why they are in care, to be disciplined appropriately, to have appropriate clothes and belongings, the right to normal activities of their choice. The statute included rights to be represented by an attorney, to have access to their records and to speak to the judge. It also includes a grievance policy to a state ombudsman and a requirement that they be notified of their rights (Ariz. Rev. Stat. § 8–529, 2023).

For my last example, I will discuss the Texas Family Code – FAM § 263.008. Foster Children's Bill of Rights (2015). Like Arizona and Pennsylvania, it provided notice requirement to foster youth as well as a formal grievance procedure through a state ombudsman. Texas Department of Family and Protective Services (TDFPS) (2023) required foster placements to keep a copy of the rights and children, caseworker and caregivers signed off on a six-page document that included the rights shortly after the child came into care.

TDFPS (2023) lists 48 individual rights for children in care under eight headings, Safety and Care, Have a Normal Life, Discipline, Plans for Me While in Care, Medical Care, Legal Representation or Courts, Records, Make Complaints. There is also a special subsection for older youth that allows them the right to attend various planning conferences, meetings and services aimed at securing them job, education, healthcare and housing services as the aged out of care (TDFPS, 2023).

The other 12 states have similar views on the rights of children in care, which purely on paper provide ample rights. However, as with many US rights problems, the differences between states can be vast. For instance, Missouri begins its statute "*In all circumstances, the best interests of the child shall be the first priority of the children's division*" Mo. Rev. Stat. § 210.564 (1), thereby subsuming children's rights into the fraught world of best interest interpretation. The Massachusetts Department of Children and Families (n.d.) details 18 comprehensive rights, but the rights are found only in policy documents for their CPS, not as a part of state law. Texas, Hawaii, Arizona, Pennsylvania and North Carolina all have language within their statute limiting foster children's ability to enforce their rights. As an example, the Hawaii statute states "*Nothing in this section shall establish a private cause of action for violation of any provision of this section*" Haw. Rev. Stat. § 587A-3.1(d).

When practicing in Texas, my clients routinely were unaware of their rights even though many were given copies of them. While I was often able to get the dependency court to rectify "rights" violations, this is not the same as having an enforceable right against the state agency. Had this existed, suing the state of Texas for violating the foster children's rights would have been full time work. Without the enforceability though, their rights were essentially meaningless.

In my experience the ombudsman process as well was rarely used unless there were complaints about a specific caseworker. Though the ombudsman's office took the complaints seriously, it was a slow process and finding resolution through the dependency court was generally a better, more reliable practice.

This system is made all the stranger when you consider that Arkansas also has a comprehensive foster child rights statute found in Ark. Code §

9–28–1003 that does not contain any limits on liability. In fact, the Arkansas court even has caselaw that supports that foster child rights under their statute can be violated, see *Stricklin v. Ark. Dep't of Human Servs. & Minor Child*, 528 S.W.3d 321, 2017 Ark. App. 441 (Ark. Ct. App. 2017). As its name implies, the city of Texarkana is located directly on the border of both Texas and Arkansas, meaning that a foster child on one side of the street might not have the rights of a foster child on the other.

For the states where the rights are not limited, the rights can be significant. California includes the rights to "*To make, send, and receive confidential telephone calls and other electronic communications, and to send and receive unopened mail, unless prohibited by court order.*" Cal. Welf. and Inst. Code § 16001.9 (13) and

> To be placed in out-of-home care according to their gender identity, regardless of the gender or sex listed in their court, child welfare, medical, or vital records, to be referred to by the child's preferred name and gender pronoun, and to maintain privacy regarding sexual orientation and gender identity and expression, unless the child permits the information to be disclosed, or disclosure is required to protect their health and safety, or disclosure is compelled by law or a court order.
>
> Cal. Welf. and Inst. Code § 16001.9 (19)

Colorado grants the right,

> to be self-sufficient during the transition to adulthood, including:**(I)** Consistent with the child's or youth's developmental level, assistance with establishing a bank account, including identifying institutions where a child or youth may open a bank account, obtaining documents necessary to open an account, learning how to spend a reasonable amount of money, and managing personal income.
>
> Colo. Rev. Stat. § 19–7–101(i) (I)

Florida recognizes the right of foster youth "*to organize as a group for purposes of ensuring that they receive the services and living conditions to which they are entitled and to provide support for one another while in the custody of the department.*" Fla. Stat. § 39.4085 (v).

Some states even include provisions encouraging aggrieved foster youth to enforce their rights via the court. The Delaware statute states, "*Any child aggrieved by a violation of this section may motion the court, through an attorney or court-appointed special advocate, for appropriate equitable relief.*" Del. Code tit. 13 § 2522 (15) (b). Colorado empowers the court itself to act and outlines the standard of proof for any denial,

> Sua sponte or upon motion, a juvenile court may issue any orders to any party to ensure the child or youth is provided the rights enumerated in subsection (2) of this section.

> A juvenile court shall not limit or deny the rights enumerated in subsection (2) of this section unless the court finds by clear and convincing evidence that there are extraordinary circumstances and the limitation or denial is necessary for the safety of the child or youth in foster care.
>
> Colo. Rev. Stat. § 19–7–101(6) & (7)

California's statute also makes clear that

> the rights described in this section are broad expressions of the rights of children in foster care and are not exhaustive of all rights set forth in the United States Constitution and the California Constitution, federal and California statutes, and case law.
>
> Cal. Welf. and Inst. Code § 16001.9 (b)

Many of the state's also include normalcy in their bills. The Nevada statute states that children have the right "*to reasonable participation in extracurricular, cultural and personal enrichment activities which are consistent with the age and developmental level of the child*" Nev. Rev. Stat. § 432.535 (2). Delaware foster youth have the right,

> To have the opportunity to participate in age-appropriate or developmentally-appropriate activities and experiences to promote healthy development, and to have those opportunities explained to them in an age- and developmentally-appropriate manner, consistent with the reasonable and prudent parent standard. Del. Code tit. 13 § 2522 (13). Texas includes the right to, participation in school-related extracurricular or community activities; interaction with persons outside the foster care system, including teachers, church members, mentors, and friends.
>
> Tex. Fam. Code § 263.008 (8) & (9)

Finally, at the federal level, the US House of Representatives recently issued its first nonbinding resolution regarding foster youth rights. Known as the Foster Youth Bill of Rights Resolution (2023) it includes ten minimum rights, including normalcy.

1. *Right to receive an education and remain in their original school, if desired;*
2. *Right to participate in extracurricular, cultural, and social activities;*
3. *Right to receive needed health services, including but not limited to medical, dental, vision, and mental health services;*
4. *Right to freedom from abuse, neglect, or corporal punishment;*
5. *Right to be represented by, and speak to, a guardian or attorney ad litem;*
6. *Right to adequate and healthy food, adequate clothing, and a safe and comfortable living environment;*
7. *Right to freedom from discrimination based on race, gender, religion, or disability;*

8. *Right to have continued contact with siblings, if desired;*
9. *Right to regular or at least reasonable contact with their assigned case worker or an employee of the agency responsible for their child welfare services; and the*
10. *Right to be informed of their rights.*

(H.Res.509, 2023)

All told, the various Foster Child Bill of Rights represent real progress at least in making the child welfare system consider the lived experiences of children in care and what basic dignities and liberties they should be entitled to. Even in the states where the rights are not enforceable, they exist as aspirational goals and have some internal grievance procedures that ensure at least minimal compliance. This is still better than the 35 states that have not articulated the rights of foster youth.

At 15 years old, Laura was on her second stay at the state psychiatric institution, an old brick building surrounded by dry grass, large parking lots and a two-meter-tall barbed wire fence. All of the furniture was round shaped and made of a tear resistance plastic foam. Laura had been cutting herself for a few years now, and her forearms were covered in scars and a few fresh cuts. She had been in multiple RTCs and generally had brief stays in juvenile psychiatric wards before moving to the next placement. The state hospital was the worst for her, though, as she was heavily medicated and monitored. She did not participate in the insufficient amount of school that was offered. She said she would go anywhere else and even was willing to return to some of the RTCs she previously left, but most places would not have her back. She was too erratic, too prone to behaviors and too likely to run. She wished she had not been born, so she would never have come into care.

Foster Care Lawsuits

One of the ways that advocates and children's rights attorneys have attempted to rectify some of the problems within the child welfare system is through the use of large lawsuits, usually class action that allege that state CPS agencies have violated the rights of children in care.

Casey Family Programs (2024) which tracks the status of class actions around the US reported that on average the cases tend to settle with judicial oversight, meaning that the CPS agency agrees to make fundamental changes to policy and practice and the court maintains jurisdiction over the case to make sure that CPS lives up to its agreement. This is generally known as a consent decree. These tend to be long and expensive lawsuits, with Casey Family Programs (2024) reporting that on average they cost the state $15 million in fees and between the lawsuit itself and the monitoring, can last at least 15 years.

The numbers are often in flux, but as of late 2023 at least 20 states were under a consent decree and CPS activities in those states were being monitored by a federal court and another 11 states had pending litigation. Another nine states completed the terms of their consent decrees within the past decade. Unfortunately, there are overlaps between the former and current litigation such as Tennessee that exited court monitoring in 2019 after a year 2000 suit alleging discrimination against Black children, but was sued again in 2023 regarding poor treatment of immigrant children (Casey Family Programs, 2024).

The majority of the suits alleged problems related to excessive caseloads for workers, the lack of mental health services for youth in care and the failure of CPS agencies to achieve stable, permanent placements (Casey Family Programs, 2024). A recent class action against the state of North Carolina focused on the lack of services and placements for disabled foster youth with the Court writing,

> Children with disabilities in North Carolina's child welfare system face significant barriers to accessing community-based placements and services, including "shortages or waitlists for intensive in home services, crisis intervention services, outpatient mental health and substance abuse services, and inadequate transportation to and from such services." However, instead of addressing these barriers and expanding community based placements and services, Defendant sends children to PRTFs (RTCs) "because it has nowhere else to put them.
>
> (Timothy B. et al. v. Kody Kinsley 1:22-cv-01046|
> US District Court for the Middle District of North Carolina
> Memorandum and Order March 29, 2024, p. 5)

Another new complaint against the state of Louisiana which mentions excessive workloads and staffing shortages wrote that,

> Louisiana is required to ensure that children are protected from actual harm and the risk of harm, according to the substantive due process clause of the Fourteenth Amendment. In addition, Courts have recognized that "the State's responsibility to protect foster children's 'general well-being' requires it 'to take steps to prevent children in state institutions from deteriorating physically or psychologically.'"
>
> Complaint at para 149. *Jacob B. and Amelia L. et al., v. Louisiana Department of Children* and Family Services et al., Case No. 3:24-cv-00289-BAJ-SDJ

Overall, the lawsuits themselves have generally been successful with only two being dismissed within the last decade (Casey Family Programs, 2024). Though the tangible results for children in care have been mixed such as the case of Texas, where a 13-year-old lawsuit and 6 years of court oversite have resulted in three findings of contempt against Texas CPS for failures to improve conditions for children in care (Harper, 2024).

Still, from a foster children's rights perspective the class action cases have been useful at providing more recognition. The Washington Supreme Court held,

> that at its core, foster children have a substantive due process right to be free from unreasonable risk of harm, including a risk flowing from the lack of basic services, and a right to reasonable safety.
>
> *Braam v. State*, 150 Wn. 2d 689, 699 (Wash, 2003)

An Illinois Court faced with an early class action extended the right of children to bring litigation holding

> that a child involuntarily placed in a foster home is in a situation so analogous to a prisoner in a penal institution and a child confined in a mental health facility that the foster child may bring a section 1983 action for violation of fourteenth amendment rights.
>
> *Aristotle P. v. Johnson*, 721 F. Supp. 1002, 1009 (N.D. Ill. 1989)

This same logic was used in the Texas litigation, where the court held that children who were in the permanent custody of the state have substantive and procedural due process rights that create a right to counsel, with the judge comparing children being sent to RTCs the same as adults being sent to psychiatric commitment.

> The Court is compelled to jealously protect the liberties of Texas' most vulnerable citizens and safeguard their right to be heard when their liberty is placed in jeopardy. DFPS can articulate no rational basis for making it more difficult for a PMC child to receive procedural due process than persons civilly committed.
>
> *M.D. v. Abbott*, CIVIL ACTION NO. 2:11-CV-84, 18 (S.D. Tex. Jan. 9, 2017)

As someone who practiced law in Texas representing foster youth, I believe that children benefited from this right to counsel.

Parents Rights vs Child Rights

Because resistance to children's rights is often tied up in discussions about the rights of parents, it is helpful to also gain some understanding of how these rights might conflict. Though the parents of foster youth usually have some or all of their rights suspended or terminated until the family is reunited, the state takes on these rights through parens patriae. So for foster children, parent's rights and state rights overlap and are in flux throughout the case.

Philosophically, Brake and Millum (2022) wrote that parental rights are grounded in moral duties to their children. Rights are granted to them as ways to uphold their responsibilities and these rights diminish over time as children come into more maturity. Though in times past, parents' rights were sometimes linked to property rights, as children were considered possessions of the father, this view is no longer the norm (Brake & Millum, 2022).

Cholbi (2017) linked parental rights to procreation rights noting that adults have a right to procreate that may not be interfered with by the state or others. Parental rights begin because they are responsible for bringing their children into being. These rights belong only to the parents of a particular child who are related to that child. The rights also come with duties to care for all of the child's needs and duties to refrain from maltreatment. Finally, these rights are not absolute and abuse or neglect of a child can result in the loss of rights. Cholbi (2017) wrote that

> These rights include the right to control a child's physical location, to guide the child's personal relationships, to exercise proxy judgment on the child's behalf, and (more controversially) to shape a child's education and to raise the child in the parent's particular religious or cultural traditions.
>
> (Cholbi, 2017, p. 16)

From the legal perspective, beginning with CRC (1989), several articles mention the importance of family and a child being raised with their family. As for rights of parents themselves, Article 3 highlights that states must respect parental rights, but the two most substantive mention of parents are in Article 5 and Article 18.

Article 5 reads in part,

> States Parties shall respect the responsibilities, rights and duties of parents or, where applicable, the members of the extended family or community as provided for by local custom, legal guardians or other persons legally responsible for the child, to provide, in a manner consistent with the evolving capacities of the child, appropriate direction and guidance in the exercise by the child of the rights recognized in the present Convention.
>
> (CRC, 1989, Article 5)

In their commentary, UN Committee on the Rights of the Child (2023) wrote that while family rights are generally thought to be upheld in multiple other international treaties, Article 5 was meant to reaffirm the family environment that is beneficial for children. The rights of parents are not absolute, but are preconditioned on the parents upholding all of the holistic rights guaranteed by the CRC and come with the understanding that as children mature more of their rights will come into play (UNCRC, 20223).

Daly (2017) wrote that this view sees parents essentially holding their children's rights in trust. Lee (2017) noted that in the UK, the CRC has been interpreted as parental responsibilities to act for the best of their children rather than as right unto itself. Though not binding, the Commission on European Family Law's Principles of European Family outline a similar idea that adults hold parental responsibility and that this responsibility can be held by more than the child's birth parents (Boele-Woelki, 2021).

Finally, the UNCRC (2023) noted that protection of family or culture or religion is not a legitimate reason for denying a child's rights, writing "*states are not required to respect the right of parents to provide direction and guidance when such direction and guidance would promote discrimination*" (p. 4).

Article 18 describes that parents have the primary duty to care for children with the first section reading,

> States Parties shall use their best efforts to ensure recognition of the principle that both parents have common responsibilities for the upbringing and development of the child. Parents or, as the case may be, legal guardians, have the primary responsibility for the upbringing and development of the child. The best interests of the child will be their basic concern.
>
> (CRC, 1989, Article 18.1)

Article 18 of course brings in the best interest standard, but Ruggiero (2022) noted that it is generally interpreted in a limited fashion as a means to protect the rights of children until their reach their full capacity. Eekelaar (2020) wrote that this subjective best interest language has the unfortunate effect of putting family courts into the role of determining if a parent is doing their best. This has relevance not only for child welfare, but also simple custody cases.

Quennerstedt (2009) argued that the vagueness of the CRC's discussion of parental rights actually hampers an understanding about how the rights or parents and children interact. Children's rights to free expression, religion, education, participation and others can often come in conflict with parental rights. This is complicated by the CRC not detailing what rights parents actually have (Quennerstedt, 2009). Added to this complexity is the notion that parents may not always act in their child's best interest, but their actions do not warrant state intervention, such as smoking indoors, allowing children too many unhealthy snacks, or even withholding love and affection.

One of the reasons the US has been reluctant to ratify the CRC is because the ideas of children's participation and autonomy embedded within it seem to weaken parental and family rights, which the US Supreme Court has routinely protected (Lee, 2017). In one international comparison study, Americans were three times more likely than Norwegians to favor parental rights over children's rights (Berrick et al., 2022). So there is some limited evidence that perhaps the US has a stronger parental rights normative perspective.

From a US legal perspective, the rights of parents have been firmly established in the jurisprudence. In a case involving a state law that required children to attend only public schools, the US Supreme Court upheld a parent's right to choose the child's education system holding,

> The child is not the mere creature of the State; those who nurture him and direct his destiny have the right, coupled with the high duty, to recognize and prepare him for additional obligations.
>
> *Pierce v. Society of Sisters*, 268 US 510, 535 (1925)

Parental rights were reaffirmed again in *Prince v. Massachusetts*, the Court wrote,

> It is cardinal with us that the custody, care and nurture of the child reside first in the parents, whose primary function and freedom include preparation for obligations the state can neither supply nor hinder.
>
> *Prince v. Massachusetts*, 321 US 158, 166 (1944)

Later in *Wisconsin v. Yoder*, the Court repeated this idea writing,

> The history and culture of Western civilization reflect a strong tradition of parental concern for the nurture and upbringing of their children. This primary role of the parents in the upbringing of their children is now established beyond debate as an enduring American tradition.
>
> 406 US 205, 232 (1972)

Later still in the *Troxel v. Granville* decision that I mentioned in Chapter 2 regarding best interest, the Court wrote

> There is a presumption that fit parents act in their children's best interests, Parham v. J. R., 442 U.S. 584, 602; there is normally no reason for the State to inject itself into the private realm of the family to further question fit parents' ability to make the best decisions regarding their children.
>
> 530 US 57, 58 (2000)

Still, even in the US parental rights are controversial and scholars have set out multiple arguments for their support or their elimination. Huntington and Scott (2020) viewed parental rights in what they termed a Child Wellbeing Framework, where parental rights are respected so long as children are not harmed. They wrote that the state has poor record of raising children better than parents and that young children especially cannot make decisions on their own. Some adult, either a parent or an agent of the state, must make decisions for young children at minimum and it is better for parents who know the child best to be in that role. Parents' rights thusly become a mechanism of protecting children from the state (Huntington & Scott, 2020).

This idea of parents' rights versus state intervention has also been used in family autonomy cases as well in support of minority and LGBTQ families

(Ryan, 2023). Children's rights are thus conversely seen as opportunities for state government to find excuses for interfering in private family life (Ryan, 2023).

Godwin (2015) argued, however, that despite the law not literally considering children the property of their parents, it effectively treats them that way regardless. Parental rights are "quasi property interest". Adults are considered to have control of themselves and their possessions and likewise parents can control their children, but not the children of others.

> The idea that parents can impose on their child what others cannot, because that child is their child and belongs to them, and not to others, amounts to a belief that parents are functionally related to their children as car owners are to their cars.
>
> (Godwin, 2015, p. 30)

The end effect, Godwin (2015) argued is that parents rights today have more in common with historical rights of husband's over their wives than with conventional human rights. This possessory right also comes into play in the law of adoption, where adults legally transfer their parental rights to another person and the child has no say. Similarly, parents name guardians in their wills leaving their children to another adult of their choosing and transferring their rights in the process (Godwin, 2015).

As a possible solution to this parent vs child rights conflict, Dailey and Rosenbury (2021) proposed a relational view of parental rights acknowledging that children need care and support from their parents, but acknowledges children as independent right holders. Parents do not have individual rights over their children like they have their own personal rights. Parental rights stem from their relationship to their children and the state has an interest in promoting that relationship and in children rights.

> A relational perspective sets some limits on parental control by bestowing equal respect on children's independent interests in people and experiences beyond the parent–child relationship. From this perspective, children are active participants in their own lives rather than passive objects of parental control.
>
> (Dailey & Rosenbury, 2021, p. 114)

They go on to argue that the law should encompass this relational view of parental and child rights by adopting dual standards. Any time that the law seeks to separate children from their families, a strict scrutiny high standard should be applied to legal decisions. However, state intervention that seeks to uphold children's rights and interests that does not threaten family separation should be met with a lesser intermediate standard of review (Dailey & Rosenbury, 2021).

Of course, regardless of the version of parental rights you ascribe to, these rights are subject to state supervision and termination so long as the state follows due process.

Children's Healthcare Rights

A youth's right to make healthcare decisions is complex enough to be worth its own chapter, but needs to be mentioned here at least in summary. Like all of the rights discussed thus far, much of the specifics depends on the place where the child lives.

The common law notion that some youth should be able to make their own health care decisions is known as the mature minor doctrine. In its original form, it allowed children of any age to bypass parental approval for medical treatment so long as the treating doctors agreed that the minor was mature enough to make an informed decision (Levesque, 2011).

As always starting with the CRC, we find health care decisions wrapped up in a number of the articles. Article 24 specifically lays out the nation's duty to provide health care for children. Article 25 provides children who have been committed the right to review their treatment. The Steering Committee for Human Rights in the fields of Biomedicine and Health (CDBIO) and the Steering Committee for the Rights of the Child (CDENF) (2024) wrote that children's right to have a say in the medical decisions concerning them are governed under Article 12 as part of their right to participation. The committees wrote,

> Children should be at the centre of the decision-making process, their views should always be sought, obtained, and given due weight. A child's age or degree of maturity does not determine the existence of their right to participate, but rather the weight that ought to be given to their view. Children should be considered as individuals, with specific characteristics and needs to be taken into account.
>
> (CDBIO & CDENF, 2024, p. 22)

US states have a hodgepodge of laws allowing youth of different ages to access different types of medical services without parent approval. For instance, Delaware allows 12-year-olds to consent to contraceptives, whereas Idaho simply does not allow it (National District Attorney Association, 2013). The U.S. Center for Disease Control (2022) reports that every US state has laws enabling youth to access sexual transmitted infections testing and treatment, but the age varies by state such that Washington state allows 14-year-olds to consent and Vermont requires youth be only 12. Nevada and New Hampshire both allow youth to consent to general medical treatment under a mature minor standard, whereas Kansas only allows mature minor consent for prenatal care (National District Attorney Association, 2013). All told, 35 states plus Washington DC have statutes that allow for minors in certain circumstances to consent to medical, dental, surgical or emergency treatment, with a few states also including mental health and substance abuse specifically (School House Connection, 2023).

In the US, youth medical decision-making has often been tied up in discussion about reproductive freedom (Levesque, 2011). Though, truly beyond the scope of this work, in very brief, the US Supreme Court in *Bellotti v. Baird* (1976) held that states must allow youth's seeking abortion against parental authority some means of judicial bypass and that this right was guaranteed by the 14th Amendment. However, even under *Bellotti* many states courts routinely denied youth petitions for judicial bypass (Advocates for Youth, 2015). How this right will fair post *Dobbs v. Jackson Women's Health Organization*, which overturned abortion rights in the US with some scholars suggesting the right will survive (Quinter & Markowitz, 2023) and others suggesting minor's rights could be further restricted (Horvath & Frietsche, 2023).

In other countries, the right to consent or refuse consent is equally jumbled. The Department of Justice of Canada (2023) reported that the common law mature minor doctrine exists, but most territories have their own legislation that applies to minors under the age of 16. Canadian youth under 16 can generally consent to healthcare so long as understand the medical treatment and the medical provider determines that the treatment is in the child's best interests (Department of Justice of Canada, 2023).

Within the EU, medical consent laws vary depending on the nation. For example, Ireland, Bulgaria and Portugal allow 16-year-old to consent to treatment. Austria allows 14-year-olds and Denmark 15-year-olds, whereas France and Italy require parental approval until the age of 18 (CDBIO & CDENF, 2024).

In the UK the mature minor doctrine has been subsumed by the famous Gillick v West Norfolk and Wisbech Area Health Authority [1986] AC 112 which involved a minor receiving sexual health counseling from an NHS physician without parental approval. This led to the test known as the Gillick Competence, which states that a minor under 16 can consent to health care if they are mature and intelligent enough to understand the nature of the treatment (Griffith, 2016). Weighing a child decision under Gillick requires medical professionals to factor maturity against the type of decision being made. Small children might be able to give consent to simple medical procedures, but may be unable to consent to more complex treatments (Griffith, 2016).

A great deal of guidance has been produced to help medical professionals make these decisions. Doctors are encouraged to assess if the child understands the consequences and alternatives for each recommended treatment (Steering Committee for Human Rights in the fields of Biomedicine and Health [CDBIO] and Steering Committee for the Rights of the Child [CDENF], 2024). They should assess if the child is actually willing to make a choice that they are not being pressured and if the child would rather an adult to decide for them. Ultimately, the final decision should fall under a best interest framework (CDBIO & CDENF, 2024).

From a neurological and psychological perspective, Grootens-Wiegers et al. (2017) argued that while maturity cannot be always be tied to a particular age, on average, children 12 and older demonstrate the required capacities to both understand and make rational choices about their own healthcare. The primary caution they write is that this is also the age of adolescence, which corresponds to more risk seeking behaviors, so adult support in decision-making is still warranted (Grootens-Wiegers et al., 2017).

As for the participation itself, various studies of child participation in health care have come back with different findings. Andersen and Dolva (2015) in Danish study wrote that children were pleased with being consulted, but their views were largely only taken in less important decisions. Coyne and Gallagher (2011) reported that children in an Irish hospital wanted to participate more, but were being held back by adults. Quaye et al. (2019) reported children in a Swedish hospital were generally included in decision-making at a higher level. Much of the difference can be related to the medical setting and methodologies of the studies, so no overall conclusions can be reached.

Where all of this intersects most clearly with the lives of children in the care system is in the use of psychotropic medication, which are used to treat emotional, behavioral and mental health disorders. Numerous studies have shown that foster children are over prescribed psychotropic medication at rates significantly higher than their peers (Keefe et al., 2023; Raghavan et al., 2005; Stambaugh et al., 2012).

In the US foster youth are covered through the federal and state healthcare program known as Medicaid, which provides health insurance for certain eligible groups generally based on income or disability. When Keefe et al. (2023) compared foster youth with their Medicaid peers, they found that not only are psychotropics given at a higher rate, foster youth are prescribed nearly twice as many types of drugs and that foster youth were more likely to be given drugs even if they did not have a mental health or developmental disability diagnosis. Stambaugh et al. (2012) also found that the type of placement affected the use of psychotropics, with children in group homes and RTCs to be on psychotropics at a higher rate and to be prescribed more types of them. Similarly, children in foster homes were more likely to be given psychotropics and be given more of them, than their peers in kinship homes or those placed with their parents (Stambaugh et al., 2012). Finally, when the US Office of the Inspector General (2018) examined foster youth in five states, reported that one third of the youth that were given psychotropic medication did not receive the medically appropriate oversight and monitoring.

In light of this overuse of psychotropic medication, the US federal government has pushed efforts for greater accountability and better use of informed consent laws to make sure that youth and their foster caregivers have a greater say in medication decisions (Mackie et al., 2022). Though for most healthcare decisions ultimately are made by CPS workers under state authority or with the permission of the parent if the case is prior to termination (Collins, 2016).

For adults, the state use of psychotropic medication against their will must be justified under a strict standard of due process as it infringes on liberty rights guaranteed by the Constitution. The state has to justify that a lesser intrusive method could not be used instead. For children in the child welfare system, case workers can make the decision to approve medication and doctors can prescribe it, so long as they believe it to be in the child's best interest (Collins, 2016).

Repeated violations of psychotropic medicine standards have led to at least one class action lawsuit and settlement against the state of Missouri (Kelly, 2019).

From a foster children's rights perspective, health care decisions are some of the thorniest issues. My clients would often complain about being on too many medications and the ways that the meds made them feel or their effects on their bodies. The court would often order CPS to perform a medication review, where doctors checked the medications being prescribed. However, so long as those prescriptions were within the recommended dosages guidelines, the reviews tended to support their usage. Because withdraw from psychotropic medications can have its own issues and because judges are not trained health care provides, the court was extremely reluctant to make changes to medications on its own.

Many of my clients simply refused to take the meds they were prescribed rather than wait for the CPS, Medicaid and dependency process to make a decision for them. This was easier done for youth in foster care placements than for those in RTCs where medication was often used as a means of control.

Simone, a 17-year-old female, had been on some form of psychotropic for nearly 12 years since she came into care with her siblings. She was diagnosed with a host of mental health disorders and was seen by multiple health care professionals. Her diagnosis would change over the years as old disorders would fall aside and new ones appear. One consistent feature was that she routinely tested near the borderline of an intellectual disability. She had been shown this result, but never thought it was accurate. Towards the end of her time in care, the court ordered that she receive a thorough psychological assessment by an independent provider outside of the normal CPS doctor list. The provider actually spent time meeting with and getting to know Simone over the course of a few days prior to asking her to submit to psychological assessments. The result was that most of Simone's mental health disorders disappeared and her intelligence was normal.

Child Participation

Of course, the right that is most discussed as it is the most controversial in implementation in foster care, is the right to participate. As noted previously, this is one of the 3Ps of categories of rights granted under the CRC and is directly related to decision-making. Participation is a broad category in that in it actively involves children in decisions affecting them in the home, in their court case and in their community. It is also the right most likely to conflict with adult ideas of best interests and with the rights of adults.

Participation is often framed as the right to be heard which is found in Article 12 of the CRC (1989) that reads,

> 1. States Parties shall assure to the child who is capable of forming his or her own views the right to express those views freely in all matters affecting the child, the views of the child being given due weight in accordance with the age and maturity of the child.

2. For this purpose the child shall in particular be provided the opportunity to be heard in any judicial and administrative proceedings affecting the child, either directly, or through a representative or an appropriate body, in a manner consistent with the procedural rules of national law.

In their general comment on Article 12, the UN Committee on the Rights of the Child (2009) wrote that to effectively implementing this right requires five stages. States must prepare children by informing them about their right and the implications of expressing their views. They must hear the child, creating an enabling and respectful environment for children to express their views. States must also perform a capacity assessment to evaluate the child's ability to form and express views. Fourth, they must give feedback providing children with information on how their views influenced the outcome. Finally, state must have mechanisms for complaints and remedies for children if their right to be heard is disregarded.

The UN Committee (2009) also wrote that the right of the child to be heard applies across various settings. In the family, parents should involve children in decision-making processes. In alternative care, children in care should express views on their placement and care. In health care, children should be included in decisions about their health and provided confidential advice. In education, participatory learning environments and school governance should involve children. In the workplace, children working illegally should be consulted and involved in policy development to eliminate child labor. In situations of violence, children should participate in developing strategies to prevent and address violence. In immigration and asylum, children's views should be considered in relevant processes. In emergency situations, children's participation in post-emergency and post-conflict resolution processes should be supported (UN Committee, 2009).

Lansdown (2022) wrote that while Article 12 is a right in of itself, like the rest of the CRC, it is meant to be read as one of complimentary rights so that rights to free expression, assembly, access to information and others are all linked with the right to participate. Backe-Hansen (2018) noted that from a child welfare perspective, Article 12 places much of the responsibility for protecting the rights of foster youth with the CPS agency and workers and requires them to balance their own oversite responsibilities with the need to allow foster families to make decisions on their own.

This is right to participation in child welfare is even more complex because it sometimes conflicts with one of the other 3Ps of the CRC, protection. Asking CPS agencies to uphold both sets of rights at the same time has been an ongoing challenge. McCafferty (2021) described a variety of reasons for this, including professional attitudes where social workers often hold ambivalent attitudes towards children's participation, viewing children as less capable than adults and thus not valuing their input. Structural barriers where organizational structures and bureaucratic processes do not always support meaningful participation. Policies for participation are often inadequate, and there is a lack of training and resources for social workers. Another reason is simple, day-to-day practical difficulties. Engaging children in decision-making is challenging due to their unique vulnerabilities and the complexities of child protection work. Social workers must balance safeguarding children with listening to their wishes, which is often difficult in high-risk situations (McCafferty, 2021). McCafferty (2017) also suggested that the habit of not listening to children ultimately reinforces the practice. Finally, Collins (2016) identified that tokenism, where participation is superficial and does not have any genuine influence on decisions, is also rampant in child welfare practice.

Collins (2016) wrote that this dichotomous view of participation versus protection ultimately undermines foster children's rights.

> While protection and survival are essential rights, a holistic understanding of child rights necessitates addressing the tensions that may be perceived between children's protection and participation. In fact, they need not be regarded as conflicting approaches, but rather complementary. Yet many international child protection workers may reflect a myopic priority of protection in practice so that participation is dismissed or ignored when dealing with complex situations, crises and/or when resources are limited.
>
> (Collins, 2016, p. 26)

Daly (2017) extended the criticism to Article 12 itself writing that the right to be heard is insufficient for child protection cases. Article 12 does not well distinguish between an individual child and children in general and does little to expel the paternalism built into best interest care proceedings. There is too much discretion built into child welfare in the ways that children are heard. The level of participation, the timing of the participation and the degree to which participation influences outcomes are all left to the whims of the care system (Daly, 2017).

Daly (2017) wrote that while Article 12 is taunted as a major accomplishment for children's rights, the text itself put those rights in jeopardy. Article 12's capable language means that courts and CPS agencies can make subjective determinations about the capabilities of a child to participate. Younger children especially are often discriminated against under this framework.

Another obstacle according to Daly (2017) is that Article 12's demand that children be heard "freely" is difficult to achieve in formal adult spaces, such as CPS offices and courtrooms. Specialty trained CPS staff and courts are required for children to actually speak freely (Daly, 2017). As mentioned before, this part is something I have witnessed in practice. Dependency cases that were held in front of elected family law judges included very little child participation. Even getting the judges to meet with the children required scheduling special times and children were not encouraged to come to regular hearings. Daly (2017) linked this sort of denial of access to judges as gatekeeping feature that is ultimately a due process denial.

Lastly, Daly (2017) argued that Article 12's language that children's views will be given "due weight", which in the context of best interest decisions leaves a lot of space for children to simply be ignored. There is no consensus on what weight to given children's desires or even what guideline might be used to determine the weight and thusly the child's views become just one of many factors to be considered in the overall case. Added to this complexity is the notion of maturity and the subjective value judgment of whether a child's wishes are considered reasonable and good. The result is that children's views are diluted and have little bearing on the final decision (Daly, 2017).

Lindkvist et al. (2023) added more criticisms noting that the right to participate and participation are not always the same, with many programs counting children's presence as a sufficient indicator of their rights being upheld. They also wrote that participation is often viewed as friendly collaboration with existing state entities rather than protest of those same government structures (Lindkvist et al., 2023).

Perhaps Lindkvist et al. (2023) sharpest criticism is that the language of Article 12 speaks of a child's age and maturity, which they wrote is unique to the CRC among human rights law. This in contrasted with human rights related to disability, which also carries some of the same concerns about capacity. The rights of people with disabilities come not from their capacity, but from existence in the world. Tying a child's participation to their capacity, maturity and age once again highlights the problems with how their participation is weighted and judged (Lindkvist et al., 2023).

While no one in US state dependency courts ever mention Article 12, these same conflicts play out. This is a setting whose primary function is the protection of children, so the balance between protection and participation are always present. Even in courts where children's participation is actively encouraged, judges still must balance the child's views with other evidence and weigh their testimony like any other party.

The Lundy Model

In the seminal paper, "Voice is not enough: conceptualizing Article 12 of the United Nations Convention on the Rights of the Child" Lundy (2007) wrote about participation in the education system, but the model has been widely adapted to the child welfare field (McCafferty, 2017; Kennan et al., 2018a; Molloy, 2024).

Lundy (2007) laid out multiple critiques for the interpretation of Article 12, noting first that the term voice often used to describe Article 12, significantly oversimplifies its full scope and intent. It suggests that merely allowing children to express their opinions is sufficient. However, Article 12 encompasses not only the right to express views but also the requirement that these views be given due weight in decision-making processes. These terms tend to focus solely on the act of speaking rather than ensuring that children's views have a substantial impact on outcomes.

Lundy (2007) also identified problems with professional beliefs, organizational barriers and tokenism that McCafferty (2017) and Collins (2016) would still cite a decade later. Because of these problems, Lundy (2007) developed a model of participation that includes four key elements: Space, Voice, Audience and Influence see Figure 6.1. These elements collectively ensure

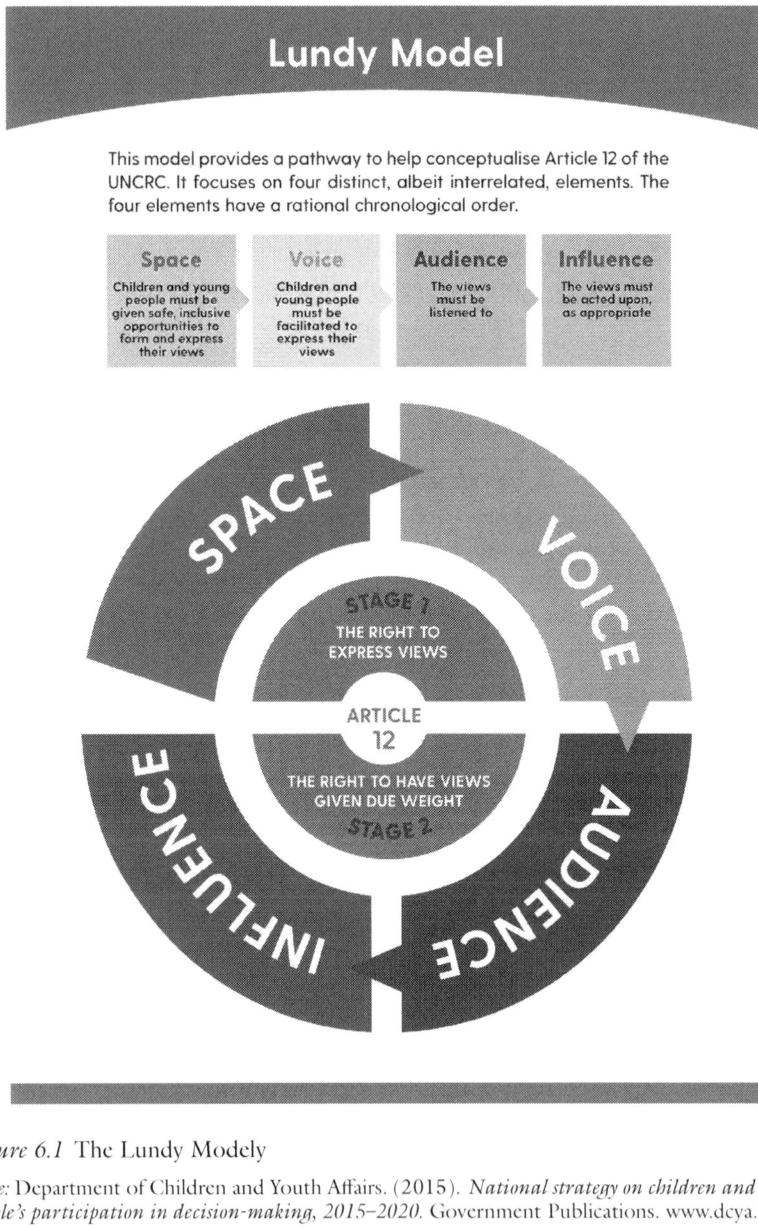

Figure 6.1 The Lundy Modely

Note: Department of Children and Youth Affairs. (2015). *National strategy on children and young people's participation in decision-making, 2015–2020*. Government Publications. www.dcya.ie

that children's right to participate is not only respected but also meaningfully integrated into decision-making processes.

Space refers to providing children with the opportunity to express their views. This involves creating environments where children feel safe and encouraged to share their thoughts and opinions. It is crucial to offer clear and structured opportunities for participation, whether in formal settings like school councils or more informal environments, such as classrooms and homes. The space must be inclusive and safe, ensuring that all children, including marginalized groups, can participate without fear of reprisal or judgment. Respecting children's preferences regarding how and on which issues they wish to engage is also essential, as this respects their autonomy and ensures the relevance of discussions (Lundy, 2007).

Voice involves facilitating the expression of children's views. It is not enough to simply provide opportunities; children must also be supported in articulating their thoughts. This means accommodating various forms of expression, such as writing, drawing, or digital media. Providing guidance and support, as outlined in Article 5 of the CRC, helps children form and express their views. Ensuring that children can express their views freely, without fear of negative consequences, is critical. Misconceptions about children's capacity to contribute must be addressed, recognizing that the right to express a view is not contingent on age or maturity but on the child's ability to form an opinion (Lundy, 2007).

Audience refers to ensuring that children's views are heard by the relevant decision-makers. Active listening is crucial, requiring adults to genuinely understand and consider children's perspectives. This involves training educators and policymakers in active listening skills and being receptive to non-verbal expressions. Establishing formal mechanisms where children's views can be communicated to those in authority, such as school councils or committees, is necessary. Avoiding tokenism is also vital as children's views should not only be collected but also seriously considered and acted upon. Effective communication channels ensure that children's voices reach those who can make decisions (Lundy, 2007).

Influence ensures that children's views have a tangible impact on decisions. Giving due weight to children's views according to their age and maturity is a core aspect of Article 12. This means that children's contributions should lead to real changes and not merely be acknowledged superficially. Providing feedback to children about how their views influenced decisions is important for validating their participation. Establishing a culture where children's views are integral to decision-making processes fosters a sense of inclusion and respect. Overcoming adult gatekeeping and ensuring that children's views are genuinely considered can transform participation from a procedural formality into a meaningful practice (Lundy, 2007).

Kennan et al. (2018a) wrote that the Lundy Model was adopted by Ireland when the government set out to develop a new national strategy for participation of children in care.

Because the Lundy Model so well encapsulates how children in care should be allowed to participate, I will come back to it and its implications on best interest, normalcy and decision-making in later chapters.

What Professionals Think

Whether children's rights are upheld depends greatly on how the adults in the child welfare system interpret and encourage participation. As I mentioned before, in my experience representing children in Florida and Texas, children's participation varied greatly depending on the caseworker, the type of meeting being held and the judge on the case.

In Skauge et al. (2021) discussion of participation and the surrounding literature, they noted that the meaning of participation in a child welfare context is not well defined, despite practitioners and researchers using the term regularly. Generally, there is some consensus on the CRC Article 12 definition, but cultural and organizational context mean that even this can be interpreted differently. Children's participation is seen as either information gathering on behalf of the caseworker, information dissemination to the child or the child as an active participant at the center of the case (Skauge et al., 2021).

In van Bijleveld et al. (2015) review of the literature, they noted that workers have different beliefs about not only what merits participation and when participation should occur, but also what weight to give children's preferences. The CPS workers also expressed concern about involving children in cases that involved serious abuse and many believed that their role to protect children would override child participation (van Bijleveld et al., 2015). This conflict between protection and participation was also identified by Kosher by Ben-Arieh (2020) who found that Israeli social workers supported the idea of participation more for social and personal choices than those involving the actual child welfare case and wrote "*their views change in accordance with the potential or actual danger they think the child might experience*" (p. 300). In the more recent systemic review, Toros (2021) echoed these findings and reported that belief that allowing participation might actually harm the child was one of the commonalities of much of the research. Children actually needed protection from the harm of participation. McTavish et al. (2022) linked this conflict to the previously discussed philosophical distinction of children as "beings" that would merit participation versus "becomings" that require protection.

In Delgado et al. (2023) scoping review, they found that children are often not meaningfully participating and that their views are not having any bearing on decision-making in their case. Children perceived as difficult or those with disabilities had lower rates of participation and in almost all the studies reviewed, children reported not being told about important case events (Delgado et al., 2023).

Woodman et al. (2023) found that Australian caseworkers generally understand that children do have rights, but levels of participation varied based on the caseworker involved. van Bijleveld et al. (2020) found that caseworkers tended to view participation as either gathering information from children or providing information to them and that even when given tools designed by children to encourage participation, they did not always use them. Vis and Fossum (2015) noted that organizational factors, such as the setting where children are encouraged to participate can impact the level of participation, with formal bureaucratic meetings sometimes encouraging less participation because children might choose to opt out. However, Vis and Thomas' (2009) research in Norway found that the more meetings that children attended, the more likely they were to be actually participatory in the case. Pölkki et al. (2012) wrote that Finnish caseworkers also express concern with their training and ability to communicate on the appropriate level with the child and thusly are fearful of allowing participation. Lastly, Kennan et al. (2018b) wrote that despite procedures to record children's voice, caseworkers tended to report children's wishes through the words and interpretation of the caseworker, thus diluting or even silencing the child's voice.

Usurpingly, cultural and legal differences also seem to play a part in how workers perceive and apply participation. In their research comparison of the USA, England and Norway, Križ and Skivenes (2017) wrote that while all of the countries generally agreed that participation was important, American and English workers were more likely to understand participation as something akin to tokenism, whereas their Norwegian counterparts were more likely to encourage more engaged forms of participation.

Berrick et al. (2015) compared workers in England, Finland, Norway and the USA on how they incorporated participation in the initial removal decision. While all of the workers agreed that the age of the child involved was a factor, the nations differed on what they considered participation. Finns prioritized providing information to children. The English were the least likely to emphasize talking to children about their wants and needs. US workers highlighted the importance of gathering information from the children. Norwegians wanted to know about a child's wishes, but did not believe that providing information was a priority (Berrick et al., 2015). In Arad-Davidzon and Benbenishty's (2008) similar study of Israeli caseworkers' removal and reunification decisions, they even found that the child's wishes had no influence at all on the workers decision.

In a literature review examining factors that facilitate participation researchers wrote that there is some evidence that children who attended family group conferences report better engagement and that those who had an independent advocate had better participation outcomes (Kennan et al., 2018b). Toros (2021) and Delgado et al. (2023) also reported that across studies caseworkers tended to agree that age was a factor in participation, with old children being involved more.

So once again, the research is telling us that caseworkers do not approach participation uniformly. The setting, the type of decision, the age of the child, their own beliefs about what participation is and their own confidence in their skills can all effect how they allow and encourage participation.

The findings regarding caseworkers' hesitancy to allow participation when they believe it runs counter to their protective role is especially relevant to this discussion. As discussed in Chapter 4, CPS agencies and caseworkers tend to be risk averse from both internal and external reasons. The safe decision will therefore be to favor protection when there is any doubt. Coupled with best interest's subjective freedom to defend any position based on the decision-makers preference, we have a system that disfavors participation and does not listen to children.

In my practice, though caseworkers met with children regularly, it was unusual for them to advocate for a child's position in the case itself. Caseworkers were more likely to fight for a child's rights in other settings, such as school or in the foster home. Participation on the CPS side mostly consisted of meetings where my clients were asked to give their thoughts.

Specialized child welfare courts with specialty trained judges were the only places where participation was taken seriously. I have seen judges change orders to case plans based on child input, but I never saw CPS make that change on their own. Often the caseworker themselves would agree with the child, but middle management would object.

What Children Think

Given the findings above regarding how caseworkers perceive and implement participation, it should not be surprising that foster children themselves have mixed reactions to their own participation. Foster children generally have mixed views of the care system itself (Wilson et al., 2020). Studies of foster children found that they viewed the initial CPS investigation and removal experience as confusing and frightening and were particularly unhappy with forms of institutionalized care. This feeling of confusion and instability often lasted throughout the case, though some children did report positive experiences of being moved to a new home. Many children also carried with them a sense of shame as being labeled a foster child (Wilson et al., 2020).

Children often report not being listened to and not feeling like they had an opportunity to participate (van Bijleveld et al., 2015). Even when children reported that adults heard them, they did not feel like their voices had any impact on decision-making. Though children did report that even if they were not heard, they valued attending meetings because they at least knew what was being said about them (van Bijleveld et al., 2015).

In McTavish et al. (2022) review of studies of how foster children perceive participation, they identified some commonalities. Children reported wanting information before a change and wanted to be given meaningful choices about changes to their lives. This involves creating an environment conducive to allowing children to speak where caseworkers value the children's voice and allow children to share power in decision-making. One critical factor for this to be successful is that children need to trust the adults around them (McTavish et al., 2022). Augsberger and Swenson (2015) wrote that children were able to build trusting relationships when their caseworkers spent more time with them, were nonjudgmental in their interactions and when there was continuity with the same worker throughout the case. Fylkesnes et al. (2021) again emphasized trust building as an essential in participation and wrote that children repeatedly asked that adults consider their perspective and that they might know what is best for themselves.

In one study, Pölkki et al. (2012) found that children reported wanting different levels of participation at different stages in the case, but at all levels they felt not fully included. Another study reported that while youth were vaguely aware that they possessed rights to protection and to care, they were unaware that they even had rights to information and participation, highlighting the need for adults to discuss in detail their rights once they entered care (Saarnik et al., 2023).

In their review, Selwyn and Riley (2015) wrote that foster youth often did not feel included in their own lives and they wanted to know more information about their case plan, the standards for the homes they are placed in and what brought them into care to begin with. They also expressed an inability to make complaints and have opportunities for making mistakes themselves or gaining new skills (Selwyn & Riley, 2015).

Apart from the fact that participation is their right, research also tells us that children in the care system benefit from participation. Children reported that participation made them feel valued even if what they wanted did not happen and could lead to a more successful placement (van Bijleveld et al., 2015). They felt closer to the adults around them and led them to feel more self-worth and more control over their lives (Vis et al., 2011). This also led to a reinforcing role where the more children participated, the more they felt valued and the more the felt the case plan reflected their input (Vis et al., 2011).

Children also reported that when they were not heard that they felt a host of negative emotions, such as sadness, helplessness and anger. Some even reported that the lack of participation could lead them to act out (van Bijleveld et al., 2015). Vis et al. (2011) even argued that the lack of participation could have long-term effects on the safety of children noting that,

> failing to include children's perspectives can have two important effects: (a) it may decrease the probability that abuse and neglect will be discovered and acted upon speedily and (b) it is more difficult for children who have not experienced participation to speak out if something is wrong.
> (p. 331)

Balsells et al. (2017) wrote that failure to promote participation also carries risks of for reunification efforts that are at the heart of the case. Essentially, the child and the family have changed as a result of the CPS removal and placement. When children are not involved in the reunification process, it can seem as if they have been uprooted once again (Balsells, 2017).

In one of the few studies to examine how foster youth actually think of and engage with their rights, Hernandez (2022) studied California foster youth about their perceptions of the California Foster Care Bill of Rights. The foster youth reported being provided with paperwork that contained their rights, but not being provided an explanation. They reported numerous rights violations such as not being safe in their placement, not having contact with their siblings, not having privacy and not having opportunities for normalcy (Hernandez, 2022).

In response to these violations, youth generally took one of three actions. Firstly, many did nothing as they reported that previous attempts to enforce their rights had failed. Secondly, some of the youth took action informally, such as talking to their caseworker or caretaker. Lastly a few of the youth took legal action by informing their attorney or the court (Hernandez, 2022). Unfortunately, the study does not compare methods to see if any produce better outcomes.

From my experience representing foster youth, legal actions tend to get better results as the power of the court can compel CPS to do many things for which they are not inclined. Compelling foster parents is a much more difficult task. They are not parties to the case, so a judge cannot order them directly. Foster parents also have the power to terminate a child's placement, so they often cannot be held accountable for rights violations for anything beyond safety issues. The continual shortage of foster homes (Kelly, 2023; Booth, 2023) means that foster parents are in constant demand. Removing a difficult foster child from their home has very few consequences because CPS will simply place another one.

This of course is a bit mercenary and most foster parents jumps through hurdles daily for the benefit of a child in their home. Still for a teenage client with a history of placement instability, there is very little bargaining with a rights violating foster home. I have unfortunately counseled clients to stay put and tolerate homes they did not like while I asked the court to order a new placement because the immediate alternative would have been a lock down RTC or sleeping in a CPS office. There are mechanisms to find appropriate placements for foster youth and to discipline foster homes, but they take time. It is a difficult choice for a young person to make to accept some rights violations because the alternative is worse.

As an attorney, my instinct for dealing with rights violations naturally goes to legal process and the court, but problems like a bad foster home or RTC are not always solvable by courts either. Getting a court to order a new placement is relatively simple. Actually, locating an appropriate home in a sometimes-limited geographic area is an ongoing challenge. So, like all things child welfare, the regular rights violations are tied to complex systemic issues, including the lack of placements.

Karen a 16-year-old female was deaf and used a cochlear implant, though not regularly. Homes for deaf children with foster parents that know ASL are notoriously difficult to locate. The only appropriate home was out of state. At the time, Karen was living in an RTC, and though she was nervous about leaving the area, she wanted free from the RTC and agreed to the move. However, within a couple of months of the move, she was fighting with the family and even ran away for a few days and was sent to a psychiatric hospital. After being located, the foster family were afraid of keeping her, and she was sent back to another RTC in her home state. Not a soul in the RTC knew ASL, and she was effectively cut off from communicating with any staff or other youth. She asked to return to the out of state foster home, but they were unwilling to take her back. A state boarding school for deaf children was also unwilling to take her because they feared she would run away from them as well, and they did not have behavioral staff. Karen aged out of care in various RTCs, none of which had properly trained staff for a youth with hearing loss.

Child Participation, Right to Counsel and the Courts

Though most of a child welfare case and the life of a foster child happens outside of the courtroom, the cases are at their core legal protection and enforcement mechanisms. At least in the US context, all of the truly important decisions and many of the everyday ones are reviewed and then decided by a judge. Because this is essentially the most important setting for decision-making and participation, it is worth examining it separately.

As discussed in Chapter 2, foster children in the US come to court through mixed representational models with some children being represented by an attorney under a direct client model, some by an attorney under a best interest model and some by hybrid representation (NACC, 2022). Additionally, while there is some research that suggest that attorney representation can have positive effects on case outcomes (Zinn & Slowriver, 2008; Washington State Center for Court Research, 2021), there is not solid evidence for which representational model works the best (Office of Program Policy Analysis and Government Accountability, 2021).

The last few decades have seen a great deal of interest from the courts, attorney groups and researchers about increasing child participation in legal representation and in the court process. The Children's Advocacy Institute (2019) which tracks the right to counsel within the US wrote that states have been making progress in providing children with attorneys in dependency cases. Giving states a grade from A to F, the institute noted that 29 states scored an A or B. States scored higher when the followed a direct representational model and provided funding for an attorney throughout the whole case (Children's Advocacy Institute, 2019). Not only does the NACC and the ABA consider direct representation the best practice, some scholars have argued that the lack of attorney counsel represents a due process violation as it denies children the right to legal advocacy and confidentiality (Good, 2014).

As for how the children themselves perceive their rights, Miller et al. (2017) surveyed current and former foster youth and found that overall, they had mixed perceptions regarding their legal representation. Youth in general were unhappy with their representation and wanted more contact with their attorneys. Those that did report more attorney involvement also reported more satisfaction with their representation and with their overall foster care experience (Miller et al., 2017). Goldfarb et al. (2021) reported similar findings in their survey of current foster youth with youth satisfaction with their attorney's communication and representation correlating with their approval of the dependency system in general.

In a follow-up study, Miller et al. (2018) asked foster youth to describe what effective representation looked like to them. The foster youth described representation in six broad clusters. They wanted an attorney with general legal skills and knowledge, but also someone that have specific training and expertise in foster care. They valued trust and a positive attorney client relationship along with someone that was actually working on their behalf. Finally, they wanted more physical contact and more frequent communication from their attorneys (Miller et al., 2018).

Closely related to legal representation are the studies that ask foster youth about their perceptions and participation within the court setting itself. Likewise with legal representation, studies have reported mixed findings for foster youth participation. Weisz et al. (2011) wrote that children generally had positive feelings about their time in court and were more comfortable talking directly to the judge hearing their case. The children came away from their hearings with a better understanding of their case and more trust in the judge and the judge's decisions (Weisz et al., 2011). However, in another study, many children reported not understanding the court process or their role within it (Block et al., 2010). Many of the foster youth reported feeling anxious about the process and most did not feel like they were able to tell the court everything they wanted to say with 37 percent reporting that they did not feel heard by the court (Block et al., 2010). Similarly, Quas et al. (2009) found that older children and those that had been in care longer reported a greater understanding of the court process and less anxiety related to it.

The ABA Center on Children and the Law in their national study wrote that in general foster youth reported wanting to participate in court hearings as a way to both have their voices heard and also to understand what was occurring in their case (Elstein et al., 2015). Some youth also reported telling the judge things that they had not told others on the case (Elstein et al., 2015). This idea of information sharing and information gathering that the youth reported mirrors some of the ideas of participation listed by caseworkers that was discussed by van Bijleveld et al. (2020).

In addition to the desires of youth to participate, there is also some argument that participatory hearings can produce better outcomes, though this not been well studied. McDonald (2014) described two specialized dependency courts where youth participation and problem solving were emphasized and noted that youth reported better trust in the courts and one delinquency court actually saw recidivism rates drop. In the ABA survey, judges in several states themselves also reported that they benefited from youth participation and made better decisions from learning facts directly from the youth in court (Elstein et al., 2015).

Better studied are the effects of quality hearings on outcomes, though none test children's participation directly. Macgill and Summers (2014) found that courts that encourage parent participation and engagement were more likely to have children placed back into the parents' home than other courts. Summers et al. (2017) found that more in-depth hearings at the beginning of the dependency case were linked to higher rates of reunification and initial placement with a kinship home or with the parents. Summers (2017) also found that better more engaged and participatory hearings that involved all the parties and were oversee by fewer judges had better outcomes for timely permanency and reunifications.

Jenkins (2008) argued that youth participation allows them to be better invested in the dependency process, promote children's rights and can even have a therapeutic benefit so that the youth can feel a greater sense of control over their fate. From the judicial side, for a hearing focused on the needs of the child, it also makes sense from a purely informational gathering perspective to have the child participate (Jenkins, 2008). Buss (2010) wrote that the benefit to children of court participation also comes from the court's enforcement powers as it is the only entity involved that can actually order CPS to provide services. For older youth, court involvement also serves additional purposes,

> it helps ensure that the youth's case plan accurately captures the needs and aspirations of the youth. Less obvious is the developmental value youth can derive from the process of participation itself. Providing youth with opportunities to take on decision-making responsibility and gain experience with self-advocacy will help them develop the skills necessary to function independently in adulthood.
>
> (Buss, 2010, p. 268)

This push to make the dependency process more participatory for children has also resulted in a lot of guidance for best practices. The NACC (2022) which issues guidelines for attorney representation wrote that attorneys have specific duties related to ensuring that their clients are guaranteed meaningful participation. Lawyers must prepare children prior to the hearings in a way commiserate with the child's ability to understand and bring all of the child's concerns before the court. To the extent possible, they should ensure that hearings are scheduled that do not conflict with school or youth activities. Throughout the court hearing, lawyers should make sure that their client understands what is being discussed. Finally, they should encourage their clients to attend all of the hearings and should only waive their attendance if the youth truly wants to be excluded (NACC, 2022).

Child participation is also mandated by federal law in some circumstances and highly encouraged by professional standards. Federal law 42 U.S.C. § 675 (1) (B) requires older children to participate in their own permanency case plan, stating

> With respect to a child who has attained 14 years of age, the plan developed for the child in accordance with this paragraph, and any revision

> or addition to the plan, shall be developed in consultation with the child and, at the option of the child, with up to 2 members of the case planning team who are chosen by the child and who are not a foster parent of, or caseworker for, the child.

The American Bar Association has issued multiple resolutions that also encourage participation. ABA Policy 115 encourages courts and lawyers to remove barriers to participation (ABA, 2020). ABA Policy 613 goes even further and

> urges federal, state, local, territorial, and tribal legislatures to enact, and courts to enforce, laws establishing a presumption of child presence in all dependency proceedings to ensure that:
>
> (1) legal decisions and practices respect and value a child's unique identity, including their racial, cultural, ethnic, linguistic, sexual orientation, and gender identities;
> (2) the child can express their individual needs and interests and meaningfully engage in a case; and
> (3) the child, in consultation with the child's attorney, has the sole right to choose not to be present and reasons such as age, disability, scheduling conflicts, lack of transportation, or perceived trauma which is not documented, are not used to rebut the presumption.
>
> (ABA, 2022, p. 1)

Likewise, courts have also adopted informal procedures and best practices for encouraging foster child participation. National Council of Juvenile and Family Court Judges (NCJCF) (2022) reported that judges should make certain that children are provided age-appropriate notice of hearings, that they are greeted by name when they come to court, that they are always asked about their preferences, allowed the opportunity to speak in chambers and given the chance to provide input about their experiences in CPS. The NCJCF actually developed bench cards to show judges how they might interact better with children of various ages in their courtrooms. These initiatives have been supported by the federal government, with HHS (2019) also issuing state guidance to promote youth voice in the dependency process.

While all of these efforts are laudable, it should be noted that there is not much research evidence to conclude that many of these changes to participation produce differences in outcomes (Summers et al., 2022).

With my bias as a former foster child lawyer acknowledged, I do believe that court participation is the most important and meaningful way that foster youth can access their rights. CPS is a bureaucracy and even the best caseworker has a supervisor and a regional manager and a state office that must be appeased. A court is the one place where a child can actually complain, tell their story, speak their truth and an adult can take immediate action to help them. As

I wrote earlier, courts are not perfect, there are real-world limits to their powers, but the courts ability to hold other adults accountable is tremendous.

Once I saw a child describe for a judge the horrors of her current placement. At the end of the hearing, the judge ordered CPS to find another home for the child posthaste. After a week passed and CPS had done nothing to find a new placement, the judge called a hearing and demanded that the local placement coordinator testify about their efforts to locate a new home. Unconvinced by CPS' excuses for delays, the judge ordered that the caseworker, supervisor and coordinator come to court every single day for a hearing to update the judge about their process. By the end of the week, CPS had managed to find a placement. While the court certainly did not take this approach to every slow CPS process, the ability to make a bureaucracy uncomfortable should not be understated.

My clients did have meaningful participation in other areas of their case and courts that did not specialize in foster care could be a bad as any CPS bureaucrat. The only place, though, where the voice and rights of children were guaranteed was in the specialized child welfare court.

Foster Youth Advisory Boards

One mechanism for participation comes from Youth Advisory Boards (YAB). These are found in each state and came into existence following the passage of the John H. Chafee Foster Care Independence Act, which provided federal funding for their creation (Forenza & Happonen, 2016). YABs consist of foster youth that usually are over the age of 14 and are generally organized by the state agency themselves, but in a few states are managed by nonprofit organizations (Havlicek et al., 2016). The organization depends on the state, with some having multiple local boards and others having one larger board serving the whole state. Membership varies from a few dozen to a few hundred youth and the youth usually have some training and a membership requirement, such as giving a speech. The larger state meetings generally occur quarterly, with the local boards meeting more often. The meetings themselves are conducted using some formal rules of procedure (Havlicek et al., 2016).

The purpose of YABs is to provide a mechanism to empower foster youth to advocate for improvements in the child welfare system and to meet directly with adults responsible for the system sometimes resulting in actual policy or legislative change (Forenza & Happonen, 2016). Recall, that members of Florida's Youth Shine board who testified before the Florida Legislature prior to the passage of Florida's normalcy law, Let Kids Be Kids (Perlmutter, 2017). Almost every board was involved in some form of advocacy with sibling rights, foster care rights, youth centered practice and normalcy being the most common themes (Havlicek et al., 2016).

Havlicek et al. (2016) in their national survey reported that board members perceived their participation as a net positive as they felt it gave them a forum to discuss issues, affect policy and also develop their own professional skills.

In a smaller qualitative study, Forenza (2018) found that YAB members perspectives on the care system and themselves changed allowing them to think critically about the causes of inequalities in the system and how their own leadership and public speaking abilities had improved.

Despite the benefits that the YAB members themselves acquire, there is not enough evidence to say that boards always have a real effect on policy or legal change (Havlicek et al., 2016). Still, Perlmutter (2017) credits the Florida youth with helping to persuade the legislature there.

The YABs also operate under different levels of adult supervision and guidance depending on the state, so there is some question about if all boards represent meaningful participation (Havlicek et al., 2018). In their study of the adult coordinators on YABs, the researchers found that only two boards out of the 42 surveyed actually had youth led boards. Two boards were completely adult led and 13 were adult-driven with youth input, where the adults viewed the foster youth more as sources of knowledge to guide state policy. The researchers noted that this adult-driven or adult-led category can be seen as symbolic representation. The remaining 16 YABs were labeled as adult and youth partnerships that sought a collaborative relationship between all the stakeholders. Organizational issues about priorities and policy between the youth and the adults still remained a challenge (Havlicek et al., 2018).

Augsberger et al. (2020) examined in-depth one board, the New England Youth Colation (NEYC), which they identified as an adult and youth partnership model where adults were there to facilitate the youth's work and provide structure and support. This collaborative model required adults with specialized training to share power with youth and establish a trusting relationship (Augsberger et al., 2020).

In their work looking broadly at youth councils created by governments and institutions to empower youth in society Taft and Gordon (2013) found that youth often were unhappy with the level of participation offered by formal youth councils. Teens reported tokenization and a lack of influence on issues they cared about. Many reported leaving their youth council as they felt they could be better agents of change in other political spaces (Taft & Gordon, 2013).

Though the evidence is mixed regarding their levels of participation, the YABs have been pushed by federal and state governments and nonprofits in the field. Casey Family Programs (2022a) wrote that CPS agencies should recruit new members on an ongoing basis and should strive to have a diverse board that is representative of the foster care population. The process to become a member should be simple and meetings should be scheduled around the youth's schedule and not the agency's. Casey Family Programs (2022b) also emphasized the importance of valuing the time of participating foster youth. This means actually paying young people to attend at the same rate that an adult expert would be paid.

Beyond the local and state level, it should also be mentioned that there are national foster care boards designed to guide policy. The National Foster

Care Youth and Alumni Policy Council and the NACC's National Advisory Council on Children's Legal Representation are both made up of foster youth or alumni with lived experience.

At minimum, YAB boards seem to have been influential in the creation of and the ongoing discussion around normalcy. Augsberger et al. (2019) described how the NEYC created the Normalcy Bill of Rights that I discussed in Chapter 3. The youth described the creation as an exercise in their collective power. Between the Normalcy Bill of Rights and the advocacy efforts in Florida, foster youth have been at the forefront of the demand for normalcy.

Rights, Participation and Children?

It would not be a stretch to say that this chapter has been the most challenging to write because children's rights, children's participation and even children themselves are not well defined or understood.

At first glance, the law seems to suggest that children are anyone under the age of 18, but then upon closer inspection the law fails us. A 12-year-old can consent to sex and be held criminally liable for a felony, but cannot buy a cigarette. A 14-year-old can receive treatment for HIV, but cannot get married without parental consent. Legally, a child seems to be whatever the particular law wants them to be with little or no overlap between the laws.

Philosophically, we are left with competing ideas about how children's rights develop and if children are fully formed people or simply on their way to becoming a person. Added to this is the parent's duty to hold children rights in trust or conversely, their rights to guide a child's development and beliefs.

What rights a child has seems to be mostly based on where they are located, both within the globe, within a country and within the context of what they seeking. Adults might allow them to participate fully in decision-making or they might be merely tokens of representation. Their rights are subsumed under the guise or parental rights or state authority and they can be passed around as if they are just chattel. Their capacity and maturity are tested at every level for making rational "good" decisions and then weighed against the competing desire of adults. How many adult decisions would survive with that level of scrutiny?

This is exacerbated for children/youth/young people in the child welfare system who have the additional pressure of a risk averse, best interest deciding state CPS agency making decisions for them that sees their duty to protect as contrary to the child's right to participate. Their rights are curtailed simply because they are in state custody.

When they have the teeth of enforceability, the various foster child Bill of Rights seem to be the best way to actually protect children in care. So long as adults can default to subjective best interest, children's rights will always be at stake. The best interest of children is fundamentally incompatible with the autonomy rights of children in the care system. I will discuss this more in Chapter 8 when I lay out my argument for a Normalcy Charter.

In my 15 years of practice, I never met a client that did not want more say in their lives, who did not want the adults to take seriously their views and who did not want more information about their case and the decisions that were made about them. If anything, the rights of children in care should be easier to accommodate as the apparatus of the court is already deeply involved in their lives. It is shameful that these rights are so often ignored in the name of best interest.

References

Advocates for Youth. (2015). *Judicial bypass procedures: Undue burdens for young people seeking safe abortion care.* Retrieved June 17, 2024, from https://www.advocatesforyouth.org/resources/policy-advocacy/judicial-bypass-procedures/

American Bar Association. (2020). *Policy resolution 115: Involvement of individuals with lived experience in legal system reform.* Retrieved June 13, 2024, from https://www.americanbar.org/groups/public_interest/child_law/resources/attorneys/#:~:text=ABA%20Policy%20Resolution%20115%20recognizes,in%20reform%20and%20advocacy%20efforts

American Bar Association. (2022). *Policy resolution 613: Presumption of child presence in dependency proceedings.* Retrieved June 13, 2024, from https://www.americanbar.org/content/dam/aba/administrative/child_law/613-report.pdf

Andersen, C. S., & Dolva, A.-S. (2015). Children's perspective on their right to participate in decision-making according to the United Nations Convention on the Rights of the Child article 12. *Physical & Occupational Therapy in Pediatrics, 35*(3), 218–230. https://doi.org/10.3109/01942638.2014.918075

Arad-Davidzon, B., & Benbenishty, R. (2008). The role of workers' attitudes and parent and child wishes in child protection workers' assessments and recommendation regarding removal and reunification. *Children and Youth Services Review, 30*(1), 107–121. https://doi.org/10.1016/j.childyouth.2007.07.003

Archard, D. (2023). Children's rights. In E. Zalta & U. Nodelman (Eds.), *The Stanford encyclopedia of philosophy* (Spring 2023 ed.). https://plato.stanford.edu/archives/spr2023/entries/rights-children/

Aristotle P. v. Johnson, 721 F. Supp. 1002, 1009 (N.D. Ill. 1989). https://law.justia.com/cases/federal/district-courts/FSupp/721/1002/1420024/

Ariz. Rev. Stat. § 8–529. (2023). Retrieved May 30, 2024, from https://www.azleg.gov/viewdocument/?docName=https://www.azleg.gov/ars/8/00529.htm

Ark. Code § 9-28-1003. https://law.justia.com/codes/arkansas/title-9/subtitle-3/chapter-28/subchapter-10/section-9-28-1003/

Augsberger, A., Springwater, J. S., Hilliard-Koshinsky, G., Barber, K., & Martinez, L. S. (2019). Youth participation in policy advocacy: Examination of a multi-state former and current foster care youth coalition. *Children and Youth Services Review, 107*, 104491. https://doi.org/10.1016/j.childyouth.2019.104491

Augsberger, A., & Swenson, E. (2015). "My worker was there when it really mattered": Foster care youths' perceptions and experiences of their relationships with child welfare workers. *Families in Society, 96*(4), 234–240. https://doi.org/10.1606/1044-3894.2015.96.34

Augsberger, A., Toraif, N., Springwater, J. S., Koshinsky, G. H., & Martinez, L. S. (2020). Strategies for engaging youth currently and formerly in foster care in child welfare policy advocacy: Lessons from the New England Youth Coalition (NEYC). *Child Welfare, 97*(6), 251–270. https://www.jstor.org/stable/48626325

Backe-Hansen, E. (2018). Formal and everyday participation in foster families: A challenge? In A. Falch-Eriksen & E. Backe-Hansen (Eds.), *Human rights in child protection: Implications for professional practice and policy* (pp. 227–244). Springer International Publishing. https://doi.org/10.1007/978-3-319-94800-3_12

Balsells, M. Á., Fuentes-Peláez, N., & Pastor, C. (2017). Listening to the voices of children in decision-making: A challenge for the child protection system in Spain. *Children and Youth Services Review*, *79*, 418–425. https://doi.org/10.1016/j.childyouth.2017.06.055

Bellotti v. Baird, 428 U.S. 132, 150. (1976). https://supreme.justia.com/cases/federal/us/428/132/

Berrick, J. D., Dickens, J., Pösö, T., & Skivenes, M. (2015). Children's involvement in care order decision-making: A cross-country analysis. *Child Abuse & Neglect*, *49*, 128–141. https://doi.org/10.1016/j.chiabu.2015.07.001

Berrick, J. D., Skivenes, M., & Roscoe, J. N. (2022). Children's rights and parents' rights: Popular attitudes about when we privilege one over the other. *International Journal of Social Welfare*, *31*(4), 449–462. https://doi.org/10.1111/ijsw.12523

Block, S. D., Oran, H., Oran, D., Baumrind, N., & Goodman, G. S. (2010). Abused and neglected children in court: Knowledge and attitudes. *Child Abuse & Neglect*, *34*(9), 659–670. https://doi.org/10.1016/j.chiabu.2010.02.003

Boele-Woelki, K. (2021). A European model for harmonizing the law on parental responsibilities: The family law perspective. In L. Bernardi & D. Mortelmans (Eds.), *Shared physical custody: Interdisciplinary insights in child custody arrangements* (pp. 51–72). Springer International Publishing. https://doi.org/10.1007/978-3-030-68479-2_4

Booth, R. (2023). Thousands of new foster carers urgently needed in England, experts say. *The Guardian*. Retrieved June 11, 2024, from https://www.theguardian.com/society/2023/dec/03/thousands-new-foster-carers-urgently-needed-england-experts

Braam v. State, 150 Wn. 2d 689, 699 (Wash. 2003).

Brake, E., & Millum, J. (2022). Parenthood and procreation. In E. N. Zalta (Ed.), *The Stanford encyclopedia of philosophy* (Spring 2022 ed.). https://plato.stanford.edu/archives/spr2022/entries/parenthood/

Bureau of Alcohol, Tobacco, Firearms and Explosives. (2022). *Does a customer have to be a certain age to buy firearms or ammunition from a licensee?* ATF. Retrieved June 15, 2024, from https://www.atf.gov/firearms/qa/does-customer-have-be-certain-age-buy-firearms-or-ammunition-licensee

Buss, E. (2010). Juvenile court for young adults? How ongoing court involvement can enhance foster youths' chances for success. *Family Court Review*, *48*, 262–276. https://doi.org/10.1111/j.1744-1617.2010.01308.x

Cal. Welf. and Inst. Code § 16001.9. https://leginfo.legislature.ca.gov/faces/codes_displaySection.xhtml?sectionNum=16001.9.&lawCode=WIC

Casey Family Programs. (2022a). What are some best practices for recruiting and working with youth advisory boards? *Strategy Brief*. Retrieved June 14, 2024, from https://www.casey.org/media/22.07-QFF_SComm-Youth-Engagement-2-YAB.pdf

Casey Family Programs. (2022b). What does it mean to value youth partners as assets? *Strategy Brief*. Retrieved June 14, 2024, from https://www.casey.org/media/22.07-QFF_SComm-Youth-Engagement-3-Value-as-Asset.pdf

Casey Family Programs. (2024). *Summary of child welfare class action litigation*. Retrieved June 4, 2024, from https://www.casey.org/class-action-summary/

Child Rights International Network. (n.d.). *Minimum ages of criminal responsibility in Europe*. Retrieved June 15, 2024, from https://archive.crin.org/en/home/ages/europe.html

Children's Advocacy Institute. (2019). *A child's right to counsel: A national report card on legal representation for abused & neglected children* (4th ed.). University of San Diego School of Law, CAI Special Reports 1. https://digital.sandiego.edu/law_cai_spec/1

Chilton, K. (2022). Did anyone ask the child?: Recognizing foster children's rights to make mature decisions through child-centered representation. *Emory Law Journal, 72*, 385. https://scholarlycommons.law.emory.edu/elj/vol72/iss2/3
Cholbi, M. (2017). How procreation generates parental rights and obligations. In M. Cholbi & J. Ahlberg (Eds.), *Procreation, parenthood, and educational rights: Ethical and philosophical issues*. Routledge.
Collins, T. M. (2016). A child's right to participate: Implications for international child protection. *The International Journal of Human Rights, 21*(1), 14–46. https://doi.org/10.1080/13642987.2016.1248122
Colo. Rev. Stat. § 19-7-101.
Cowden, M. (2012). Capacity, claims and children's rights. *Contemporary Political Theory, 11*(4), 362–380. https://doi.org/10.1057/cpt.2011.43
Coyne, I., & Gallagher, P. (2011). Participation in communication and decision-making: Children and young people's experiences in a hospital setting. *Journal of Clinical Nursing, 20*(15–16), 2334–2343. https://doi.org/10.1111/j.1365-2702.2010.03582.x
Cramer, M. (2020). When are you really an adult? *New York Times*. Retrieved June 15, 2024, from https://www.nytimes.com/2020/01/18/us/usa-legal-age.html
Dailey, A., & Rosenbury, L. (2021). The new parental rights. *Duke Law Journal, 71*, 75–165. https://scholarship.law.duke.edu/dlj/vol71/iss1/7
Dallman, S., & Nath, A. (2020). *Education clauses in state constitutions across the United States*. Federal Reserve Bank of Minneapolis. Retrieved May 30, 2024, from https://www.minneapolisfed.org/article/2020/education-clauses-in-state-constitutions-across-the-united-states
Daly, A. (2017). *Children, Autonomy and the courts: Beyond the right to be heard*. Brill|Nijhoff. https://doi.org/10.1163/9789004355828
Del. Code tit. 13 § 2522 (15).
Delgado, P., Carvalho, J. M. S., & Alves, S. (2023). Children and young people's participation in decision-making in foster care. *Child Indicators Research, 16*(1), 421–445. https://doi.org/10.1007/s12187-022-09979-5
Department of Children and Youth Affairs. (2015). *National strategy on children and young people's participation in decision-making, 2015–2020*. Government Publications. www.dcya.ie
Department of Justice of Canada. (2023). *Article 12 of the convention on the rights of the child and children's participatory rights in Canada*. Government of Canada. Retrieved June 17, 2024, from https://www.justice.gc.ca/eng/rp-pr/other-autre/article12/toc-tdm.html
Eekelaar, J. (2020). Do parents know best? *The International Journal of Children's Rights, 28*(3), 613–631. https://doi.org/10.1163/15718182-02803002
Elstein, S. G., Kelly, K., & Trowbridge, S. (2015). *Engaging youth in court: A national analysis*. National Youth Engagement Project, American Bar Association Center on Children and the Law. https://www.americanbar.org/content/dam/aba/administrative/child_law/youthengagement/NationalAnalysisFinal.authcheckdam.pdf
European Union Agency for Fundamental Rights. (2017). *Consent for sexual activity with an adult*. EUFRA. Retrieved June 15, 2024, from https://fra.europa.eu/en/publication/2017/mapping-minimum-age-requirements/consent-sexual-activity-adult#:~:text=All%20Member%20States%20establish%20a,at%2018%20years%20%E2%80%93%20in%20Malta
Feinberg, J. (1980). A child's right to an open future. In W. Aiken & H. LaFollette (Eds.), *Whose child? Parental rights, parental authority and state power* (pp. 124–153). Littlefield, Adams, and Co.
Fla. Stat. § 39.4085. https://www.flsenate.gov/laws/statutes/2018/39.4085
Forenza, B. (2018). Awareness, analysis, engagement: Critical consciousness through foster youth advisory board participation. *Child and Adolescent Social Work Journal, 35*(2), 119–126. https://doi.org/10.1007/s10560-017-0515-3

Forenza, B., & Happonen, R. G. (2016). A critical analysis of Foster Youth Advisory Boards in the United States. *Child & Youth Care Forum*, *45*(1), 107–121. https://doi.org/10.1007/s10566-015-9321-2
Fylkesnes, M., Larsen, M., Havnen, K., Christiansen, Ø., & Lehmann, S. (2021). Listening to advice from young people in Foster Care: From participation to belonging. *The British Journal of Social Work*, *51*(6), 1983–2000. https://doi.org/10.1093/bjsw/bcab138
Geneva Declaration of the Rights of the Child. (1923). *UN documents: Gathering a body of global agreements*. Retrieved June 8, 2024, from http://www.un-documents.net/gdrc1924.htm
Godwin, S. (2015). Against parental rights. *Columbia Human Rights Law Review*, *47*, 1–83.
Goldfarb, D., Tashjian, S. M., Goodman, G. S., Bederian-Gardner, D., Hobbs, S. D., Cordón, I. M., Ogle, C. M., Bakanosky, S., Narr, R. K., & Chae, Y. (2021). After child maltreatment: The importance of voice for youth in Foster Care. *Journal of Interpersonal Violence*, *36*(13–14), NP7388–NP7414. https://doi.org/10.1177/0886260519825884
Good, B. (2014). A child's rights to counsel in removal proceedings. *Stanford Journal of Civil Rights and Civil Liberties*, *10*, 109.
Griffith, R. (2016). What is Gillick competence? *Human Vaccines & Immunotherapeutics*, *12*(1), 244–247. https://doi.org/10.1080/21645515.2015.1091548
Grootens-Wiegers, P., Hein, I. M., van den Broek, J. M., & de Vries, M. C. (2017). Medical decision-making in children and adolescents: Developmental and neuroscientific aspects. *BMC Pediatrics*, *17*(1), 120. https://doi.org/10.1186/s12887-017-0869-x
H.Res.509 – Foster Youth Bill of Rights Resolution. 118th Congress. (2023). https://www.congress.gov/bill/118th-congress/house-resolution/509/text
Harper, K. (2024). Child welfare officials move to reduce Texas judge's oversight of embattled foster system. *The Texas Tribune*. Retrieved June 4, 2024, from https://www.texastribune.org/2024/02/21/texas-foster-care-lawsuit/
Havlicek, J., Curry, A., & Villalpando, F. (2018). Youth participation in foster youth advisory boards: Perspectives of facilitators. *Children and Youth Services Review*, *84*, 255–270. https://doi.org/10.1016/j.childyouth.2017.12.016
Havlicek, J., Lin, C.-H., & Villalpando, F. (2016). Web survey of foster youth advisory boards in the United States. *Children and Youth Services Review*, *60*, 109–118. https://doi.org/10.1016/j.childyouth.2015.11.023
Haw. Rev. Stat. § 587A-3.1. https://law.justia.com/codes/hawaii/title-31/chapter-587a/section-587a-3 1/
Hernandez, J. (2022). Foster youth perspectives: How Foster youth navigate and mobilize their rights within the foster care system. *Humanity & Society*, *46*(2), 249–270. https://doi.org/10.1177/0160597621991546
Herring, J. (2023). Vulnerability and children's rights. *International Journal for the Semiotics of Law: Revue internationale de Sémiotique juridique*, *36*(4), 1509–1527. https://doi.org/10.1007/s11196-022-09951-0
Horvath, S., & Frietsche, S. (2023). Judicial bypass for minors post-Dobbs. *Womens Health (Lond)*, *19*, 17455057231219601. https://doi.org/10.1177/17455057231219601
Human Rights Watch. (2022). How do US states measure up on child rights? Challenging US States to meet international child rights standards for child marriage, corporal punishment, child labor, and juvenile justice. *Human Rights Watch*. Retrieved May 30, 2024, from https://www.hrw.org/feature/2022/09/13/how-do-states-measure-up-child-rights
Huntington, C., & Scott, E. S. (2020). Conceptualizing legal childhood in the twenty-first century. *Michigan Law Review*, *118*(7), 1371–1457. http://www.jstor.org/stable/45285778

The Interstate Commission for Juveniles. (2024). *Age matrix*. Retrieved June 15, 2024, from https://juvenilecompact.org/age-matrix

Jacob B. and Amelia L. et al., v. Louisiana Department of Children and Family Services et al., Case No. 3:24-cv-00289-BAJ-SDJ.

Jenkins, J. J. (2008). Listen to me! Empowering youth and courts through increased youth participation in dependency hearings. *Family Court Review*, *46*(1), 163–179. https://doi.org/10.1111/j.1744-1617.2007.00190.x

Kara B. v. Dane County, 205 Wis. 2d 140, 158 (Wis. 1996).

Keddell, E. (2018). The vulnerable child in neoliberal contexts: The construction of children in the Aotearoa New Zealand child protection reforms. *Childhood*, *25*(1), 93–108. https://doi.org/10.1177/0907568217727591

Keefe, R. J., Cummings, A. D. L., Smith, A. E., Greeley, C. S., & Van Horne, B. S. (2023). Psychotropic medication prescribing: Youth in Foster Care compared with other medicaid enrollees. *Journal of Child Adolescence Psychopharmacology*, *33*(4), 149–155. https://doi.org/10.1089/cap.2022.0092

Kelly, J. (2019). Potential 'landmark' settlement reached on use of psychotropic drugs in foster care. *The Imprint*. Retrieved June 18, 2024, from https://imprintnews.org/child-welfare-2/potential-settlement-reached-on-use-of-psychotropic-drugs-in-foster-care/36384

Kelly, J. (2023). Number of youth in formal foster care continues to decline, imprint survey finds. *The Imprint*. Retrieved June 11, 2024, from https://imprintnews.org/subscriber-content/fewer-foster-youth-homes-2023-imprint-survey-finds/246470

Kennan, D., Brady, B., & Forkan, C. (2018a). Space, voice, audience and influence: The lundy model of participation (2007) in child welfare practice. *Practice*, *31*(3), 205–218. https://doi.org/10.1080/09503153.2018.1483494

Kennan, D., Brady, B., & Forkan, C. (2018b). Supporting children's participation in decision making: A systematic literature review exploring the effectiveness of participatory processes. *The British Journal of Social Work*, *48*(7), 1985–2002. https://doi.org/10.1093/bjsw/bcx142

Kosher, H., & Ben-Arieh, A. (2020). Social workers' perceptions of children's right to participation. *Child & Family Social Work*, *25*(2), 294–303. https://doi.org/10.1111/cfs.12685

Kosher, H., Ben-Arieh, A., & Hendelsman, Y. (2016). The history of children's rights. In *Children's rights and social work* (pp. 9–18). Springer International Publishing. https://doi.org/10.1007/978-3-319-43920-4_2

Križ, K., & Skivenes, M. (2017). Child welfare workers' perceptions of children's participation: A comparative study of England, Norway and the USA (California). *Child & Family Social Work*, *22*(S2), 11–22. https://doi.org/10.1111/cfs.12224

Lansdown, G. (2022). Article 12: The right to be heard. In Z. Vaghri, J. Zermatten, G. Lansdown, & R. Ruggiero (Eds.), *Monitoring state compliance with the UN Convention on the Rights of the Child: An analysis of attributes* (pp. 41–48). Springer International Publishing. https://doi.org/10.1007/978-3-030-84647-3_5

Lee, S. J. (2017). A child's voice vs. a parent's control: Resolving a tension between the convention on the rights of the child and U.S. Law. *Columbia Law Review*, *117*, 687–728.

Levesque, R. J. R. (2011). Mature minor doctrine. In R. J. R. Levesque (Ed.), *Encyclopedia of adolescence* (pp. 1659–1660). Springer. https://doi.org/10.1007/978-1-4419-1695-2_683

Lindkvist, L., Adami, R., Kaldal, A., & Aspán, M. (2023). Chapter 7: The rights of the child: Legal, political and ethical challenges. In *Five problems with children's participation rights* (pp. 151–163). Brill|Nijhoff. https://doi.org/10.1163/9789004511163_016

Lundy, L. (2007). 'Voice' is not enough: Conceptualising Article 12 of the United Nations Convention on the Rights of the Child. *British Educational Research Journal*, *33*(6), 927–942. https://doi.org/10.1080/01411920701657033

Macgill, S., & Summers, A. (2014). Assessing the relationship between the quality of juvenile dependency hearings and foster care placements. *Family Court Review, 52*(4), 678–685. https://doi.org/10.1111/fcre.12120

Mackie, T. I., Schaefer, A. J., Palatucci, J. S., Leslie, L. K., Crystal, S., Gusmano, M., & Karpman, H. E. (2022). The role of formal policy to promote informed consent of psychotropic medications for youth in child welfare custody: A national examination. *Administration and Policy in Mental Health, 49*(6), 986–1003. https://doi.org/10.1007/s10488-022-01212-3

Malempati, S. (2014). Ethics, advocacy, and the child client. *Cardozo Public Law, Policy, and Ethics Journal, 12*, 633. http://dx.doi.org/10.2139/ssrn.2318020

Massachusetts Department of Children and Families. (n.d.). *Foster child bill of rights.* Retrieved May 30, 2024, from https://www.mass.gov/doc/foster-child-rights-0/download

McCafferty, P. (2017). Implementing Article 12 of the United Nations Convention on the Rights of the child in child protection decision-making: A critical analysis of the challenges and opportunities for social work. *Child Care in Practice, 23*(4), 327–341. https://doi.org/10.1080/13575279.2016.1264368

McCafferty, P. (2021). Children's participation in child welfare decision making: Recognising dichotomies, conceptualising critically informed solutions. *Child Care in Practice, 30*(2), 112–129. https://doi.org/10.1080/13575279.2021.1896990

McDonald, C. (2014). Collaborative courts: Implementation with AB12 foster youth to ensure meaningful participation and positive outcomes post-emancipation. *University of San Francisco Law Review, 48*(4), Article 4. https://repository.usfca.edu/usflawreview/vol48/iss4/4

McTavish, J. R., McKee, C., & MacMillan, H. L. (2022). Foster children's perspectives on participation in child welfare processes: A meta-synthesis of qualitative studies. *PLoS One, 17*(10), e0275784. https://doi.org/10.1371/journal.pone.0275784

M.D. v. Abbott, CIVIL ACTION NO. 2:11-CV-84, 18 (S.D. Tex. January 9, 2017).

Miller, J. J., Duron, J., Washington, E., & Donohue-Dioh, J. (2017). Exploring the legal representation of individuals in foster care: What say youth and alumni? *Children and Youth Services Review, 78*, 142–149. https://doi.org/10.1016/j.childyouth.2017.05.010

Miller, J. J., Duron, J. F., Donohue-Dioh, J., & Geiger, J. M. (2018). Conceptualizing effective legal representation for Foster youth: A group concept mapping study. *Children and Youth Services Review, 91*, 271–278. https://doi.org/10.1016/j.childyouth.2018.06.031

Mo. Rev. Stat. § 210.564 The National Association for Counsel of Children. (2022). *Recommendations for legal representation of children and youth in neglect and abuse proceedings.* https://nacchildlaw.org/wp-content/uploads/2024/01/NACC-Recommendations-Final.pdf

Molloy, S. (2024). The Committee on the Rights of the Child and Article 12: Applying the Lundy model to treaty body recommendations. *Leiden Journal of International Law*, 1–25. https://doi.org/10.1017/S0922156524000098

National Conference of State Legislatures. (2019). Foster care bill of rights. *NCSW.* Retrieved May 30, 2024, from https://www.ncsl.org/human-services/-foster-care-bill-of-rights#table1

National Council of Juvenile and Family Court Judges. (2022). Judges' roles in promoting youth-centered legal permanency. *Judge's Action Alert.* Retrieved June 13, 2024, from https://www.ncjfcj.org/wp-content/uploads/2022/10/youth-centered-permanency-1.pdf

National District Attorney Association. (2013). *Minor consent to medical treatment laws.* Retrieved June 17, 2024, from https://ndaa.org/wp-content/uploads/Minor-Consent-to-Medical-Treatment-2.pdf

Nev. Rev. Stat. § 432.535.

Nicini v. Morra, 212 F.3d 798, 808 (3d Cir. 2000).

Noogle, R. (2018). Children's rights. In A. Gheaus, G. Calder, & J. Wispelaere (Eds.), *The Routledge handbook of the philosophy of childhood and children*. https://doi.org/10.4324/9781351055987

Office of Inspector General, U.S. Department of Health and Human Services. (2018). *Treatment planning and medication monitoring were lacking for children in foster care receiving psychotropic medication*. https://oig.hhs.gov/documents/evaluation/3074/OEI-07-15-00380-Complete%20Report.pdf

Office of Program Policy Analysis and Government Accountability. (2021). *Literature review of studies on the effectiveness of advocacy models for children in dependency*. https://oppaga.fl.gov/Documents/Reports/21-07.pdf

Pennsylvania Statute Title 11 Chapter 35. (2010). Children in Foster Care Act. Retrieved May 30, 2024, from https://casetext.com/statute/pennsylvania-statutes/statutes-unconsolidated/title-11-ps-children/chapter-35-children-in-foster-care-act/section-2633-children-in-foster-care

Perlmutter, B. (2017). "Letting kids be kids": Youth voice and activism to reform foster care and promote "normalcy". *Studies in Law, Politics, and Society*, *72*. Retrieved March 5, 2024, from https://repository.law.miami.edu/cgi/viewcontent.cgi?article=1210&context=fac_books

Pierce v. Society of Sisters, 268 U.S. 510, 535 (1925).

Pölkki, P., Vornanen, R., Pursiainen, M., & Riikonen, M. (2012). Children's participation in child-protection processes as experienced by foster children and social workers. *Child Care in Practice*, *18*(2), 107–125. https://doi.org/10.1080/13575279.2011.646954

Prebeck, N. (2023). Virginia legal ages laws. *FindLaw*. Retrieved June 15, 2024, from https://www.findlaw.com/state/virginia-law/virginia-legal-ages-laws.html

Preventing Sex Trafficking and Strengthening Families Act of 2014 (H.R. 4980). *Congress.gov*. Retrieved March 7, 2024, from https://www.congress.gov/bill/113th-congress/house-bill/4980/text

Prince v. Massachusetts, 321 U.S. 158, 166 (1944).

Quas, J. A., Wallin, A. R., Horwitz, B., Davis, E., & Lyon, T. D. (2009). Maltreated children's understanding of and emotional reactions to dependency court involvement. *Behavioral Sciences & the Law*, *27*(1), 97–117. https://doi.org/10.1002/bsl.836

Quaye, A. A., Coyne, I., Söderbäck, M., & Hallström, I. K. (2019). Children's active participation in decision-making processes during hospitalisation: An observational study. *Journal of Clinical Nursing*, *28*(23–24), 4525–4537. https://doi.org/10.1111/jocn.15042

Quennerstedt, A. (2009). Balancing the rights of the child and the rights of parents in the convention on the rights of the child. *Journal of Human Rights*, *8*(2), 162–176. https://doi.org/10.1080/14754830902897270

Quinter, J., & Markowitz, C. (2023). Judicial bypass and parental rights after Dobbs (November 18, 2022). *Yale Law Journal*, *132*, 1908. http://dx.doi.org/10.2139/ssrn.4280735

Raghavan, R., Zima, B. T., Andersen, R. M., Leibowitz, A. A., Schuster, M. A., & Landsverk, J. (2005). Psychotropic medication use in a national probability sample of children in the child welfare system. *Journal of Child Adolescent Psychopharmacology*, *15*(1), 97–106. https://doi.org/10.1089/cap.2005.15.97

Reiss, F. (2021). Child marriage in the United States: Prevalence and implications. *Journal of Adolescent Health*, *69*(6s), S8–S10. https://doi.org/10.1016/j.jadohealth.2021.07.001

Reno v. Flores, 507 U.S. 292, 309 (1993).

Reyes, J. (2012). *Child welfare bills of rights for foster children*. American Bar Association. Retrieved May 30, 2024, from https://www.americanbar.org/groups/public_

interest/child_law/resources/child_law_practiceonline/child_law_practice/vol_31/december_2012/child_welfare_billsofrightsforfosterchildren0/

Ruggiero, R. (2022). Article 18: Rights concerning parental responsibility. In Z. Vaghri, J. Zermatten, G. Lansdown, & R. Ruggiero (Eds.), *Monitoring state compliance with the UN Convention on the Rights of the Child: An analysis of attributes* (pp. 153–162). Springer International Publishing. https://doi.org/10.1007/978-3-030-84647-3_17

Ryan, C. (2023). Are children's rights enough? *American University Law Review*, University of Alabama Legal Studies Research Paper No. 4448878. https://ssrn.com/abstract=4448878

Saarnik, H., Sindi, I., & Toros, K. (2023). 'Well, the child can't choose, right?': Foster children's participation experiences of child protection removal practices. *Child and Adolescent Social Work Journal*. https://doi.org/10.1007/s10560-022-00911-y

Sacotte, K., Tomlin, B., Judkins, A., & Brunelli, L. (2023). A brief history of children's rights. In *The evolution of global child rights: Protecting the vulnerable* (pp. 1–11). Springer Nature Switzerland. https://doi.org/10.1007/978-3-031-45520-9_1

School House Connection. (2023). *State laws on minor consent for routine medical care*. State Policy. Retrieved June 17, 2024, from https://schoolhouseconnection.org/article/state-laws-on-minor-consent-for-routine-medical-care#:~:text=Any%20minor%20who%20is%2014,no%20other%20person%20shall%20be

Selwyn, J., & Riley, S. (2015). *Children and young people's views on being in care a literature review*. Hadley Centre for Adoption and Foster Care Studies, Coram Voice. Retrieved June 10, 2024, from https://coramvoice.org.uk/wp-content/uploads/2021/01/Childrens-views-lit-review-FINAL-2.pdf

Skauge, B., Storhaug, A. S., & Marthinsen, E. (2021). The what, why and how of child participation: A review of the conceptualization of "child participation" in child welfare. *Social Sciences*, *10*(2), 54. https://www.mdpi.com/2076-0760/10/2/54

Stambaugh, L. F., Leslie, L. K., Ringeisen, H., Smith, K., & Hodgkin, D. (2012). *Psychotropic medication use by children in child welfare*. OPRE Report #2012-33. Office of Planning, Research and Evaluation, Administration for Children and Families, U.S. Department of Health and Human Services.

Steering Committee for Human Rights in the fields of Biomedicine and Health & Steering Committee for the Rights of the Child. (2024). *Guide to children's participation in decisions about their health*. Council for Europe. Retrieved June 17, 2024, from https://www.coe.int/en/web/bioethics/guide-to-children-s-participation-in-decisions-about-their-health

Stricklin v. Ark. Dep't of Human Servs. & Minor Child, 528 S.W.3d 321, 2017 Ark. App. 441 (Ark. Ct. App. 2017).

Summers, A. (2017). *Exploring the relationship between hearing quality and case outcomes in New York*. New York State Unified Court System Child Welfare Court Improvement Project. https://ww2.nycourts.gov/sites/default/files/document/file

Summers, A., Gatowski, S., Richards, T., & Fromknecht, A. (2022). *Measuring child welfare court performance: Review of resources*. Children's Bureau, Administration for Children and Families, U.S. Department of Health and Human Services. Retrieved June 13, 2024, from https://www.americanbar.org/content/dam/aba/administrative/child_law/cw-court-performance-resource-review.pdf

Summers, A., Gatowski, S. I., & Gueller, M. (2017). Examining hearing quality in child abuse and neglect cases: The relationship between breadth of discussion and case outcomes. *Children and Youth Services Review*, *82*, 490–498. https://doi.org/10.1016/j.childyouth.2017.10.018

Taft, J. K., & Gordon, H. R. (2013). Youth activists, youth councils, and constrained democracy. *Education, Citizenship and Social Justice*, *8*(1), 87–100. https://doi.org/10.1177/1746197913475765

Texas Department of Family and Protective Services. (2023). CPS rights of children and youth in foster care. *Form 2530*. Retrieved May 30, 2024, from https://www.dfps.texas.gov/Child_Protection/Foster_Care/Childrens_Rights.asp

Texas Family Code – FAM § 263.008. *Foster children's bill of rights*. Retrieved May 30, 2024, from https://statutes.capitol.texas.gov/Docs/FA/htm/FA.263.htm#263.008

Timothy, B. et al. v. Kody Kinsley 1:22-cv-01046|U.S. District Court for the Middle District of North Carolina Memorandum and Order March 29, 2024.

Toros, K. (2021). Children's participation in decision making from child welfare workers' perspectives: A systematic review. *Research on Social Work Practice*, *31*(4), 367–374. https://doi.org/10.1177/1049731520984844

Troxel v. Granville, 530 U.S. 57, 58 (2000).

UN Committee on the Rights of the Child. (2009). *General comment No. 12: The right of the child to be heard*. CRC/C/GC/12 20 July 2009. Retrieved June 6, 2024, from https://www.refworld.org/legal/general/crc/2009/en/70207

UN Committee on the Rights of the Child. (2023). *Statement of the Committee on the Rights of the Child on article 5 of the Convention on the Rights of the Child*. Retrieved June 15, 2024, from https://www.ohchr.org/sites/default/files/documents/hrbodies/crc/statements/CRC-Article-5-statement.pdf

United Nations Convention on the Rights of the Child. (1989). https://www.ohchr.org/en/instruments-mechanisms/instruments/convention-rights-child

United Nations General Assembly. (2010). *Guidelines for the alternative care of children (A/RES/64/142)*. Retrieved May 27, 2024, from https://resourcecentre.savethechildren.net/pdf/5416.pdf/

U.S. Center for Disease Control and Prevention. (2022). *State laws that enable a minor to provide informed consent to receive HIV and STD services*. CDC. Retrieved June 17, 2024, from https://www.cdc.gov/hiv/policies/law/states/minors.html

U.S. Department of Education. (n.d.). *Eligibility requirements*. Federal student Aid Office. Retrieved June 15, 2024, from https://studentaid.gov/understand-aid/eligibility/requirements

U.S. Department of Health & Human Services (HHS), Administration for Children and Families, Administration on Children, Youth and Families, Children's Bureau. (2019). *Log No: ACYF-CB-IM-19-03*. Retrieved June 13, 2024, from https://www.acf.hhs.gov/sites/default/files/documents/cb/im1903.pdf

U.S. Department of Health & Human Services, Administration for Children and Families, Administration on Children, Youth and Families, Children's Bureau. (2023). *Legislation*. Retrieved May 30, 2024, from https://www.acf.hhs.gov/cb/laws-policies/federal-laws/legislation

U.S. Department of Health & Human Services Assistant Secretary for Planning and Evaluation. (2004). *Statutory rape: A guide to state laws and reporting requirement*. Retrieved June 15, 2024, from https://aspe.hhs.gov/reports/statutory-rape-guide-state-laws-reporting-requirements-1

U.S. Department of Labor. (n.d.). *Age requirements*. Retrieved June 15, 2024, from https://www.dol.gov/general/topic/youthlabor/agerequirements

Usa.gov. (n.d.). Requirements to join the U.S. military. *USAGOV*. Retrieved June 15, 2024, from https://www.usa.gov/military-requirements 42 U.S.C. § 675.

van Bijleveld, G. G., Bunders-Aelen, J. F. G., & Dedding, C. W. M. (2020). Exploring the essence of enabling child participation within child protection services. *Child & Family Social Work*, *25*(2), 286–293. https://doi.org/10.1111/cfs.12684

van Bijleveld, G. G., Dedding, C. W. M., & Bunders-Aelen, J. F. G. (2015). Children's and young people's participation within child welfare and child protection services: A state-of-the-art review. *Child & Family Social Work*, *20*(2), 129–138. https://doi.org/10.1111/cfs.12082

Vis, S. A., & Fossum, S. (2015). Organizational factors and child participation in decision-making: Differences between two child welfare organizations. *Child & Family Social Work*, *20*(3), 277–287. https://doi.org/10.1111/cfs.12076

Vis, S. A., Strandbu, A., Holtan, A., & Thomas, N. (2011). Participation and health: A research review of child participation in planning and decision-making. *Child & Family Social Work, 16*(3), 325–335. https://doi.org/10.1111/j.1365-2206.2010.00743.x

Vis, S. A., & Thomas, N. (2009). Beyond talking: Children's participation in Norwegian care and protection cases. *European Journal of Social Work, 12*(2), 155–168. https://doi.org/10.1080/13691450802567465

Vissing, Y. (2023). *Children's human rights in the USA: Challenges and opportunities.* Springer International Publishing. https://doi.org/10.1007/978-3-031-30848-2_14

Washington State Center for Court Research. (2021). *Evaluation of the Washington State dependent child legal representation program.* Administrative Office of the Courts.

Weisz, V., Wingrove, T., Beal, S. J., & Faith-Slaker, A. (2011). Children's participation in foster care hearings. *Child Abuse & Neglect, 35*(4), 267–272. https://doi.org/10.1016/j.chiabu.2010.12.007

Wilson, S., Hean, S., Abebe, T., & Heaslip, V. (2020). Children's experiences with child protection services: A synthesis of qualitative evidence. *Children and Youth Services Review, 113*, 104974. https://doi.org/10.1016/j.childyouth.2020.104974

Wisconsin v. Yoder, 406 U.S. 205, 232 (1972).

Woodman, E., Roche, S., & McArthur, M. (2023). Children's participation in child protection: How do practitioners understand children's participation in practice? *Child & Family Social Work, 28*(1), 125–135. https://doi.org/10.1111/cfs.12947

Zinn, A. E., & Slowriver, J. (2008). *Expediting permanency: Legal representation for foster children in Palm Beach County.* Chapin Hall Center for Children at the University of Chicago.

7 Best Interest vs Normalcy

How Professionals Respond

The intersection of best interest, normalcy, children's rights and decision-making plays out every day in jurisdictions across the world. While courts are the place where big decisions are made and disputed decisions are resolved, most decisions about the life of a child in care start at a lower level, with the caseworker or the foster parent. It is at this level that I wanted to study how various foster care professionals might respond to the requests of a foster youth.

I will spoil the ending by saying that I did not get the results that I hoped I might, but I did find some interesting results nevertheless. As this whole book thus far has discussed the surrounding literature, I will omit that section from the following discussion.

Research Question

As mentioned in earlier chapters, one of the frustrating things about representing foster children is being told so often by so many professionals that the very thing my client desired, was not in their best interest. This was of course, subject to the dozens of factors we now know influence child welfare decision-making, such as the internal beliefs of the caseworker, the organization they worked for, their own sense of risk aversion and sometimes even the facts of the case itself.

With that in mind, this study examined the basic question of would a normalcy framework make professionals more likely to agree to the request of a foster child. To put it another way, do we value children's voice more if we think about it in a different legal context?

Methods

The data for this preregistered study was collected from an anonymous survey sent to various groups of child welfare professionals between August 2022 and July 2023. Participants were recruited using direct solicitation emails to various state CPS professional groups, foster parent groups, to state and local CASA organizations and to foster care non-profit organizations asking them to distribute the survey internally. Participants were also recruited using

DOI: 10.4324/9781003510253-7

targeted solicitations to various membership restricted social media groups, such as Facebook groups of US child welfare professionals or former foster youth. These groups had closed membership that required some level of verification prior to joining. Finally, many participants were recruited through the helpful distribution onto social media channels by a foster parent social media influencer, who sent the survey to her Facebook and Instagram followers.

The survey had no material reward or prize for completion, so it seems unlikely that anyone outside of these child welfare groups would have participated. Unfortunately, because of the type of distribution, a response rate cannot be calculated.

All told, I was able to recruit more than 1100 participants, but after excluding incomplete responses, I was left with a total of 803 for analysis. The numbers broken down by role and demographics are shown in Tables 7.1–7.5.

The roles are reasonably self-explanatory. Within the organizations, such as CASA, CPS and nonprofit, there are obviously numerous jobs that a person might have, such as an intake worker versus a state supervisor. As noted in Chapter 5, these individual roles within an organization or agency can affect decision-making but for the purposes of this study that was comparing the greater roles themselves, these roles are left broad. The categories Nonprofit and Other Foster Care Job are probably the most ill-defined and might include

Table 7.1 Participants by Role

Role	*Percentage*
State CPS employee	10.7%
CASAGAL	15.8%
Other state agency	1.1%
Foster parent	34.5%
Foster alumni	6.3%
Nonprofit	6.8%
Religious organization	0.8%
Kinship Parent	4.5%
Other Foster Care Job	6.1%
Social Work Student	2.7%
Self-employed	1.3%

Table 7.2 Participants by Race

Race	*Percentage*
Black	5.3%
White	86.8%
Hispanic	4.95%
American Indian	1.21%
Asian	1.51%
Native Hawaiian or Pacific Islander	0.12%

Table 7.3 Participants by Education Level

Education Level	*Percentage*
Less than high school degree	0.4%
High school graduate (high school diploma or equivalent)	8.0%
Some college but no degree	17.2%
Associate degree in college (2-year)	6.9%
Bachelor's degree in college (4-year)	24.8%
Master's degree	26.7%
Doctoral degree	9.1%
Professional degree (JD, MD)	5.4%

Table 7.4 Participants by Years of Experience

Experience Level	*Percentage*
0–3 years	15.3%
3–6 years	12.3%
6–9 years	12.6%
9–12 years	12.3%
12–15 years	10.2%
15–18 years	7.0%
18+ years	8.6%

Table 7.5 Participants by Age

Age Group	*Percentage*
Under 18	0.1%
18–24 years old	4.0%
25–34 years old	15.5%
35–44 years old	17.3%
45–54 years old	21.3%
55–64 years old	15.4%
65+ years old	4.7%

some overlap, but were included in the survey to capture participants that work along with, but not necessarily for the child welfare system. This could be someone that coordinates foster care for a school district, someone that works for a youth homeless shelter or a therapist for foster youth. The jobs that touch foster care are simply too numerous to mention, so some aggregation of roles was necessary. Finally, for most of this book I have generally used the term care experienced to describe adults that were once part of the foster care system. For the survey, I used the term foster alumni, so I will use that term throughout this chapter.

Approximately 91 percent of the participants are female, with less than 5 percent male and only about 1.5 percent identifying as non-binary. The participants are also predominately White. While the numbers are still a bit skewed, for purposes of this study the number of White female participants is less problematic because of the nature of the child welfare field workforce. Women make almost up 90 percent of social workers (Salsberg et al., 2020), the majority of foster parents (Kirby, 1997) and the majority of CASA volunteers (Cooley et al., 2019).

The survey was distributed nationally throughout the US and there was at least one participant from all but three states, Manie, Rhode Island and Hawaii. The highest number of participants were from Florida at 19.92 percent, California at 7.82 percent, Missouri at 6.31 percent and Texas at 5.93 percent. Though Missouri is a bit of an outlier in representation, California, Florida and Texas are the three most populous states, so their inclusion within the top spots is encouraging.

Prior to distributing the survey, I conducted five qualitative interviews with child welfare professionals in three US states to vet the vignette, the survey questions and the research question. Changes were made to the survey to make it more universally understandable.

The survey itself consisted of nine demographic questions followed by one of three randomized instructions, a control, a best interest prompt and a normalcy prompt. Participants were told that they would read a short vignette about a hypothetical foster child named Morgan and that they would be asked a series of questions related to Morgan's wishes. They were told they were given the final authority to make the decision and what they decide will be the final outcome.

For the control group, that was the extent of the instructions. For the best interest group, they were told to make the decisions based on Morgan's best interest and were given the following definition,

> Best interest refers to factors related to the child's stability in their placement, their time in the child welfare system, their physical, emotional and living needs, their safety considerations, their wishes and the individual characteristics that are important to their identity.

The normalcy group was told to make the decision that they believed would best promote normalcy for Morgan and were given this definition,

> Normalcy is the ability of a child in care to live as normal a life as possible, including engaging in childhood activities that are suitable for children of the same age, level of maturity, and developmental level as determined by a reasonable and prudent parent standard.

Following the instructions, participants saw one of eight vignettes about Morgan, a 15-year-old female who had been in foster care for three years. Her age, gender and time in care were the same throughout all of the vignettes, though there could be some interesting differences in how people respond to those potential variables, I chose to make them consistent as they were not the effect I wanted to test. Vignette are commonly used in social science and in child welfare research with the idea that researchers can use them to test real-life scenarios with under experimental circumstances controlled by the researchers (Keddell & Hyslop, 2018; Middel et al., 2022; Taylor, 2005; Stokes & Schmidt, 2012).

The eight vignettes had three randomized moving pieces regarding the stability of her current placement, the number of placements since she came into care and her current case goal. This was an attempt to better reflect the reality of actual foster youth. The result is that each vignette has an overall stability ranking reflecting essentially how stable Morgan was in foster care, with vignette one being the most stable and vignette eight being the least. This ranking was also discussed and approved by all five child welfare professionals during the qualitative interview process.

I have mentioned the importance of stability in prior chapters, but again it relates to the idea of whether the child is moving from placement to placement at a frequent pace or having their placement disrupted by multiple stays in a psychiatric hospital. Older youth are more likely to experience instability (Rubin et al., 2007; Liming et al., 2021; Stenason & Romano, 2023). Instability is linked with behavioral and mental health disorders (Konijn et al., 2019; Maguire et al., 2024), health disorders (Asif et al., 2024), juvenile delinquency (Maguire et al., 2024) and overall placement satisfaction (Stenason & Romano, 2023). Perhaps most importantly the lack of stability negatively affects permanency making it less likely that a foster youth will achieve a permanent home either through reunification or adoption (Stott & Gustavsson, 2010; Akin, 2011).

Following the vignette, participants were then given eight short questions regarding Morgan's desires and how they would respond. These questions were again chosen after qualitative interviews with professionals to identify common real-life instances where foster youth often expressed their wishes. Though some of the questions touch on some controversial topics, the defining feature of them is their banality for people with experience in child welfare. The order of the questions was randomized, but each participant was shown each question. For each answer, participants were given a six-point Likert question rating from being strongly opposed to the child's request to being strongly supportive. The questions are listed in numbered paragraphs below.

1. Morgan identifies as LGBTQ. Morgan's foster family has religious objections to LGBTQ relationships. Morgan requests to be allowed to participate in local LGBTQ activities and groups despite foster family objections. **How strongly would you support or oppose Morgan being allowed to participate in LGBTQ activities?**
2. Morgan has a diagnosis of ADHD, but she wants to stop taking her medication for it, claiming that it causes illness and she cannot think clearly. **How strongly would you support or oppose Morgan's request to stop taking her medication?**

3. Morgan has been in individual counseling since coming into care. Her therapist recommends that counseling continue. Morgan says the counseling is a waste of time and would like to stop going. **How strongly would you support or oppose Morgan's request to discontinue individual counseling?**
4. Morgan is in family counseling with her biological father and her two younger siblings. Recently, the counseling sessions have become emotionally difficult. She has requested that she no longer be required to participate. **How strongly would you support or oppose Morgan's request to stop family therapy sessions?**
5. Morgan has begun to communicate on social media with her biological mother, who lost legal parenting rights early in the case after allegations of drug abuse and neglect. Morgan has requested that supervised visits be allowed. Biological mother would also like to visit with her. **How strongly would you support or oppose Morgan's request to have supervised visits with her mother?**
6. Morgan has recently had some trouble at school. Her grades have been going down and she has received some punishment from school staff for poor behavior. Morgan says the problem is the school environment and that she would do better in a different school. There are other high schools she could attend, though it would require a longer bus ride for her and she would have to get up earlier. She requests to be allowed to transfer schools. **How strongly would you support or oppose Morgan's request to transfer schools?**
7. Morgan is having serious trouble in school despite receiving appropriate school supports. She tells you she does not enjoy school and would prefer to take vocational classes instead and get her diploma through a vocational training program. **How strongly would you support or oppose Morgan's request to withdraw from school and enroll in vocational training courses?**
8. Morgan's foster family is of a different race and ethnicity as Morgan and live in an area with little ethnic/racial diversity. Morgan requests to be placed with a different family because of her racial/ethnic identity. **How strongly would you support or oppose the idea of Morgan being placed with another family?**

Finally, participants were given the Dalgleish Scale (2010). This questionnaire consists of eight paired statements where participants must choose one statement from each pair. After making their choices, participants are asked to rank the strength of the statement they selected. These statements include options, such as "Work should be focused on keeping the family together" or "Child protection workers should be willing to be an advocate for the child". The outcome is a score that sorts participants along a spectrum from prioritizing child safety with higher scores to favoring family preservation with lower scores. Previous research has identified this measure as moderately reliable, with a Cronbach's alpha of 0.664 (Fluke et al., 2016). The scale has been used to test child protection workers beliefs on child safety and family preservation and their relationship with numerous other child welfare metrics.

I discussed research related to the Dalgleish Scale in Chapter 5. It represents the fundamental question about child welfare of family preservation versus child safety. Also given what we know about risk aversion that I discussed in Chapter 4, where risk aversion leads to decisions centered on the child's physical safety alone, the Dalgleish Scale also serves a second purpose. Scores closer to family preservation are arguably more risk tolerant as the "safest" decision is often going to be removal from the family.

My hypotheses for the survey were as follows:

1. The normalcy prompt would lead to participants giving more supportive answers (higher Likert scores) for the questions in comparison to the control or the best interest prompt.
2. Higher stability vignettes would lead to more supportive answers (higher Likert scores) for the questions regardless of the prompt.
3. Higher Dalgleish scores representing child safety beliefs would correspond to less supportive answers (lower Likert scores).
4. Lower Dalgleish scoress representing family preservation beliefs would correspond to more supportive answers (higher Liker scores).

Results

The data was analyzed using structural equation modeling (SEM) in Stata to determine if the treatment variables had any effect on the final Likert answers. Table 7.6 below describes the central tendencies of the questions as a whole before being divided by treatment group. As can be seen, the participants were the most supportive of the LGBTQ questions and were the least supportive of the individual counseling request. For ease of understanding, I will explain the results per question and treatment effect first and then discuss the demographic differences and the Dalgleish Scale.

Table 7.6 Central Measures

Question	*Mean*	*Median (50%)*	*Standard Deviation*
LGBTQ	5.24	6.00	1.15
ADHD	3.74	4.00	1.22
Individual Counseling	2.63	3.00	1.13
Family Counseling	3.89	4.00	1.30
Bio Mom Visit	4.79	5.00	1.12
New School	4.54	5.00	1.12
Vocational	4.41	5.00	1.30
Race	4.82	5.00	1.05

Using the control as the baseline, Table 7.7 below shows the treatment effects for each question. As noted before, none of the treatments produced any significant effects and the few p-values of significance should be considered cautiously as they do not show any consistent pattern across the data and are most likely false positives. To check if a simpler model might show results, I also analyzed the data again with the stability groups combined. In one analysis, I combined the stability treatment into just four groups representing just four levels of stability. Finally, I combined the groups into a binary stable or not stable group and ran the analysis again. Neither combination of the stable variable resulted in any change to the findings. So I was unable to reject the null hypothesis for my first and second hypothesis.

Table 7.7 Treatment Effects per Question

Category	*Prompt Type*	*Coefficient*	*p-value*	*Statistically Significant*
LGBTQ	Best Interest	0.0088	0.928	No
LGBTQ	Normalcy	-0.0796	0.423	No
LGBTQ	Stable8	0.394	0.016	Yes, but possible false positive
ADHD	Best Interest	-0.1735	0.093	No, possible marginal
ADHD	Normalcy	0.1634	0.118	No
ADHD	Stable3	–	–	Probably False Positive
Individual Counseling	Best Interest	-0.0286	0.769	No
Individual Counseling	Normalcy	0.1000	0.312	No
Individual Counseling	Stability Vignettes	–	–	No
Family Counseling	Best Interest	-0.0058	0.959	No
Family Counseling	Normalcy	0.1036	0.361	No
Family Counseling	Stability Vignettes	–	–	No
Biological Mom Visit	Best Interest	-0.1319	0.167	No
Biological Mom Visit	Normalcy	-0.014	0.884	No
Biological Mom Visit	Stability Vignettes	–	–	No
New School	Best Interest	0.0434	0.650	No
New School	Normalcy	0.0644	0.507	No
New School	Stability Vignettes	–	–	No
Vocational School	Best Interest	-0.0917	0.411	No
Vocational School	Normalcy	0.0312	0.783	No
Vocational School	Stability Vignettes	–	–	No
Race	Best Interest	-0.0445	0.619	No
Race	Normalcy	0.0202	0.824	No
Race	Stability Vignettes	–	–	No

Dalgleish Scale

Moving on to the Dalgleish Scale where each participant receives a total score between -40 and 40. Higher scores represent a more child safety orientation, while lower scores indicate a preference for family preservation. Unlike the treatment, a participants Dalgleish Scale score, did seem to have some bearing on some of the responses as can be seen in Table 7.8.

All of these effect sizes are reasonably small, but they do point in some interesting directions. The responses suggest that participants with higher Dalgleish scores, who favor child safety seem to be slightly more supportive of Morgan's request to participate in LGBTQ activities, to terminate family counseling and to change foster homes because of her race. This is the opposite effect of what I expected in my hypotheses where I believed that child safety would lead to less supportive answers. How these effects might play out in the real world is more complicate and would require further study, but it does at minimum suggest that internal beliefs are playing some small part even if it is in a different direction than what I would have initially thought.

In addition to the Dalgleish Scale's potential relationship with certain participant answers, this study also found important differences among child welfare professional in how they scored on the Dalgleish itself (Trail, 2024). I report these findings in detail along with another study in a separate paper, but will discuss them briefly here also as they are relevant to this discussion. Because some of the roles did not have sufficient participants for analysis, they were left out of this subset.

As can be seen in Table 7.9, the role of participants within the child welfare system seems to have an effect on how they perceive the role of child welfare as a child safety or a family preservation agency (Trail, 2024).

State CPS employees have statistically significant lower scores than every other child welfare professional. Though they still fall within the child safety range of scores, they tend to score closer to family preservation than any other role possibly representing their dual purpose within the system to protect children but also promote reunification (Trail, 2024). The study also found significant differences between some of the other pairs, but none as striking as the difference between CPS workers the rest.

Table 7.8 Dalgleish Scores and Question Relationships

Category	*Coefficient*	*p-value*	*Significance*
LGBTQ	0.0181404	0.000	Highly statistically significant
Individual Counseling	–0.0043318	0.118	Not significant
Family Counseling	0.0081727	0.010	Statistically significant
Bio Mom Visit	–0.0048368	0.078	Possible weak significance
New School	0.0050233	0.065	Possible weak significance
Vocational	.0033007	0.293	Not significant
Race	.0081175	0.001	Statistically significant
ADHD	–.0046858	0.112	Not significant

Table 7.9 Dalgleish Scores by Participant Role

Role	*Participant Count*	*Mean*	*Median*
CASA	147	23.86	26.0
Foster Alumni	59	26.32	30
Foster Parent	335	22.22	25.0
Kinship	41	25.34	30.0
Nonprofit	66	19.89	24.0
Other Foster	57	18.89	22.0
State CPS	103	14.68	16.0
Student	23	26.52	31.0

Child Welfare Roles

Related to the findings that different roles had different Dalgleish scores, participant roles also possibly affected their answers to the survey questions. Not every question and role showed significance, but the results suggest that some participant's role within child welfare played a part in how specific questions were answered. The Family Counseling and the Vocational School questions had no statistical significance attached to any specific role, but for the other six questions, at least one child welfare role stood out. For purposes of this analysis, I excluded any findings for roles with fewer than 20 participants.

For the LGBTQ question, being a state CPS worker seemed to have some correlation with more supportive answers with a positive coefficient of 0.4528 and p-value of 0.002.

For the individual counseling question, nonprofit employees with a coefficient of 0.2989 and a p-value of 0.058 showed some correlation with Morgan quitting counseling compared to the other roles. Because this role category is rather vague and could include dozens of jobs, I would be hesitant to interpret this result.

For the Bio Mom Visit question, both state CPS workers with a negative coefficient of -0.4047 and a p-value of 0.006 and CASA workers who had a negative coefficient of -0.3221 and a p-value of 0.027 were less likely of supporting Morgan's desire to visit her terminated mother.

For the ADHD question, CASA recorded a negative coefficient of -0.3741 and p-value of 0.015, whereas foster alumni had a positive coefficient of 0.3889 and a p-value of 0.032. Working for the CASA organization is correlated then with less support for Morgan to come off her ADHD medications. Foster alumni of the other hand were more likely to support this, perhaps because of their own experience being on psychotropic medication.

For the new school question, CASA and Foster alumni once again came out on opposite sides. CASA's negative coefficient of -0.4477 with an accompanying p-value of 0.002 compares to the foster alumni positive coefficient 0.3572 with a p-value of 0.036. CASA workers tend to want Morgan to stay in her current school, while foster alumni are more supportive of her transferring to a new school, again perhaps because of their own experience.

Perhaps the most interesting difference is regarding the race question. CASA and Foster alumni once more come out on opposing sides; however, other Foster workers also score significantly on this question. CASA had a negative coefficient of -0.2685 with a p-value of 0.046 and likewise other Foster workers displayed a negative coefficient of -0.4689 and a p-value of 0.006, suggesting that participants of both groups were more reluctant to move Morgan based on race compared to foster alumni with a positive coefficient 0.2916 and p-value of 0.066. Though not quite traditional significance, I include it here because of how close it is and how it seems to follow the same trend as the prior questions.

Finally, age, education and experience level were also tested for all of the questions, but none resulted in any significance to the participants' answers.

Discussion

Firstly, just looking at the overall means of each question, it is obvious that different questions that represent different issues generated different levels of support. The LGTBQ question in particular generated the most supportive answers, which was heartening given the hurdles that LGBTQ foster youth face. The Child Welfare Information Gateway (2021) noted that many states still have laws that restrict LGBTQ rights regarding fostering, so youth may feel they are unable to express their sexuality to people in the care system. Additionally, LGBTQ youth are overrepresented within foster care with some studies finding that they are 2.5 times more likely to end up in care compared to their peers (Fish et al., 2019). They also report lower levels of overall well-being than their foster youth peers and were more likely to experience sexual assault (Kaasbøll et al., 2022).

The only question to have overall disapproval was the question involving Morgan quitting her individual counseling sessions. There is an interesting dynamic within this question as foster youth are known to have significant mental health issues (Engler et al., 2022) with some studies suggesting that as much as 80 percent of foster youth have mental health needs (Szilagyi et al., 2015). However, multiple studies of the mental health interventions used to treat foster children have found most of them to not be evidenced based and to be generally ineffective (Leathers et al., 2009; Hambrick et al., 2016).

These findings confirm with my personal experience that my clients were often ordered to attend counseling because of their mental health issues, but very few ever reported the sessions being helpful to them and most grew weary of telling their stories to someone new every time they moved placement or their therapist changed. I suspect that the participants are aware of the mental health issues of foster youth, but are perhaps less aware of the ineffectiveness of their treatment provided.

Also, as individual counseling is a medical issue, possibly the participants did not feel qualified to give a supportive answer. In my experience, child welfare professionals were perhaps wisely hesitant to counter any advice given by a health care professional even when they did not agree. Given that the two other lower scoring questions about ADHD medication and family counseling also relate to health care aspects, this could be a reason behind these lower scores.

Moving on to the treatments, I will admit some disappointment that I did not find any effects. However, a null result does still have some value as it suggests some items that are not influencing decision-making. So, within the context of these particular questions regarding these issues, it does not appear that asking participants to decide using a normalcy or a best interest framework has any effect on their final decisions.

There are a few possible explanations for this. Firstly, as discussed throughout this book, best interest is the pervasive legal standard throughout child welfare. It is ubiquitous in all conversations about children in care and the phrase is repeated ad nauseum every time someone makes a decision. Because of this reason, it is likely that participants in the control group have a default internal setting to making decisions in a child's best interest. They have made potentially thousands of best interest decisions already in their work. The participants that received the best interest prompt were essentially just being told to do what they already were intending to do, that is, make a decision using the best interest framework.

As for the participants that received the normalcy prompt, it did ask them to think of the question differently that just best interest. Still, because normalcy also included the reasonable prudent parent standard, which contains the idea of best interests as a liability waiver, it is possible that participants still had an internal best interest mindset for answering the questions.

While the questions themselves reflect common occurrences in child welfare, they do not all fit into a traditional example of a normalcy activity. This was of course, the purpose of the research to see if thinking about normalcy makes us more likely to support a child's wishes. The questions are also not central to the child welfare case itself, such as reunification, termination, adoption or permanency. The questions were intended to be challenging, but everyday issues nonetheless. Since they did not all align with a common normalcy example, it is possible that participants just reverted to their default of best interest.

It is also possible that the prompts themselves and the participants numbers were not sufficient to produce a measurable effect. The degree to which people can be primed to change their decision-making is contested (Cesario, 2014; Lee, 2021), though priming effects are better seen in within subjects designed experiments than between subject designs (Sherman & Rivers, 2021). Because of the uncertainty inherent in recruiting non-paid participants specifically from child welfare professionals and the limitation in time needed for them to complete the survey, this study used a between subjects approach. It is possible that a more robust within subjects study could still find a difference between these prompts, but that is a topic for future research.

As for the stability treatments, I was again surprised but pleasantly this time to see that Morgan's stability or instability did not have an effect on the answers. I had expected that the most stable version or Morgan might get more supportive answers than the least stable. In fact, the one possible finding from the stability vignettes was the opposite. In the LGBTQ question the least stable version of Morgan was slightly more likely to garner participant support. As this was the only question where this effect was observed, I am hesitant to place any weight to this finding. It could simply be a false positive, but it could also indicate that at least for the LGBTQ issue a very unstable Morgan was better listened to. Perhaps participants believed that access to LGBTQ activities would improve her stability in her placement. Though again, this finding should be treated with a hefty measure of skepticism.

Because the questions do not go to the core issues of permanency, it is possible that participants did not see them as particularly important. Again, because of the limitations in recruiting participants, each participant was only exposed to one stability vignette. A within subjects design might show if stability changes participant decision-making.

Moving on to the Dalgleish Scale's effects on the participant answers, the LGBTQ, the family counseling and the race questions all showed significant effects related to the Dalgleish. These are small positive coefficients, so the effect size might be minimal. Overall though these results suggest that the Dalgleish score is a significant predictor of support for each of these requests by Morgan in the vignette, with higher scores that indicate a focus on child safety being associated with greater support.

In these questions, Morgan wants to participate in LGBTQ activities, end family counseling and change foster homes to one that better fits her racial identity. How these are related into marginally higher beliefs about child safety are difficult to explain. Any theory I proposed would be pure speculation, but the strength of the relationship in the findings do point to some connection. This is worth potential further research.

The most interesting of the Dalgleish Scale results come from the differences found between the different roles within child welfare. Though the Dalgleish Scale has been used often in research, this was the first time that participants outside of a CPS agency were ever tested (Trail, 2024) so it provides some novel insight into how the roles of participants correlate with their beliefs about child safety and family preservation.

As I wrote before, CPS agency workers scored consistently lower than any other child welfare role perhaps because of their dual job within child welfare that includes reunification, but why the other roles scored higher is less clear (Trail, 2024). CASA, foster parents, kinship parents, foster alumni and social work university students all have high child safety related scores.

Either the role itself or the people that chose that role tend to cluster around child safety. Foster and kinship parents obviously have the important job of taking care of a child that has been removed from a home, therefore their role is literally to provide a safe home for children, which could explain their scores (Trail, 2024).

It is also not terribly surprising that CASA, the organization that is designed around serving the best interest of children should score higher on child safety, possibly as a result of the complex cases to which they are assigned (Trail, 2024).

The fact that social work students who might someday become CPS workers scored highest might reflect the influence of experience. In prior studies involving CPS workers, more experienced workers tended to score lower on child safety and higher on family preservation than their less experienced coworkers (Clark et al., 2021; Middel et al., 2024). This is also a relatively small sample of students within the dataset, so it is possible that this is not representative.

Perhaps the most surprising Dalgleish score comes from the foster alumni group, who scored the second highest on the scale, which is possibly related to their own sense of trauma (Trail, 2024). The exact reason for their high score is unclear. Most of my clients expressed deep dissatisfaction with CPS, their removal and their lives in foster care; however, some studies have suggested foster youth have positive experiences with care (Chapman et al., 2004; Augsberger & Swenson, 2015). It is possible that the foster alumni, now as grown adults have a different perspective on care than when they were younger.

As for the roles effect on the questions themselves, again something about the role itself or the participants within certain roles seem to have a correlation with how some of the questions are answered. CPS workers were more likely than other roles to be supportive of Morgan participating in LGBTQ activities, perhaps reflecting a more sophisticated understanding of is the issues faced by LGBTQ foster youth. Certainly, CPS workers in many states have mandated policies and programs for serving LGBTQ youth (Capacity Building Center for States, 2016), but this is also true for foster parents (Child Welfare Information Gateway, 2021b) and CASA (CASA of Tarrant County, 2024). Why CPS workers alone would have higher scores is unclear and worth further research.

CPS and CASA were both less supportive of Morgan's request to visit her biological mother. In this vignette, Morgan's mother would not have any legal rights remaining after court ordered termination. This generally involves a no contact order with the child placed on the offending parent. CPS would always have a role in termination recommendations and hearings and this is often true of CASA guardians as well. Both roles also report to the court regularly about the status of the case, so it is perhaps not surprising that these two roles would be less inclined to thwart a potential court order. In the real world, when this happens the child will need court permission before CPS will allow visits again.

Perhaps the most interesting difference in the roles comes from the opposite answers given by CASA and Foster alumni on the ADHD, new school and race questions. Without delving too deeply into the research regarding CASA as an organization, it should be noted that CASA workers and volunteers who are appointed by the court as a child's guardian ad litem are almost entirely made of White, middle-aged women, most of whom have at least a college degree (Caliber Associates, 2004).

Whether having CASA assigned to a case is helpful or harmful is a contested issue. Some research has found that having a CASA guardian actually reduces a child's odds of achieving permanency, especially through reunification or kinship placement, (Osborne et al., 2020) though CASA are assigned on more complicated cases potentially skewing these results and making causality difficult (Osborne et al., 2019). Other studies have shown that having CASA guardians on a case can improve outcomes, such as reducing the time children spend in out-of-home placements and hastening permanency (Crane et al., 2023). Still, given the demographic makeup of CASA guardians and the foster children they represent some have argued that racial bias is inherent in their work as well off White women make judgments about the best interests of impoverished minority children (Mulzer & Urs, 2017).

That is all preface to say that given the given these differences between CASA guardians and foster alumni, it is perhaps not surprising that some differences would be seen in their responses. Foster alumni would have direct experience with both being forced to take medications and with struggling with school that are most likely foreign to the average CASA guardian that is using a subjective best interest standard. Likewise, the issue of race in which the demographic differences are distinctly on display are perhaps more salient for participants in the foster alumni group.

These role related results are in keeping with the findings of Britner and Mossler (2002) that found that different child welfare professionals came to different conclusions and emphasized different factors when given the same removal vignette. I discussed their results in detail in Chapter 5, but given the similarities it is worth mentioning here again.

Decision-Making Ecology

Using the framework of the DME to help understand these results we see little influence for the stability related case factors influencing participants final decisions, though this could be a result of the experimental design. Certainly, though, her gender, time in care, age and stability of Morgan have some effect on decision-making as we would expect to see different results for a differently described child.

As this was simply a survey of questions following a vignette it seems unlikely that organizational factors played a significant role in participant decision-making. The survey made it clear that participants in this case were the final decision-makers. External factors also should play little role for the same reason, though it is arguable here that the laws codifying best interests in the participants jurisdictions could be of some influence.

So it seems likely that the participants were mostly making decisions using their own internal factors, which is in keeping with how best interest decisions are made. Because best interest is so dominate in child welfare decision-making it is the default framework that participants would have been familiar with and might reach for.

Since this was just a vignette study, the outcomes of decision-making do not come into play, but if we imagine Morgan as a child in the real world, these small requests might have larger consequences. Though none of the questions specifically reference the big issues of permanency, they each could have repercussions on just that issue. Participating in LGBTQ issues might make Morgan happier and thus improve her mental health. Stopping counseling could do the opposite and affect her stability in her home. Leaving a high school where she is struggling to attend a vocational program could be the start of Morgan's career or it could be a failure and set her education back further.

They are all on their own small issues, but they each carry risk and opportunity that is tied up to the ultimate outcome of the case. From the DME, we know that these outcomes would feed back into future decisions and Fluke et al. (2022) remind us that different stakeholders have different perceptions of what the best decision might be. We see this not only in the ways that different child welfare roles answered the questions, but especially in the large differences in how the groups scored on the Dalgleish Scale.

Limitations

Like all vignette studies, the findings really only tell us how respondents responded to the particular issue presented in the vignette and the question asked. It is impossible to say if any of the responses could be generalized to other settings. It is likely that had the age, gender or circumstances of Morgan changed then the responses would have changed as well. I would expect different answers for a 5-year-old or perhaps even for a boy. Morgan's race was not mentioned in the vignette, so it is unclear if racial perceptions played any part in the participants decision-making.

As mentioned beforehand, the absence of treatment effects could have much to do with the experimental design chosen. A shorter within subjects experiment with a more consistent set of participants could be a better approach to this particular research question. If a better designed survey could be given to child welfare professionals as part of a workforce training event that required more consistent participation, it is possible that some treatment effects regarding normalcy, best interest and stability might be seen.

In its current form, the final model when all of the variables are included has a high risk of multicollinearity. Because I did not detect any treatment effects, this was less of an issue in the final analysis, but any future experiments along this line of inquiry would need to consider this problem. Future research would benefit from using a simpler experimental design with fewer randomized parts.

Conclusion

Though this study failed to show any effects from the best interest and normalcy prompts nor the stability rankings, it did show some intriguing differences in how different roles within child welfare respond and how the internal beliefs about the purpose of child welfare as represented through the Dalgleish Scale have some influence on decision-making as well. To what extent the participants bring their beliefs to a role or if the role shapes their beliefs or a mixture of the two is unknown, but does point us towards the need for further research.

The study also implies that best interest is the default decision-making framework even when it is not explicitly referenced. This is not surprising given the ubiquity of best interest language in child welfare, but it does suggest that if advocates wished to change that relationship, a new legal decision-making framework would need to be spelled out in a way that explicitly rejects or limits best interests. This is something I will try to articulate in Chapter 8.

References

Akin, B. A. (2011). Predictors of foster care exits to permanency: A competing risks analysis of reunification, guardianship, and adoption. *Children and Youth Services Review*, *33*(6), 999–1011. https://doi.org/10.1016/j.childyouth.2011.01.008

Asif, N., Breen, C., & Wells, R. (2024). Influence of placement stability on developmental outcomes of children and young people in out-of-home care: Findings from the pathways of care longitudinal study. *Child Abuse & Neglect*, *149*, 106145. https://doi.org/10.1016/j.chiabu.2023.106145

Augsberger, A., & Swenson, E. (2015). "My worker was there when it really mattered": Foster care youths' perceptions and experiences of their relationships with child welfare workers. *Families in Society*, *96*(4), 234–240. https://doi.org/10.1606/1044-3894.2015.96.34

Britner, P. A., & Mossler, D. G. (2002). Professionals' decision-making about out-of-home placements following instances of child abuse. *Child Abuse & Neglect*, *26*(4), 317–332. https://doi.org/10.1016/S0145-2134(02)00311-3

Caliber Associates. (2004). *Evaluation of CASA representation: Final report.* Retrieved July 3, 2024, from https://www.improvechildrep.org/Portals/0/PDF/Articles,%20Reports,%20CVs,%20etc/Evaluation%20of%20CASA%20Representation_Caliber.pdf

Capacity Building Center for States. (2016). Toolkit to support child welfare agencies in serving LGBTQ children, youth, and families. *The Children's Bureau.* Retrieved July 3, 2024, from https://capacity.childwelfare.gov/states/resources/toolkit-agencies-lgbtq-children-youth-families

CASA of Tarrant County. (2024). *Supporting LGBTQ+ youth in child welfare systems.* Court Appointed Special Advocates for Children. Retrieved July 3, 2024, from https://www.speakupforachild.org/advocate-impact/2024/6/14/supporting-lgbtq-youth-in-child-welfare-systems

Cesario, J. (2014). Priming, replication, and the hardest science. *Perspectives on Psychological Science*, *9*(1), 40–48. https://doi.org/10.1177/1745691613513470

Chapman, M. V., Wall, A., Barth, R. P., Child, N. S. O., & Group, A. W.-B. R. (2004). Children's voices: The perceptions of children in foster care. *American Journal of Orthopsychiatry*, *74*(3), 293–304. https://doi.org/10.1037/0002-9432.74.3.293

Child Welfare Information Gateway. (2021a). *Frequently asked questions from LGBTQ+ prospective foster and adoptive parents.* U.S. Department of Health and Human Services, Administration for Children and Families, Children's Bureau.

Child Welfare Information Gateway. (2021b). *Supporting LGBTQ+ youth: A guide for foster parents.* U.S. Department of Health and Human Services, Administration for Children and Families, Children's Bureau.

Clark, S., Byers, K., Akin, B. A., Dunkerley, S., Wright, K., & McCall, S. (2021). *Child safety and family preservation: Investigating the relationships between tenure, type of employment, and values influencing decision making among child welfare professionals* [Conference session]. 25th Annual Society for Social Work and Research Annual Conference, Social Work Science for Social Change. Retrieved October 25, 2023, from https://socwel.ku.edu/child-safety-and-family-preservation-investigating-relationships-between-tenure-type-employment-and

Cooley, M. E., Thompson, H. M., & Colvin, M. L. (2019). A qualitative examination of recruitment and motivation to become a Guardian ad Litem in the child welfare system. *Children and Youth Services Review*, *99*, 115–124. https://doi.org/10.1016/j.childyouth.2019.01.031

Crane, D., Bailey, E., Doogan, N., Mack, A., Schnitzler, N., Dudsak, A., & Price-Spratlen, T. (2023, August 30). *Ohio CASA evaluation*. Ohio Colleges of Medicine Government Resource Center. Retrieved July 3, 2024, from https://ohiocasa.org/wp-content/uploads/2023/10/CASA-Evaluation-Final-Report-8-31-23.pdf

Dalgleish, L. (2010). *Balance of work focus in child welfare*. Unpublished manuscript.

Engler, A. D., Sarpong, K. O., Van Horne, B. S., Greeley, C. S., & Keefe, R. J. (2022). A systematic review of mental health disorders of children in foster care. *Trauma, Violence, & Abuse*, *23*(1), 255–264. https://doi.org/10.1177/1524838020941197

Fish, J. N., Baams, L., Wojciak, A. S., & Russell, S. T. (2019). Are sexual minority youth overrepresented in foster care, child welfare, and out-of-home placement? Findings from nationally representative data. *Child Abuse Neglect*, *89*, 203–211. https://doi.org/10.1016/j.chiabu.2019.01.005

Fluke, J. D., Bauman, D. J., Dalgleish, L. I., & Kern, H. D. (2022). Decisions to protect children: A decision-making ecology. In R. D. Krugman & J. E. Korbin (Eds.), *Handbook of child maltreatment* (pp. 611–626). Springer International Publishing. https://doi.org/10.1007/978-3-030-82479-2_31

Fluke, J. D., Corwin, T. W., Hollinshead, D. M., & Maher, E. J. (2016). Family preservation or child safety? Associations between child welfare workers' experience, position, and perspectives. *Children and Youth Services Review*, *69*, 210–218. https://doi.org/10.1016/j.childyouth.2016.08.012

Hambrick, E. P., Oppenheim-Weller, S., N'zi, A. M., & Taussig, H. N. (2016). Mental health interventions for children in foster care: A systematic review. *Children and Youth Services Review*, *70*, 65–77. https://doi.org/10.1016/j.childyouth.2016.09.002

Kaasbøll, J., Pedersen, S. A., & Paulsen, V. (2022). What is known about the LGBTQ perspective in child welfare services: A scoping review. *Child & Family Social Work*, *27*(2), 358–369. https://doi.org/10.1111/cfs.12894

Keddell, E., & Hyslop, I. (2018). Role type, risk perceptions and judgements in child welfare: A mixed methods vignette study. *Children and Youth Services Review*, *87*, 130–139. https://doi.org/10.1016/j.childyouth.2018.02.017

Kirby, K. (1997). Foster parent demographics: A research note. *The Journal of Sociology & Social Welfare*, *24*(2), Article 10. https://doi.org/10.15453/0191-5096.2421; https://scholarworks.wmich.edu/jssw/vol24/iss2/10

Konijn, C., Admiraal, S., Baart, J., van Rooij, F., Stams, G.-J., Colonnesi, C., Lindauer, R., & Assink, M. (2019). Foster care placement instability: A meta-analytic review. *Children and Youth Services Review*, *96*, 483–499. https://doi.org/10.1016/j.childyouth.2018.12.002

Leathers, S. J., Atkins, M. S., Spielfogel, J. E., McMeel, L. S., Wesley, J. M., & Davis, R. (2009). Context specific mental health services for children in foster care. *Child Youth Services Review*, *31*(12), 1289–1297. https://doi.org/10.1016/j.childyouth.2009.05.016

Lee, S. W. S. (2021). "Social priming" through the lens of sociology of science: Fuzzy boundary, personal experience, and broader atmosphere. *Psychological Inquiry*, *32*(1), 41–44. https://doi.org/10.1080/1047840X.2021.1889842

Liming, K. W., Akin, B., & Brook, J. (2021). Adverse childhood experiences and foster care placement stability. *Pediatrics*, *148*(6). https://doi.org/10.1542/peds.2021-052700

Maguire, D., May, K., McCormack, D., & Fosker, T. (2024). A systematic review of the impact of placement instability on emotional and behavioural outcomes among children in foster care. *Journal of Child & Adolescent Trauma*, *17*(2), 641–655. https://doi.org/10.1007/s40653-023-00606-1

Middel, F., Fluke, J., & Hahn, A. (2024). *The effect of child protection attitudes on child protection decision-making: The mediating role of stereotypes* [Manuscript in Preparation, University of Groningen].

Middel, F., López, M., Fluke, J., & Grietens, H. (2022). Racial/ethnic and gender disparities in child protection decision-making: What role do stereotypes play? *Child Abuse & Neglect*, *127*, 105579. https://doi.org/10.1016/j.chiabu.2022.105579

Mulzer, A., & Urs, T. (2017, March). However kindly intentioned: structural racism and volunteer CASA programs. *CUNY Law Review*, *20*, 23. https://ssrn.com/abstract=2924920

Osborne, C., Warner-Doe, H., & Lawson, J. (2019). Who gets a CASA? Selective characteristics of children appointed a CASA advocate. *Children and Youth Services Review*, *98*, 65–71. https://doi.org/10.1016/j.childyouth.2018.12.020

Osborne, C., Warner-Doe, H., LeClear, M., & Sexton, H. (2020). The effect of CASA on child welfare permanency outcomes. *Child Maltreatment*, *25*(3), 328–338. https://doi.org/10.1177/1077559519879510

Rubin, D. M., O'Reilly, A. L., Luan, X., & Localio, A. R. (2007). The impact of placement stability on behavioral well-being for children in foster care. *Pediatrics*, *119*(2), 336–344. https://doi.org/10.1542/peds.2006-1995

Salsberg, E., Quigley, L., Richwine, C., Sliwa, S., Acquaviva, K., & Wyche, K. (2020). The social work profession: Findings from three years of surveys of new social workers. A report to the Council on Social Work Education and the National Association of Social Workers, Fitzhugh Mullan Institute for Health Workforce Equity. Retrieved October 16, 2023, from https://www.cswe.org/CSWE/media/Workforce-Study/The-Social-Work-Profession-Findings-from-Three-Years-of-Surveys-of-New-Social-Workers-Dec-2020.pdf

Sherman, J. W., & Rivers, A. M. (2021). There's nothing social about social priming: Derailing the "train wreck". *Psychological Inquiry*, *32*(1), 1–11. https://doi.org/10.1080/1047840X.2021.1889312

Stenason, L., & Romano, E. (2023). Number of placement changes among young people in care: Youth and caregiver associations. *Children and Youth Services Review*, *144*, 106737. https://doi.org/10.1016/j.childyouth.2022.106737

Stokes, J., & Schmidt, G. (2012). Child protection decision making: A factorial analysis using case vignettes. *Social Work*, *57*(1), 83–90. http://www.jstor.org/stable/2371995

Stott, T., & Gustavsson, N. (2010). Balancing permanency and stability for youth in foster care. *Children and Youth Services Review*, *32*(4), 619–625. https://doi.org/10.1016/j.childyouth.2009.12.009

Szilagyi, M. A., Rosen, D. S., Rubin, D., Zlotnik, S., Szilagyi, M., Harmon, D., Jaudes, P., Jones, V. F., Lee, P., Nalven, L., Prock, L., Sagor, L., Schulte, E., Springer, S., Tonniges, T., Braverman, P. K., Adelman, W. P., Alderman, E. M., Breuner, C. C., . . . Williams, P. G. (2015). Health care issues for children and adolescents in foster care and kinship care. *Pediatrics*, *136*(4), e1131–e1140. https://doi.org/10.1542/peds.2015-2655

Taylor, B. J. (2005). Factorial surveys: Using vignettes to study professional judgement. *The British Journal of Social Work*, *36*(7), 1187–1207. https://doi.org/10.1093/bjsw/bch345

Trail, M. (2024). Dalgleish scores difference amongst professional roles within the greater child welfare community. *Child Protection and Practice*, *2*, 100047. https://doi.org/10.1016/j.chipro.2024.100047

8 Normalcy Charter

Recall if you will late April 2020, a month or so into the first COVID lockdown. All of the myriad activities that once constituted a full life were constrained and restricted. Multiple stories began to appear in media and journals at the time about the collective loss of normalcy and its effects on our mental health (Berinato, 2020; Jones, 2020) with many authors connecting the loss with feelings of actual grief (Micsky, 2020; Walsh, 2020; Weir, 2020).

> The loss of a sense of normalcy is widespread. Life as we have known it has been derailed. Life forward is on hold, the future uncertain, and the road ahead unclear. There is much talk about the "old normal" and the "new normal." Yet, like the aftershocks of an earthquake, the ground keeps shifting, and nothing feels normal.
>
> (Walsh, 2020, p. 901)

There was so much discussion about returning to normal, the UK based magazine The Economist (2021) began a "normalcy index" to track how 50 nations around the world were slowly returning to pre-pandemic life using measures, such as retail activity, public transportation usage, sports attendance, going to the cinema and taking flights.

Since the end of the pandemic, researchers have tried to pin down the effects of the loss of normalcy on the population. Some research has found that mental health disorders increased for adults worldwide (Pedrosa et al., 2020; Penninx et al., 2022; Kupcova et al., 2023) and that lockdown in the US led to an increased usage of psychiatric facilities (Ferwana & Varshney, 2024) and a drastically increased rate of substance abuse (Abramson, 2021; Conway et al., 2022; Roberts et al., 2021).

Likewise, children and youth dealt with their own impacts from the lockdown. Children reported higher rates of anxiety depression, mental illness and emotional disorders (Anand et al., 2024; Luiten et al., 2021; Panchal et al., 2023; Pustake et al., 2022) and these effects were especially felt by children with preexisting mental health or developmental disorders (Lopez-Serrano et al., 2023).

The effects on children's education were even more severe. In the US, Kuhfeld et al. (2022) examined 5.4 million students and tracked their test scores

DOI: 10.4324/9781003510253-8

throughout the three years of the pandemic. They found large drops in both reading and math scores and that these drops were more pronounced for children from poor households. In another analysis, Dorn et al. (2021) found that children lost at least five months of math and four months of reading. A systematic review and meta-analysis by Betthäuser et al. (2023) demonstrated that this educational loss was found in children from nations around the world and that the income gap between children from wealthy and poorer families was also routinely observed.

While the death, sickness and fear of infection are certainly unique to the pandemic and cannot be directly compared, I hope the parallel I am drawing about the lockdown experience is clear at this point. The entire population of the planet got to experience what the loss of normalcy can do to our mental health and stability. The small things that we considered our normal lives were gone and many of us struggled greatly to cope. We grieved and we raged both individually and collectively about the loss small things like trips to the store or spending time with friends. Now take that memory of the loss of normalcy and apply it to children in care, especially those in RTCs and other restricted environments. For some, every day is April 2020. The loss of normalcy is not small things, because all those small things are life.

Alternatives to Best Interest

If it is not abundantly clear already, I believe best interest as a legal decision-making framework is a terrible, horrible, no good, very bad idea. Normalcy as it is currently understood is a better place to start, but also does not quite get us to a place where we really value the child and their wishes. Before I get to my proposal, there are three more concepts that I need to discuss as I will be incorporating some of their ideas into my Normalcy Charter.

Least Detrimental Alternative

In 1973 Goldstein, Freud and Solnit produced the first of what would eventually be three volumes outlining their concerns with the current state of best interest decision-making in the US child welfare system. The authors argued that the focus of all child welfare should be on the child's developmental needs and that these needs could best be met by what they referred to as the psychological parent, the adult to which the child was most strongly attached. They argued that children in most cases should not be removed from their parents because they would suffer harm and that best interest of the child had been subsumed to truly mean the competing interest of adults (Goldstein et al., 1973).

Goldstein et al. (1973) therefore argued for the creation of a new standard "the least detrimental alternative for safeguarding the child's growth and development" which they defined as

> that specific placement and procedure for placement which maximizes, in accordance with the child's sense of time and on the basis of short term

> predictions given the limitations of knowledge, his or her opportunity for being wanted and for maintain on a continuous basis a relationship with at least one adult who is or will become his psychological parent.
> (p.53)

The authors were especially concerned with the time element that so often delays resolution of a case and they believed that returning children to a stable placement should be a matter of utmost urgency with the goal of days instead of weeks or months (Goldstein et al., 1973). They wrote that the term itself with the word detrimental in the title would be a reminder to decision-makers that the children in dispute have already been harmed in some way. The decision-makers must make tough choices about the "available alternatives" to remind them that their choices are limited and subject to uncertainty.

> It should reduce the likelihood of their becoming enmeshed in the hope and magic associated with "best", which often mistakenly leads them into believing that they have greater power for doing "good" than "bad".
> (p. 63)

Between the time of its first publication and through parts of the 1990s, the least detrimental alternative, was widely discussed and influential in US child welfare legal circles (Batt, 1992; Taub, 1984; Spinak, 2007) and even some courts wrote the standard into their decisions (McKeown, 1992). However, the book's influenced waned and few people today reference least detrimental alternative in their decision-making.

Like Mnookin's criticism of best interest discussed at length in Chapter 3, it is heartening to see that scholars more than 50 years ago already identified fundamental flaws in best interest, but it is depressing to know that all of those flaws continue to exist and best interest language is now global. Still, the principles of the least detrimental alternative remain as needed as ever. It forces decision-makers to recognize their own capacity for causing harm to children in care and does away with the notion that there is some best decision. There is often only a less bad one. It embraces uncertainty and risk and places the child's needs at the center. It is a good start.

Autonomy Principle

A final alternative to traditional best interest decision-making comes from Daly (2017) who conceived of the children's autonomy principle, which emphasized the idea that all humans should have as much say in their lives as possible. Daly (2017) defined the concept thusly,

> In legal decisions in which the best interest of the child is the primary consideration, children should get to choose – if they wish – how they

> are involves (process autonomy) and the outcome (outcome autonomy) unless it is likely that significant harm will arise from their wishes.
>
> (p.10)

Daly's (2017) position is that the right to be heard in Article 12 of the CRC is vague and that best interest hearings force relationships and outcomes onto children that they do not want and can be harmed by. In order to make sure that children have autonomy in court proceedings, they should also be provided with "autonomy support" in the form of an impartial adult that can help them express themselves and make decisions.

Daly (2017) argued that court proceedings that decide the inner aspects of the lives of children are special places where the fundamentals of their lives are at stake.

> It is the element of state interference which is the key driver of the children's autonomy principle which I am proposing. The court may think that it is taking the place of the parent in the best interest decisions, but it is not. Unlike parents, courts have the force of law behind them.
>
> (p.12)

The language of autonomy also invokes a more active participant, someone with actual stakes in the decision-making. Though the CRC envisions more than simply being listened to, the language of the right to be heard in contrast is passive (Daly, 2017).

Though Daly (2017) does not completely reject the CRC's ideal of best interest, she does argue that as it is commonly applied it is little more than substitute judgment. Even the text of the CRC, which requires courts to weigh children's views essentially adds another subjective layer onto the best interest determination.

Continuing on, Daly (2017) wrote that in other areas of law that involve people with disabilities, there are strict legal hurdles that must be overcome before the government will take decision-making power away from them. Yet for children, the default stance is that they cannot make decisions and that they merely have the right to be heard (Daly, 2017).

The connection between children's rights and disability rights is especially interesting. In US disability law, there has been a growing push over the last couple of decades to reduce court appointed guardianships, which effectively strip a person of their rights and allow a guardian to make decisions on behalf of an adult with disabilities. Instead, a model called supportive decision-making has been encouraged. This modifiable legal agreement allows adults with disabilities to appoint a person or people that they trust to help with decision-making, while they themselves still retain all of their legal rights. This is a similar idea to Daly's supportive autonomy for children.

I believe Daly is also correct in emphasizing the special nature of children and courts being different than everyday scenarios. Courts have the power to make life altering decisions on behalf of children. The government is directly intervening in their lives in ways that can be demonstrably harmful to them and yet, they are often denied their due process rights in the name of best interest. They are the only subset of the population to be subjected to this standard.

Neurodevelopment

It is undeniable that children have different cognitive and developmental capacities than adults and this underlines why the law treats them differently. In the Center for Law, Brain & Behavior at Massachusetts General Hospital's guide for attorneys and courts, Insel et al. (2022) note that brain development continues into our early to mid-twenties and that there are differences in decision-making even between 18-year-olds and 22-year-olds. So our idea of adulthood is also hazy.

Research shows that teenagers tend to be much more prone to impulsive behavior and risk taking than adults even with life threatening risks like dangerous driving (Insel et al., 2022). By the age of 16, youth generally have the cognitive capacities to make reasoned decisions similarly to adults, but they still have impulse control issues related to their emotional regulation (Icenogle et al., 2019; Insel et al., 2022). They are less future oriented, with a present focus and worse at delaying gratification (Icenogle et al., 2019; Insel et al., 2022).

Though brains are malleable throughout our lives, Brown and Ward (2013) note that stressful times during child and adolescent development can have negative effects on the brain. This can include both maltreatment or neglect at home or the instability and trauma of removal (Brown & Ward, 2013).

As noted in Chapter 5, at least in the context of health care decision-making, some researchers have suggested that 12-year-olds have capacity to make decisions regarding health issues affecting their lives, though this should be accompanied by adult support (Grootens-Wiegers et al., 2017).

So from a neurodevelopment side, it seems that youth and certainly older youth have the capacity to be informed and make decisions. It also seems likely that even older youth would benefit from adult support in the decision-making process. This is in keeping with Daly's recommendation that children have supportive autonomy. Now if only there was a profession whose job included counseling clients about important decisions involving the court system and making sure that their position is advocated before the bench.

The Problem

Before moving into my suggestions for how we might make a better, more child rights and participation-based child welfare system, let's recap briefly the lessons from the last chapters to see how we got here.

We know there are millions of children in care around the world and we know that their outcomes are often poor across multiple measures of health, mental health, education, poverty, criminal activity, homelessness and career, especially those that that spend time in RTCs and those that age out of system. We know that they are harmed not only by the possible maltreatment they experienced in their home, but also by the removal and subsequent instability of foster care. We also know that the child welfare system disproportionately affects poor families and minority families,

The child welfare system itself operates on a best interest framework that is embedded in the CRC. However, decades worth of scholars and researchers and I have argued that this framework is deeply flawed, that it is entirely subjective, biased, indeterminate, inconsistent and that it strips away the rights of children in favor of adult expediency. It is a relic of centuries worth of jurisprudence that overlap with a time that only adult males were thought of to have any real family rights.

It also allows and perhaps even encourages a risk aversion that runs through child welfare practice in multiple countries. This risk aversion further limits the rights of children by prioritizing physical safety above all else. This is not only harmful for children but also creates a damaging work culture for child welfare professionals that punishes them for mistakes and drives many out of the field.

We also know that decision-making in child welfare is extremely complex and involves not only case factors but also organizational factors and internal beliefs of the decision-maker. The result is that any two caseworkers, or foster parents or even judges might come to very different results based on the same case. My research, though just preliminary, hints that different positions within the child welfare field also have different levels of support for the core beliefs about the purpose of the foster care system and they come to different conclusions about issues related to child participation.

In some contrast to best interest, we have a child rights and child participation-based approach. However, beyond the generally agreed upon right to be heard found within the CRC, there are significant disagreements about what constitutes participation, what age do rights begin and what even is a child in the first place.

Complicating the decision-making process is the fact that a child's rights vary from jurisdiction to jurisdiction. This is somewhat understandable between different nations, but even between states these rights fluctuate. The right to participate is only as strong as the belief of the judge hearing the case. Best interest allows all of this as individual decision-makers can contort best interest to align with whatever outcome they please.

Though not envisioned to compete with best interest, the recent legal framework of normalcy is about letting children and youth in care have normal lives. It is about empowering adult decision-makers to allow children more participation and more say in their daily lives. It is premised on the understanding that risk is an inherent part of growing up and simply being alive. It also comes with liability protection embedded which allows caregivers the ability make a riskier decision.

Because it also has best interest embedded within its legal structure, normalcy alone is not the sole answer as the arbitrary risk averse best interest seems to permeate even normalcy decisions. This is means that we need to go further.

Isiah a 14-year boy had been in care for eight years. His parents' rights were terminated, but because his mom made efforts on her case plan the final termination was delayed multiple times so Isiah had only been a permanent ward of the state for about half that time. He was a big kid for his age and looked older. He liked cars and wrestling. He had serious behavioral issues that made him quick to anger. He got in lots of fights, had stayed multiple times in the youth psychiatric hospital and had spent a few months in a juvenile detention facility. He had been bounced around to more than two dozen placements. He was years behind in school as every new placement meant a new school and often, he was schooled in RTCs or at alternative learning centers. His disabilities were never accommodated by the various school districts because they never had him long enough to properly assess him. He wanted to live with his grandmother, but CPS was worried given his behavior that she would not be able to manage him, so he continued his journey from one RTC to the next. He wanted to take auto mechanic classes when he started high school, but he was moved to a different school district that did not have the program.

The Normalcy Charter

Over the rest of this chapter, I will lay out what I believe is necessary to truly allow children in the child welfare system to fully participate and to experience something closer to a normal life. I am calling it the Normalcy Charter, but it encompasses more than normalcy as it is currently practiced. It entails a great number of changes to how we envision and practice child welfare, but nothing that I am suggesting would need to be created from whole cloth as better scholars than me have already given us the building blocks.

The Normalcy Charter would consist of the following elements,

1. Clearly delineated and defined enforceable rights for children in the care system including rights related to normalcy and participation.
2. Direct representation by an attorney for all children in care for every stage of the dependency process.
3. When required the substitute judgment standard will be applied instead of best interest.
4. Risk tolerance built into the formulation of rights.

Rights

Children in general, but foster children especially need to have spelled out rights beyond the broad but vague ones laid out in the CRC. The foster children bill of rights found in many states are a good place to start. These rights must be explicit and spelled out to prevent them from being subsumed by risk averse best interest decisions. The rights must also be specifically enforceable in court.

Aspirational documents or even rights laid out in administrative rules do not allow children to formally complain when their rights are violated. As I have written throughout this book, courts are the ultimate and final decision-makers in child welfare. They are far from perfect and subject to any number of biases themselves, but they are the only place where government agencies can be held accountable. The judge is the only person in the child welfare system that can force CPS to take or refrain from an action. Foster youth need the ability to hold accountable the government agency that controls every aspect of their lives.

Ideally, foster youth and care experienced adults would be heavily involved in the creation and drafting of these rights along with social work experts and children's rights attorneys. Youth Advisory Boards and the National Foster Care Youth & Alumni Policy Council would be good places in the US to recruit members. Similar care experienced groups in other nations should be used for local input.

Though I am certain others could conceive of different and perhaps better lists, I will outline what I factors I believe should at minimum be included.

1. All rights are enforceable by the dependency court hearing the case and can be appealed. As parents have the right to appeal removal and termination decisions, it seems only appropriate that children, who are the center of the case, should also have that right. The dependency court is appropriate for this as well as it is the one already handling the case.
2. Children rights are not to be abrogated based on the best interest of the child. I fear that even if a tiny window was open to the idea that these rights could or should be balanced against the child's best interest, then best interest will be used to deny children's rights. I do believe there is a safety exception that can be made, but I will discuss it in another section below.
3. All foster children should have the right to be represented by an independent attorney, in a direct capacity. As every other party to the case has an independent attorney, this should also be provided for children.
4. Children have a right to normalcy. For this right, I would include the entirety of the NEYC Normalcy Bill of Rights that I discussed in Chapter 3 as these basically lay out all of the important aspects of normalcy as identified by current foster youth.
5. Children have a right to the least restrictive placement setting available and RTCs should be highly disfavored. In a better world, there would be far fewer RTCs and they would be the actual treatment centers that their name suggests, but too often now they are used because they are the only places with an open placement.
6. Children's behavior should not be used against them to restrict their rights. Too often traumatized children with diagnosed behavioral disorders are

restricted from normal life activities and from better placements and told that they must behave better to earn a better life all the while being provided by CPS with the bare minimum of substandard behavioral and mental health services.

7. Children should be allowed to have personal possessions and private places for their possessions. Children are often moved from placement to placement with just a plastic bag filled with clothes. Sometimes even those are left behind.
8. Children should have the right to participate in all hearings on their case and speak to the judge in private if they chose. Though all the adults are loath to remove a child from school, missing a few days a year of class is less important that children missing a hearing where their future is determined.
9. Children should have the right to consent to the medications or health treatment they are prescribed and consult with another physician for a second opinion. Bodily autonomy exists for children as well as adults and being forced onto unwanted medications after questionable diagnosis is a violation of children's bodies.
10. Children should have the right to refuse or request counseling or other mental health and behavioral services. While we would prefer that child be able to talk through their issues, children cannot choose their own counselors or even the type of counseling they are prescribed. It should be available, but not forced onto anyone.
11. Children should have the right to participate in all of their case planning and service planning meetings if they chose. Like the courts, these meeting are when CPS makes important decisions about the life of the child and children should have a say.
12. Children should have the right to obtain current copies of all of their case records. Other parties on the case have a right to records and a child's attorney even in a guardian capacity would have the right of access. This should include medical records as I have had many clients completely unaware of their case history or medical diagnosis.
13. Children should have the right to visit with their siblings if they are placed apart and all siblings agree or the court orders otherwise. Siblings are often separated because of placement restrictions, such as a foster home only takes in one gender or one age range and busy CPS worker schedules make arranging visits complicated.
14. Children should have the right to be free from discrimination based on their ethnicity, culture, sexual or gender identity or religious beliefs. Given the disproportionality of children in care, allowing them a safe space to express who they are is a necessity.
15. Children should have the right to an education in a traditional public school with a trained, certified teacher. Children being educated at an RTC facility or being taught online will be presumed to be in violation of this right. Too many children in care are denied the opportunity to attend

a regular school with their peers because their placement restrictions make it easier for adults to watch them in the RTC setting.

16. Children should have the right to private communication with other people so long as this does not violate a court order. This is related to their right to have private relationships with people they choose.
17. Children should have the right to reasonable freedom of movement and should not be locked in facilities or rooms. We generally think of people being locked away as prisoners, yet youth can be locked away for the crime of being removed from their parents and exhibiting symptoms of trauma.
18. Children should be made aware of these rights by CPS, the court and their attorney. All the parties to the case should be instructed to make sure that children know their rights, and this should be told to children in an age-appropriate manner.

Again, this is just a start. Many of these rights already exist in certain locations under a hodgepodge of laws from the federal level down to local policy guidance. This hodgepodge status, though, means that there is no clear statement of all of the rights that children in care can or should possess. The children I represented in the specialized child protection courts had many of these rights because the judges demanded them, but the children across the street in the traditional family law courts had fewer because the judges did not. Likely there are other rights that should be included, but at minimum, this would go a long way towards ensuring normalcy and participation.

Participation

Many of the rights I describe above as well as the ones listed in the NEYC Normalcy Bill of Rights come down to children being able to participate in their own lives and this participation is more than just adults giving them time to express their opinions.

Using the Lundy Model (2007) as our guide, with actual enforceable rights in place, Space, Voice, Audience and Influence are easier to achieve. To begin with, the rights above guarantee space for children to participate, space not only in CPS planning meetings, but more importantly in the court setting. The formalized space of court means that children have the same opportunity as the adult parties to present their arguments, wishes and preferred outcomes. Rights also guarantee the equally important space in the community and home, where the majority of normalcy decisions are made.

A rights-based approach also ensures that children have a voice. I believe that children empowered by rights and with the assistance of adult legal counsel will be in a better position to express their wishes and make complaints when their rights have been violated. Fear of court intervention would likely motivate CPS workers to better seek out children's opinions. Older youth might be able to express themselves without any adult assistance, but trusted legal counsel can make certain that younger children or less confident ones also have their voices heard.

Likewise, rights guarantee an audience. Case planning meetings generally require multiple parties to be present so that a comprehensive plan can be developed. Of course, courts provide the same with the added bonus that the judge has true decision-making power. However, as Lundy (2007) noted the audience often requires special training to engage appropriately with children, which is more of a workforce policy development issue and cannot be guaranteed by rights alone.

Finally, influence is where a rights-based approach perhaps performs the best. Enforceable, appealable rights means that children's views have to be an integral part of all decision-making processes. Court opinions and orders would actually reference children's rights as they already do for the rights of adults.

Daly's (2017) autonomy principle also comes into play here in the court setting. Children's rights would essentially force courts to start their deliberations from a rights-based perspective that emphasizes autonomy rather than best interest. Additionally, the idea of supportive autonomy that I argue should be from direct attorney representation, means that a trained advocate is always available to ensure that rights are protected.

Risk Tolerance

One of the best parts of normalcy is the acknowledgment that not all activities that children do are risk free. Nothing that any of us do is actually risk free and we all hover somewhere between strength and vulnerability our whole lives. Still, for an organization that often has the words "child protection" in their title, it is a heavy lift to suggest that too much safety might be detrimental to children as well.

Even with normalcy rules in place, we know that there are lots of barriers to children that prevent them from participating. Some of these are logistical, but many come from a sense of risk aversion that plagues CPS decision-making.

I believe a children's rights-based normalcy would go a long way to developing a more risk tolerant child welfare system. For one, enforceable rights means that there are fewer scenarios that CPS workers and foster parents can say no. Denying participation is easy when it is ultimately just another type of best interest decision. Even with liability protection built into normalcy, the safest choice that poses the least risk of physical harm to a child is to say no. Foster parent license and CPS worker careers are at stake if something happens to a child under their watch.

By taking best interest out of the decision-making process and focusing on the enforcement of rights, much of the decision-making wiggle room is taken away. Though we obviously want child welfare professionals to have discretion when they make decisions, given the risk averse organizational constraints that the face currently, it seems their discretion is already quite limited. The punishment, blame and often media attention that accompany any CPS mistake means that CPS workers and foster parents are pilloried and second guessed for any perceived errors.

Rights force child welfare workers into a more risk tolerant stance by default. Denying a child's right that can be taken directly to the court hearing the case is more difficult than denying a request.

Not only would a rights-based, risk tolerant system be good for the children in care, but it would also benefit CPS and other child welfare professionals. Risk aversion and a culture of blame have really negative consequences for the child welfare workforce regarding job turnover and work satisfaction. Good workers are pushed out and decisions transform into what is best for the agency not the child.

Because children's rights carry risks, CPS workers could potentially operate in a system that does not punish every mistake and does not create a culture of fear. This might help CPS agencies to retain happier employees.

Legal Representation

Foster children in dependency hearings should have the right to direct legal representation just like all of the other parties to the case. This seems like it should be a common sense statement, but as discussed in prior chapters, it is surprisingly controversial.

Biological parents are entitled to representation because they have significant due process interest related to their parental rights. Courts take these rights so seriously that they on occasion can borderline into farcical. I have attended hearings involving children from multiple fathers and presumptive fathers. Sometimes attorneys represented men whose names we were not certain were correct, who may not have even been the father of one of the children and who were never located throughout the proceedings. The attorneys often had very little work to do in the case, but their clients' rights were protected. Certainly, if an unknown presumptive father requires attorney representation to protect his rights, the child in which the entire case revolves might also have rights.

Recall that the US Supreme Court, In re Gault (1967) case that established that juvenile defendants in juvenile justice proceeding are required to be represented by legal counsel and the right to cross examine witnesses. This is a constitutional right guaranteed by the 14th Amendment. The court wrote,

> Due process of law is the primary and indispensable foundation of individual freedom. It is the basic and essential term in the social compact which defines the rights of the individual and delimits the powers which the state may exercise.
>
> *In re Gault*, 387 US 1, 20 (1967)

Due process for a child in dependency, thus requires legal representation because it is a hearing involving state power and affects the fundamental individual rights of a child.

There are other parallels found in the *In re Gault* decision that can be drawn with foster care. The court in discussion of sentencing wrote,

> A boy is charged with misconduct. The boy is committed to an institution where he may be restrained of liberty for years. It is of no constitutional consequence – and of limited practical meaning – that the institution to which he is committed is called an Industrial School. The fact of the matter is that, however euphemistic the title, a "receiving home" or an "industrial school" for juveniles is an institution of confinement in which the child is incarcerated for a greater or lesser time. His world becomes "a building with whitewashed walls, regimented routine and institutional hours . . . ." Instead of mother and father and sisters and brothers and friends and classmates, his world is peopled by guards, custodians, state employees.
>
> *In re Gault*, 387 US 1, 27 (1967)

This exact same scenario happens in the child welfare system. Children for reasons completely beyond their control, can be taken from family and placed sometimes hundreds of miles away or even taken out of state. They can be placed in RTCs or state hospitals surrounded by barbed wire fence. They are not free to leave the facility. They are not free to even attend a public school in some cases. They are not free to invite friends back to their rooms. They are not free to make phone calls to anyone beyond their caseworker. They are simply not free in any conceivable way. Sometimes they are placed in a facility because of their behaviors, but sometimes they are placed there because there are simply not enough foster homes.

Though the *In re Gault* court only briefly mentioned best interest in their historical analysis, the court did discuss at length "*parens patriae*", the notion of the state intervening as a parent would on behalf of protecting a child. The court noted that under the doctrine, a child did not have liberty rights and ultimately rejected this idea because paternalistic ideas of protecting children did not comply with due process guarantees of the 14th Amendment. The court wrote,

> In view of this, it would be extraordinary if our Constitution did not require the procedural regularity and the exercise of care implied in the phrase "due process." Under our Constitution, the condition of being a boy does not justify a kangaroo court.
>
> *In re Gault*, 387 US 1, 27–28 (1967)

The reasoning of *In re Gault* logically continues into the dependency court. Best interest and the child safety, risk aversion built into it acts essentially the same as *parens patriae*. It strips rights from children on the grounds that a wise adult will do what is best for the child's safety.

Direct Representation

I believe the rights of children not only require legal representation throughout the entirety of the dependency process, but this must come in the form of direct representation. Children's rights cannot be guaranteed under a best interest model of representation. There are too many ways in which best interest can thwart the actual interest of a child client for it to be appropriate.

Best interest representation can put attorneys at odds with their clients. In any other attorney/client relationship this would be grounds for the attorney to withdraw and the client to find new representation. Imagine if attorneys in other areas advocated for legal positions based solely on what they thought was best for their client; criminal defendants pled guilty by their attorney who thinks some time in prison would set them straight, divorce pleadings dismissed because the attorney thinks the couple should work it out, wills ignored because the attorney believes the distribution was not fair, or contracts changed because the attorney thinks the business should order more widgets. The entire notion is absurd for every other type of legal representation, yet for children somehow this is allowed.

The paternalism baked into best interest representation is made all the more ridiculous when we think for a bit about the legal positions that adult clients take. Adults come to attorneys wanting a myriad of remedies that are often legally impossible or so difficult, costly and unlikely to achieve that they may as well be impossible. One of the primary jobs of an attorney is to counsel clients about their options, what the law allows and what a court is likely to do. Talking clients out of rash or unwise decisions is an integral part of the job and applies to adult and child clients equally.

I have counseled adults in divorce proceedings that the visitation schedule they want will not be approved by the court no matter how much they hate their soon to be ex-spouse and I have counseled foster children that the court is not going to approve of them leaving their foster home to move in with their paramour. It is simply part of the job.

The best interest representational model is premised like all of best interest on the vulnerability and reduced capacity of children. However, as discussed in Chapter 6, depending on the law, the context and the jurisdiction society has extremely divergent beliefs on what children are capable of, from the age they can work, to the age they can consent to sex, to the age they can commit an adult crime.

As noted in Chapter 1, there is a large overlap between foster youth and juvenile delinquency and these children are often referred to as dual status. It is not a stretch to say that their dependency cases and their delinquency cases are often intertwined, enough so that some jurisdictions have special dual status courts just for this population. Still under a best interest model, there are places where children have one lawyer representing them in delinquency as direct representation while perhaps across the hallway their dependency attorney only acts in their best interests.

As Mnookin (1973) pointed out more than 50 years ago, attorneys are neither trained nor qualified to act in a client's best interest. It is a direct conflict with the rights of our clients.

I acknowledge that direct representation of children can come with challenges and is not possible in all circumstances. I have been appointed to represent, infants, toddlers and children with disabilities that severely limited their ability to communicate. Under these scenarios, attorneys should use the substitute judgment model promoted by the National Association of Children Counsel. Substitute judgment recall is not best interest, though I will admit that the distinction can be subtle at times and there are overlaps.

Substitute judgment asks that the attorney represent the child client in a manner that puts them into the position of imagining what the client would want if they could express it themselves. Though like all human decision-making it will be imperfect and subject to biases and heuristics, it at least puts the attorney into the child's mind rather than have them dictate decisions from the outside.

When to invoke substitute judgment would be somewhat an individual case matter. As I discussed earlier, the law envisions 12-year-olds with the capability to consent in many ways, such as crime and sex. Some neuroscience also suggest that this age is appropriate for making informed health decisions. So at the absolute minimum, children 12 and older should be presumed to have direct representation.

I would argue, though, that perhaps there should be no age minimum for direct representation. Many young children can express which home they prefer, what activities they enjoy, what teacher they want, what scares them and which people they want to live with. These simple questions are often enough to direct representation on the more fundamental issues of a case. It is also possible that children will be able to direct representation on some issues but not others so an attorney might sometimes use substitute judgment and sometimes direct representation. Direct representation needs to be the default position, though, to guarantee children's rights.

The Role of the Court

One of the most common and perhaps understandable criticisms of a rights-based approach with direct attorneys' representation is that it could endanger the child. I would argue this comes from the same deep risk aversion that plagues all of child welfare, but it is worth addressing as no one wants a child to be hurt.

The argument usually starts with the idea that if children have rights and zealous attorneys helping them enforce those rights then they might take positions that put themselves in danger, such as demanding to stay with an unsafe relative or leaving a treatment program before they are ready. There is a deep-seated fear that foster youth with lawyers will wreck the protections inherent in the child welfare system. Best interest is the only legal doctrine that allows us to keep children safe.

Putting aside the data that I discussed in Chapter 1–4 that suggest that children's well-being is not particularly well served by the current child welfare system, this belief is erroneous in that it also ignores the role of the court. Attorneys make arguments but courts make decisions.

I worked under a direct representational model and often took legal positions on behalf of my clients that I did not always agree with and which I did not expect to prevail on in court. On occasion I would be surprised and the judge would go along with my argument regardless, but I was never the only attorney in the room. CPS was always represented and often a parent's attorney or a CASA volunteer were part of the hearing. The point being that there are always other adults with other positions available to make an argument against a child's position. A child having rights and an attorney does not mean that they win every hearing and get everything they want. This is how almost all hearings in every other court in almost every other area of law work.

A criminal defense attorney might best the prosecution and a guilty person returns to the street. A lawyer might persuade a court that a business owner was within their rights to terminate a person with a disability. An attorney might convince a jury that a negligent driver is not liable for an accident that killed another person. Though we might wish the outcomes were otherwise, we accept them because we respect that people have due process rights and we entrust courts to make difficult choices.

Under the autonomy principle, Daly (2017) argued that we should listen to children's wishes unless there will be significant harm done to them. No rights that adults have are absolute. There are always restrictions on how and when rights can be implemented. There are also always standards for when the state can intervene to supersede a right. So the idea that children have rights should not also eliminate the possibility that sometimes the state with the approval of the court can intervene if there is great danger of significant harm.

While I am concerned that a significant harm doctrine could be bent to be used the same as best interests is now, with the establishment of enforceable rights and direct counsel, I think there is a better chance that courts can still protect the children that most need it while upholding the rights of everyone in the system.

The CRC

The CRC continues to be the most influential document in the world when it comes to the rights of children and the rights enumerated within it are broad enough to encompass the more specific rights for foster children that I have suggested, though as discussed in Chapter 3, the more recent concept of normalcy does not as neatly fold into the CRC as rights to participation and counsel.

Under the CRC's Article 12 participation rights are guaranteed, but the right to counsel is not. The UN Committee on the Rights of the Child (2009) allows for the child to have representation and while this can be an attorney, it is also sufficient for a social worker or even parent to be the child's representative.

In UNICEF's manual for implementing the CRC, it is explained that states are to use their own procedural rules for ensuring that children participate and are properly represented (Hodgkin & Newell, 2007). Tempesta (2019) wrote that jurisdictions internationally interpret this obligation in a multitude of ways with some courts using views of the child reports, judicial interviews, guardian ad litems, or amicus curiae to meet Article 12's requirement.

However, Article 12 is referring to all children and not just those in the child welfare system and its concept of participation is broader than just the court setting. On its face, it does not preclude direct legal representation, but it does not require it either.

The other problem of course with the CRC is its fundamental embrace of best interest. Recall that Article 3 states that best interest of the child is of "paramount consideration". In theory there are some limitations to best interests within the CRC. The UN Committee (2009) wrote that

> The best interests of the child, established in consultation with the child, is not the only factor to be considered in the actions of institutions, authorities and administration. It is, however, of crucial importance, as are the views of the child.
>
> (p.18)

This seems to suggest the traditional balance of weighing child participation and best interest as equals for decision-making. In the UNICEF guide, it is noted that,

> best interests of children or use of the principle cannot trump or override any of the other individual rights guaranteed by other articles in the Convention.
>
> (Hodgkin & Newell, 2007, p. 35)

So there is some understanding at least on paper that best interest cannot simply overwhelm and subsume the rights of the child. In practice given the realties and uncertainties of the child welfare field, coupled with its systemic risk aversion, the discretionary nature of best interests allows it to disfavor child rights and favor safety and paternalism.

The CRC's use of best interest is to my mind, its fatal flaw. As I mentioned in Chapter 2, some of the guidebooks developed by governments for NGOs and social workers to interpret best interests are hundreds of pages long reflecting the incredible confusion that this phrase invokes.

While I am not expecting a CRC 2.0 to sweep the world and do away with best interest language, I do think the current version is inadequate especially when it comes to the lives and rights of children in the care system. Foster children have unique status within the state apparatus and this status should come with additional protections for their rights. This is not unheard of within international law. For instance, the 1951 Convention Relating to the Status of

Refugees and the United Nations Convention on the Rights of Persons with Disabilities both grant special status, obligations and rights to people within that class.

An international child welfare, Normalcy Charter, could accomplish something similar for the care system. It would not need to supersede the CRC, it would merely work in addition to it, spelling out specifically the rights of children in care.

Trey was almost 17 when he and his family came into care. For a time, he and his younger brother lived together with family, while his sisters were placed into foster homes. Soon his kinship placement also broke down, and he was moved to an RTC separated from his brother who was also moved to a different RTC. He was always even tempered and quick with a joke. He liked sports, especially football and tried to play for the high school team, but was too late coming to the new school to start with the team. He wanted to learn boxing, and we even found a community program that would accept him, but the logistics of transportation were too complicated for him to attend given his RTC's restrictions. He occasionally had phone calls with his sisters, but had not seen them except for one brief visit since they were removed. He asked me about them whenever we would meet. When he aged out of care, he had no interest in extending his time. His only immediate option was an RTC, and he had long since grown frustrated with the lack of freedom in those places. He couch-surfed for a while and never finished high school. He was shot and killed at a party about six months after he turned 18.

A Better Way Forward

Throughout this book, I have tried to tie together the various threads that make up the current system along with scientific research, history, legal thought, the law and philosophy. Each issue is complex enough to be its own volume, but I hope by demonstrating the connection between these often-siloed issues that we can think more holistically about the system. Best interest feeds into risk aversion. Normalcy promotes better outcomes. Normalcy can only be guaranteed by rights. Small decisions can sometimes be as important as big ones. Neither the law or philosophy can truly define a child, and all of our thoughts about capacity and vulnerability are not applicable to children alone.

It is easy to see evidence that the foster care system has been in some form of crisis for decades. One needs only search the phrase or something similar on the internet to find stories from the 1970s and '80s describing ongoing issues with the care systems from countries around the world. A shortage of foster homes, a shortage of workers, children sleeping in offices or hotels, care experienced adults becoming homeless or going to jail, too many cases per worker, too many children removed, too many minority families impacted, too many native children pulled into White homes, children mistreated while in the care system, children sent to institutions instead of homes, children drugged by psychotropic medications, whole communities under state surveillance. Different years bring different crisis into light, but the common theme is the broken state of child welfare and its failure to serve families and children in need.

The drumbeat of crisis and reform and new crisis and reform has even led to some advocates to call for the abolition of the child welfare system in its entirety. Given the years of poor outcome this is not entirely unwarranted, but the system is in place because there are instances of abuse and maltreatment severe enough that children do require state intervention. My research study suggested that care experienced adults have some of the highest scores for child safety, so even people that have been through the often-criticized system seem to see its need. I have had clients chained to their bed, that were beaten with coat hangers, that were not fed for a week, that were locked in closets, that were beaten so severely that they needed hospitalization, that were sexually assaulted for years, that were trafficked into prostitution, all by their birth parents. These children need help.

They also need a functioning child welfare system that respects their rights as full-fledged human beings with thoughts and desires of their own. I would not suggest that best interests is by itself responsible for all of the myriad flaws in the system, but the numerous flaws inherent in best interest decision-making allow for the maintenance of the status quo. Reforms may come to the system, but so long as they are always couched within the best interest context, then decision-making for all of the critical and minor issues of a dependency case will always be the same.

Foster children's rights, normalcy and the right to direct counsel that I have advocated for in my Normalcy Charter, I believe gives us the best way forward to a care system that treats children as the true center of the case that they always should have been. We cannot claim to be working in their best interest when we deny them basic rights available to every other party in the case. We cannot claim to be working in their best interest when we deny them the freedom of a normal life. Children's rights and normalcy do not reduce child safety, it adds protections to them from abuses by the state and offers an opportunity for their true interests to be paramount.

References

Abramson, A. (2021). *Substance use during the pandemic*. American Psychological Association Monitor on Psychology. Retrieved July 5, 2024, from https://www.apa.org/monitor/2021/03/substance-use-pandemic

Anand, P., Patil, R. S., Puri, P., & Patil, S. (2024). The psychosocial effects of lockdown due to the COVID-19 pandemic on children in 2021. *Cureus*, *16*(2), e53614. https://doi.org/10.7759/cureus.53614

Batt, J. (1992). Child custody disputes and the beyond the best interests paradigm: A contemporary assessment of the Goldstein/Freud/Solnit position and the group's painter v. Bannister jurisprudence. *Nova Law Review*, *16*(2), Article 3. https://nsuworks.nova.edu/nlr/vol16/iss2/3

Berinato, S. (2020). That discomfort you're feeling is grief. *Harvard Business Review*. Retrieved July 5, 2024, from https://hbr.org/2020/03/that-discomfort-youre-feeling-is-grief

Betthäuser, B. A., Bach-Mortensen, A. M., & Engzell, P. (2023). A systematic review and meta-analysis of the evidence on learning during the COVID-19 pandemic. *Nature Human Behaviour*, *7*(3), 375–385. https://doi.org/10.1038/s41562-022-01506-4

Brown, R., & Ward, H. (2013). Decision-making within a child's timeframe: An overview of current research evidence for family justice professionals concerning child development and the impact of maltreatment Working Paper 16 Second Edition Decision-making within a child's timeframe. https://doi.org/10.13140/2.1.2953.8884

Conway, F. N., Samora, J., Brinkley, K., Jeong, H., Clinton, N., & Claborn, K. R. (2022). Impact of COVID-19 among people who use drugs: A qualitative study with harm reduction workers and people who use drugs. *Harm Reduction Journal*, *19*(1), 72. https://doi.org/10.1186/s12954-022-00653-1

Daly, A. (2017). *Children, autonomy and the courts: Beyond the right to be heard*. Brill|Nijhoff. https://doi.org/10.1163/9789004355828

Dorn, E., Hancock, B., Sarakatsannis, J., & Viruleg, E. (2021). *COVID-19 and education: The lingering effects of unfinished learning* (p. 27). McKinsey & Company.

Economist. (2021). The global normalcy index: Is the world returning to pre-pandemic life? Find out with our interactive tracker. *The Economist*. Retrieved July 5, 2024, from https://www.economist.com/graphic-detail/tracking-the-return-to-normalcy-after-covid-19?utm_medium=pr&utm_source=us-e

Ferwana, I., & Varshney, L. R. (2024). The impact of COVID-19 lockdowns on mental health patient populations in the United States. *Scientific Reports*, *14*(1), 5689. https://doi.org/10.1038/s41598-024-55879-9

Goldstein, J., Freud, A., & Solnit, A. (1973). *Beyond the best interest of the child*. The Free Press.

Grootens-Wiegers, P., Hein, I. M., van den Broek, J. M., & de Vries, M. C. (2017). Medical decision-making in children and adolescents: Developmental and neuroscientific aspects. *BMC Pediatrics*, *17*(1), 120. https://doi.org/10.1186/s12887-017-0869-x

Hodgkin, R., & Newell, P. (2007). *Implementation handbook for the United Nations Convention on the Rights of the Child* (3rd ed.). UNICEF. https://www.unicef.org/lac/media/22071/file/Implementation%20Handbook%20for%20the%20CRC.pdf

Icenogle, G., Steinberg, L., Duell, N., Chein, J., Chang, L., Chaudhary, N., Di Giunta, L., Dodge, K. A., Fanti, K. A., Lansford, J. E., Oburu, P., Pastorelli, C., Skinner, A. T., Sorbring, E., Tapanya, S., Uribe Tirado, L. M., Alampay, L. P., Al-Hassan, S. M., Takash, H. M. S., & Bacchini, D. (2019). Adolescents' cognitive capacity reaches adult levels prior to their psychosocial maturity: Evidence for a "maturity gap" in a multinational, cross-sectional sample. *Law Human Behavior*, *43*(1), 69–85. https://doi.org/10.1037/lhb0000315

In re Gault, 387 U.S. 1, 87 S. Ct. 1428 (1967).

Insel, C., Tabashneck, S., Shen, F., Edersheim, J., & Kinscherff, R. (2022). White paper on the science of late adolescence: A guide for judges, attorneys, and policy makers. https://doi.org/10.13140/RG.2.2.10160.64008

Jones, R. (2020). *Grieving the loss of normalcy*. The University of New Mexico Health & Health Sciences Newsroom. Retrieved July 5, 2024, from https://hsc.unm.edu/news/news/grieving-the-loss-of-normalcy.html

Kuhfeld, M., Soland, J., & Lewis, K. (2022). Test score patterns across three COVID-19-impacted school years. *Educational Researcher*, *51*(7), 500–506. https://doi.org/10.3102/0013189x221109178

Kupcova, I., Danisovic, L., Klein, M., & Harsanyi, S. (2023). Effects of the COVID-19 pandemic on mental health, anxiety, and depression. *BMC Psychology*, *11*(1), 108. https://doi.org/10.1186/s40359-023-01130-5

Lopez-Serrano, J., Díaz-Bóveda, R., González-Vallespí, L., Santamarina-Pérez, P., Bretones-Rodríguez, A., Calvo, R., & Lera-Miguel, S. (2023). Psychological impact during COVID-19 lockdown in children and adolescents with previous mental health disorders. *Spanish Journal of Psychiatry and Mental Health*, *16*(1), 32–41. https://doi.org/10.1016/j.rpsm.2021.04.002

Luiten, M. A. J., van Muilekom, M. M., Teela, L., Polderman, T. J. C., Terwee, C. B., Zijlmans, J., Klaufus, L., Popma, A., Oostrom, K. J., van Oers, H. A., & Haverman, L. (2021). The impact of lockdown during the COVID-19 pandemic on mental and social health of children and adolescents. *Quality of Life Research*, *30*(10), 2795–2804. https://doi.org/10.1007/s11136-021-02861-x

Lundy, L. (2007). 'Voice' is not enough: Conceptualising Article 12 of the United Nations Convention on the Rights of the Child. *British Educational Research Journal*, *33*(6), 927–942. https://doi.org/10.1080/01411920701657033

McKeown, S. (1992). The least detrimental alternative: Bottom line best interest. *Journal of Juvenile Law*, *13*, 144–152.

Micsky, T. (2020). Uncertain times: Coping with loss during the COVID-19 pandemic. *Social Work Today*. Retrieved July 5, 2024, from https://www.socialworktoday.com/archive/exc_042420.shtml

Mnookin, R. H. (1973). Foster care: In whose best interest? *Harvard Educational Review*, *43*(4), 599–638. https://doi.org/10.17763/haer.43.4.unm6691p3u1n450v

Panchal, U., Salazar de Pablo, G., Franco, M., Moreno, C., Parellada, M., Arango, C., & Fusar-Poli, P. (2023). The impact of COVID-19 lockdown on child and adolescent mental health: Systematic review. *European Child & Adolescent Psychiatry*, *32*(7), 1151–1177. https://doi.org/10.1007/s00787-021-01856-w

Pedrosa, A. L., Bitencourt, L., Fróes, A. C. F., Cazumbá, M. L. B., Campos, R. G. B., de Brito, S. B. C. S., & Simões e Silva, A. C. (2020). Emotional, behavioral, and psychological impact of the COVID-19 pandemic. *Frontiers in Psychology*, *11*. https://doi.org/10.3389/fpsyg.2020.566212

Penninx, B. W. J. H., Benros, M. E., Klein, R. S., & Vinkers, C. H. (2022). How COVID-19 shaped mental health: From infection to pandemic effects. *Nature Medicine*, *28*(10), 2027–2037. https://doi.org/10.1038/s41591-022-02028-2

Pustake, M., Mane, S., Ganiyani, M. A., Mukherjee, S., Sayed, M., Mithbavkar, V., Memon, Z., Momin, A. S., Deshmukh, K., Chordia, A., Parida, S., Johnson, A., Warghade, S., Varma, D., & Bhagwat, A. (2022). Have the COVID-19 pandemic and lockdown affected children's mental health in the long term? A repeated cross-sectional study. *BMJ Open*, *12*(7), e058609. https://doi.org/10.1136/bmjopen-2021-058609

Roberts, A., Rogers, J., Mason, R., Siriwardena, A. N., Hogue, T., Whitley, G. A., & Law, G. R. (2021). Alcohol and other substance use during the COVID-19 pandemic: A systematic review. *Drug Alcohol Depend*, *229*(Pt A), 109150. https://doi.org/10.1016/j.drugalcdep.2021.109150

Spinak, J. (2007). When did lawyers for children stop reading Goldstein, Freud and Solnit? Lessons from the twentieth century on best interests and the role of the child advocate. *Family Questionnaire*, *41*, 393. https://scholarship.law.columbia.edu/faculty_scholarship/2503

Taub, N. (1984). *Assessing the impact of Goldstein, Freud, and Solnit's proposals: An introductory overview*. New York University Review of Law & Social Change. Retrieved July 5, 2024, from https://socialchangenyu.com/review/assessing-the-impact-of-goldstein-freud-and-solnits-proposals-an-introductory-overview/

Tempesta, C. (2019). *Legal representation as a critical aspect of the realization of the child's right to be heard*. Leiden University Faculty of Law. Retrieved July 12, 2024, from https://www.universiteitleiden.nl/binaries/content/assets/rechtsgeleerdheid/instituut-voor-privaatrecht/jeugdrecht/legal-representation-as-a-critical-aspect-of-the-childs-right-to-be-heard.pdf

UN Committee on the Rights of the Child. (2009). *General comment No. 12: The right of the child to be heard.* CRC/C/GC/12 20 July 2009. Retrieved June 6, 2024, from https://www.refworld.org/legal/general/crc/2009/en/70207

Walsh, F. (2020). Loss and resilience in the time of COVID-19: Meaning making, hope, and transcendence. *Family Process, 59*(3), 898–911. https://doi.org/10.1111/famp.12588

Weir, K. (2020). *Grief and COVID-19: Mourning our bygone lives.* American Psychological Association. Retrieved July 5, 2024, from https://www.apa.org/news/apa/2020/grief-covid-19

Index

Note: Page numbers in *italic* indicate a figure and page numbers in **bold** indicate a table on the corresponding page.

abuse 6–7
adult outcomes 11–14
African Charter on the Rights and Welfare of the Child 25–26, 124
agency 101–103
Alabama Code 21–22
American Bar Association (ABA) 29–30, 151–154
Annie E. Casey Foundation 10, 13, 56, 59, 106
Arizona Supreme Court 22–23
attorneys: best interest 28–29
Australia, State of Victoria, Department of Health and Human Services 65
autonomy principle 189–191, 197, 202

barriers 131; to normalcy 53–55, 58–60
behavioral science 104–105
best interest 1–2, 8–9, 15, 21–23; alternatives to 188–191; bias 39–44; childhood well-being 76–78; child protection vs child welfare 78; children's rights and participation 122–124, 127, 134–135, 138–143, 146–148, 157–158; child welfare roles 177–178; child welfare system and risk aversion 78–80; courts and attorneys 28–29; CPS errors and culture of fear 80–84; Dalgleish Scale 176–177, **176–177**; decision-making 92, 109–111; Decision-Making Ecology 178–183; discretion 38–39; discussion 178–183; history 26–28; inconstancy 38–39; indeterminacy 36–38; international perspective 23–26; limitations 183; methods 168–174, **169–170**; normalcy 52–55, 58, 67; Normalcy Charter 192–194, 197–205; reasonable prudent parent standard 72–74; as representational model 29–34; results 174–183, **174–175**; risk assessments 84–85; risk aversion 74–87; why best interests may not be the best 34–36
Best Interest of the Child Questionnaire (BIC-Q) 32
Best Interest of the Child Self-Report Questionnaire (BIC-S) 32
best interest representation 8, 29, 200
bias 35–44, 83–86, 94–96, 1103–105, 192–194

California Penal Code 6
CalYOUTH 11–13
Canada, Supreme Court of 37–38
caseworker 101–103
Casey Family Programs 11, 81, 105, 130–131, 156
Charter of Fundamental Rights of the European Union 24
Child Abuse and Prevention Act (CAPTA) 29
Child Abuse and Treatment Act 6
childhood well-being 76–78
child protection 78
Child Protective Services (CPS) 1–9, 13–14; and best interest 22, 27–28, 34–35, 41–44, 168–169, 176–177, 180–181; children's rights and participation 122, 125–127, 130–131, 139–142, 146–150, 153–157; and culture of fear 80–84;

and decision-making 92–93, 96, 98–103, 105–107, 109–111; and normalcy 52–55, 58–63; and Normalcy Charter 193–198, 202; and risk 72–75, 78–86
Children's Advocacy Institute 151
children's healthcare rights 137–143
children's participation 33–34, 52–53, 57–59, 72–74, 157–158, 202–203; children's healthcare rights 137–143; children's rights in the US 124–126; Foster Care Bill of Rights 126–130; foster care lawsuits 130–136; Foster Youth Advisory Boards 155–157; international children's rights 122–124; Lundy Model 143–146, *144*; and normalcy 63–64; Normalcy Charter 191–193, 196–197; philosophy 118–122; right to counsel and the courts 151–155; what children think 148–151; what professionals think 146–148
children's rights 77, 157–158; best interest 26–27, 32–34, 42–44; children's healthcare rights 137–143; Foster Care Bill of Rights 126–130; foster care lawsuits 130–136; Foster Youth Advisory Boards 155–157; international children's rights 122–124; Lundy Model 143–146, *144*; Normalcy Charter 190–194, 197–201, 205; philosophy 118–122; right to counsel and the courts 151–155; in the US 124–126; what children think 148–151; what professionals think 146–148
Child Rights International Network 119
Child Welfare Information Gateway (CWIG) 4–5, 7, 21, 178, 181
child welfare professionals *see* professionals
child welfare researchers 32–34; *see also* research
child welfare roles 177–178
child welfare system 1–2, 14–15; abuse and neglect 6–7; adult outcomes 11–14; court case 7–10; foster children 2–5; homes 5–6; leaving the care system 10–11; and risk aversion 78–80
child welfare vs child protection 78
COE Parliamentary Assembly 41
conflicting rights 41–43
Congressional Research Service (CRS) 3
Convention on the Rights of the Child (CRC) 25–27, 32, 77, 87, 118, 192–193, 202–204; Article 2 24; Article 3 24, 124–125, 133, 203; Article 4 26; Article 5 133, 145; Article 9 24, 42, 124; Article 12 137, 140–146, 190, 202–203; Article 18 24, 125, 133–134; Article 19 77, 125; Article 20 24, 123; Article 21 124; Article 24 137; Article 25 124, 137; Article 31 65–67, 74; Article 37 24
Council of Europe (COE) 24–26, 41, 80
counsel, right to 151–155
Court Appointed Special Advocates (CASA) 202; 1, 8–9, 14–15; best interest of children 27, 34–35, 40, 44; decision-making 92, 96–98, 10, 105, 109–111; response of professionals 168–171, 177–184
court cases 7–10, 22, 38–39, 140
Court of Justice of the European Union (CJEU) 38
courts: and child participation 151–155; role of 201–202; view on best interest 28–29
CPS *see* Child Protective Services (CPS)
culture of fear 80–84

Dalgleish Scale 102, 173–174, 176–177, **176–177**, 180, 183–184
decision-making 1–2, 92, 110–111; behavioral science 104–105; best interest 21–26, 33–35, 38, 39, 45; bias and heuristics 103–104; children's rights and participation 137, 139–148, 151–153, 157; group 105–107; investigation 93; judicial 105; normalcy 56–57; Normalcy Charter 188–192, 197, 201–205; removal 95–98; response of professionals 168–169, 179–184; reunification and permanency 100–103; risk 72–75, 80–87; substantiation 93–95; termination 98–100; *see also* Decision-Making Ecology (DME)
Decision-Making Ecology (DME) 107–110, *108*, 182–183
dependency 1–2, 14–15; abuse and neglect 6–7; adult outcomes 11–14; court case 7–10; foster children 2–5;

homes 5–6; leaving the care system 10–11
developmentally appropriate freedoms (DAG) 57–58; *see also* normalcy
direct representation 29–31, 44, 151, 193, 200–202
disability 4–5, 11–13; best interest of children 39–41; children's rights and participation 129–131, 139–140, 143; decision-making 98–100; normalcy 59–60, 64–68; Normalcy Charter 190, 201–204
discretion 38–39
disproportionality 85, 94–98, 195

ecology, decision-making 107–110, *108*
errors, CPS 80–84
European Asylum Support Office (EASO) 25
European Convention on the Exercise of Children's Rights 124
European Court of Human Rights (ECtHR) 26, 29, 38
European Union Agency for Fundamental Rights 24, 119
Every Student Succeeds Act 23

Family Group Decision-Making (FGDM) 106
fear, culture of 80–84
Finland, Supreme Court of 29
Foster Care Bill of Rights 126–130, 150
foster care lawsuits 130–136
foster care system (general) 2–5; *see also* child welfare system
foster children (general) 2–5
Foster Youth Advisory Boards 155–157
Foster Youth Bill of Rights Resolution 129–130

General Assessment and Decision-Making Model (GADM) 108
Geneva Declaration of the Rights of the Child 122–123
Georgia Code 98
group decision-making 105–107; *see also* decision-making

healthcare rights 137–143
heuristics 103–104
history: best interest child welfare 26–28
homes of children coming into care 5–6
Human Rights Watch 125
hybrid representation 29, 151

inconsistency 38–39
indeterminacy 36–38
Inter-American Convention on the Rights of the Child 124
international perspective: best interest 23–26; children's rights 122–124; normalcy 64–67
Interstate Commission for Juveniles 119
investigation 93

judicial decision-making 105; *see also* decision making

lawsuits *see* foster care lawsuits
least detrimental alternative 188–189
least restrictive placement 22, 126, 194
leaving the care system 10–11
legal representation 198–199
Let Kids Be Kids 53–54, 63, 77, 155
LGBTQ community: best interest of children 35, 40–43; children's rights and participation 135; normalcy 52, 55, 59–60; response of professionals 172, 174–178, 180–181, 183
Lundy Model 143–146, *144*, 196

Massachusetts Department of Children and Families 127
methods 168–174, **169–170**
Michigan Code 98
Michigan Department of Health and Human Services 22
Michigan Supreme Court 38
Midwest Study 11–12

National Association of Counsel for Children (NACC) 8, 151, 153, 157
National Conference of State Legislatures 126
National Council of Juvenile and Family Court Judges (NCJCF) 154
National Council on Disability (NCD) 5, 41
National Foster Care Youth and Alumni Policy Council 77–78
National Survey of Child and Adolescent Well-Being (NSCAW II) 94
neglect 6–7
neurodevelopment 191
New England Youth Coalition (NEYC) 56–58, 63, 67–68, 156–157, 194, 196
normalcy 1–2, 52, 110, 123–124, 129, 155–157; barriers 58–60; child

protection vs child welfare 78; child welfare roles 177–178; child welfare system and risk aversion 78–80; childhood well-being 76–78; CPS errors and culture of fear 80–84; Dalgleish Scale 176–177, **176–177**; Decision-Making Ecology 178–183; discussion 178–183; international 64–67; limitations 183; methods 168–174, **169–170**; origins 52–54; participation 63; Preventing Sex Trafficking and Strengthening Families Act 54–55; reasonable prudent parent standard 72–74; and research 60–63, *61*; results 174–183, **174–175**; risk assessments 84–85; risk aversion 74–87; what is normal 67–68; why normalcy 55–58
Normalcy Charter 2, 157, 187–188; alternatives to best interest 188–191; autonomy principle 189–191; better way forward 204–205; CRC 202–204; direct representation 200–201; least detrimental alternative 188–189; legal representation 198–199; neurodevelopment 191; participation 196–197; the problem 191–193; rights 193–196; risk tolerance 197–198; role of the court 201–202
North Carolina Supreme Court 42
Norwegian Supreme Court 28–29

Oregon Statute 21
outcomes 11–14

parental rights 10–11, 98, 198; and the best interest of children 22, 26–27, 42; and children's participation 125, 157; child rights vs 132–136
participation *see* children's participation
Pennsylvania Children in Foster Care Act 126
permanency 9–10, 153; and the best interest of children 22, 26–28; and decision-making 98–103, 106; and normalcy 60–61; response of professionals 180–183
Philadelphia Department of Human Services (PDHS) 74
philosophy: children's rights 118–122
Preventing Sex Trafficking and Strengthening Families Act (PSTSFA) 54–55, 58, 63, 72, 126
professionals 32–34; children's rights and participation 146–148; child welfare roles 177–178; Dalgleish Scale 176–177, **176–177**; Decision-Making Ecology 178–183; discussion 178–183; limitations 183; methods 168–174, **169–170**; results 174–183, **174–175**

race 3–7, 11, 40; decision-making 94, 99–100; response of professionals 173–176, 178, 180–183
reasonable prudent parent standard (RPP) 53–55, 59, 72–74, 87, 179
removal 5–9, 12–13; best interest of children 35, 40; children's rights and participation 147–149; decision-making 92–98, 102–106, 109; Normalcy Charter 191–194; response of professionals 181–182
representational model, best interest as 29–34
research: child welfare researchers 32–34; child welfare roles 177–178; Dalgleish Scale 176–177, **176–177**; Decision-Making Ecology 178–183; discussion 178–183; how professionals respond 168–184; limitations 183; methods 168–174, **169–170**; and normalcy 60–63, *61*; results 174–178, **174–175**
residential treatment facility (RTS) 2, 14
reunification 10–11; best interest of children 21, 31, 38–40; children's rights and participation 149, 153; decision-making 92, 106–111; and permanency 100–103; response of professionals 172, 176, 179–182; risk 86–87
rights 157–158; conflicting 41–43; to counsel 151–155; Normalcy Charter 193–196; *see also* children's rights; parental rights
risk: childhood well-being 76–78; child protection vs child welfare 78; child welfare system and risk aversion 78–80; CPS errors and culture of fear 80–84; reasonable prudent parent standard 72–74
risk assessments 83–85, 95
risk aversion 35, 58, 72–76, 81–83; best interest as 85–87; children's rights and participation 148, 157; and the child welfare system 78–80;

decision-making 96, 104; Normalcy Charter 192–194, 197–204; response of professionals 168, 174
risk tolerance 76, 111, 193, 197–198
roles, child welfare 177–178

sex trafficking *see* Preventing Sex Trafficking and Strengthening Families Act
structural equation modeling (SEM) 174
substantiation 93–96, 103, 107

Team Decision-Making (TDM) 106
Teen Success Agreement 58
Tennessee Supreme Court 22
termination 9–10, 81; best interest of children 22, 26, 37, 42–43; children's rights and participation 136, 139; decision-making 98–100, 103, 109–110; response of professionals 176–177, 179–181
Texas Department of Family and Protective Services (TDFPS) 127
Texas Family Code 6, 127
Texas Youth Permanency Study (TYPS) 60–61, 78

UK National Minimum Standards (NMS) 64
UN Committee on the Rights of the Child (UNCRC): 2009 141, 202–203; 2013 2, 65–66, 74; 2023 133–134
UN Guidelines for the Alternative Care of Children 124
UN High Commissioner for Refugees (UNHCR) 25
UNICEF 3, 77, 203
United States Department of Health and Human Services (HHS) 2–7, 60, 93, 119, 126, 154
U.S. Center for Disease Control 137
US Supreme Court 23, 29, 37–38, 41, 119, 124–125, 134–135, 138, 198–199

Virginia Administrative Code 6

Washington Supreme Court 132
welfare *see* child welfare system
well-being *see* childhood well-being

Youth Law Center 7, 55, 63

Made in the USA
Las Vegas, NV
19 September 2026

76325e2e-5240-4409-93bf-fdf193bf09b1R01